T0036920

CRACKING THE WALNUT

CRACKING
THE
WALNUT

THICH
NHAT
HANH

Understanding
the Dialectics
of Nagarjuna

PALM LEAVES
PRESS

Published by Palm Leaves Press
an imprint of Parallax Press

Parallax Press
2236B Sixth Street
Berkeley, California 94710
parallax.org

Parallax Press is the publishing division of
Plum Village Community of Engaged Buddhism

Copyright © 2023 by
Plum Village Community of Engaged Buddhism
All Rights Reserved
Printed in Canada

Previously published in Vietnamese as
Đập Vỡ Vỏ Hồ Đào
by Sách Phuông Nam, 2014
Translation from Vietnamese to English
by Annabel Laity (Chan Duc, True Virtue)

Cover design by Katie Eberle
Text design and composition by Maureen Forys
Printed on recycled-content paper

Non-English terms are in Sanskrit unless otherwise indicated.

ISBN: 978-1-952692-46-8
E-book ISBN: 078-1-952692-47-5

Library of Congress Cataloging-in-Publication
Data is available upon request

1 2 3 4 5 MARQUIS 27 26 25 24 23

CONTENTS

PREFACE   vii

1. EXAMINATION OF CONDITIONS   1

2. EXAMINATION OF COMING AND GOING   63

3. EXAMINATION OF THE FOUR
   NOBLE TRUTHS   175

4. EXAMINATION OF BEING AND
   NONBEING   199

5. EXAMINATION OF FIRE AND FUEL   239

6. EXAMINATION OF NIRVĀṆA   317

APPENDIX   365

PREFACE

Just as Einstein's outstanding intellect excelled at physics, so did Nāgārjuna's heart excel at comprehending the teachings of the Buddha. Not only the intellect knows how to reason; so does the heart. Both intellect and heart can see and understand. Yet the heart can go farther than the intellect, because of its greater intuition. The dialectics of Nāgārjuna that follow are a transcendent kind of reasoning—a reasoning that destroys all notions, allowing the truth to reveal itself. The language of dialectics can do this in ways the language of mathematics cannot.

Nāgārjuna was born at a time when the doors of the Mahāyāna—the Great Vehicle of Buddhism—were beginning to open. Through this crack in the door, Nāgārjuna was able to access the jewels hidden in the Source Buddhist sutras.* He understood the essence of the Buddhist teachings. Letting go of dualistic views, Nāgārjuna touched reality—a reality that cannot be accessed by someone caught in notions. Science now struggles

---

* The sutras of the Nikāyas and Āgamas.

to transcend dualism. Birth/death, being/nonbeing, production/destruction, coming/going, inside/outside, object/subject, all of these are dualistic notions. Śākyamuni Buddha taught: "There is a not-born, a not-become, a not-made, a not-compounded. If there were not the not-born, not-become, not-made, not-compounded, there could be no escape from that which is born, become, made, compounded."[*] We can only touch what is not born and does not die—that which is neither subject nor object—when we transcend the snare of dualistic notions. The dialectics of the Middle Way, as applied by Nāgārjuna, allow us to look with clarity and, in doing so, to transcend the snare of dualism. According to Nāgārjuna, this is the key to Buddhist study.

Nāgārjuna's Mūlamadhyamakakārikā (Verses on the Middle Way) is *the* exemplary work of the intellect and of the heart in Buddhist studies. And yet, Nāgārjuna did not refer to the emerging Mahāyāna sutras to establish his Dharma door; instead, he based his dialectics only on the traditional Source Buddhist sutras and, in the Verses on the Middle Way, cites the Kaccānagottasutta.[†]

Just as Einstein discovered the Theory of Relativity, so Nāgārjuna used the theory of "reciprocity" 相待

---

[*] Udāna 8.3.

[†] SN 12.15 and SA 301迦旃延

(literally "waiting for each other"). In Buddhism, reciprocity means: this is present because that is present; this is absent because that is absent. Wherever there is wisdom there is the potential for ignorance, wherever there is left there is right, wherever there are lotuses there is mud. That is reciprocity: if there is this, there has to be that. Reciprocity means that *things wait upon each other so that they can manifest together.* Short and long have to arise together. There is being because there is nonbeing. There is birth because there is death. There is impurity because there is purity. There is dark because there is light. The Sattadhātu Sutta (SN 14.11 and SA 456) shows us that there is light because there is darkness, impurity because there is purity; there is space because there is matter, there is nonbeing because there is being, there is death because there is birth. These sutras are the source of the insight of reciprocity.

Despite its pairing of seemingly opposite concepts, reciprocity in the dialectics of Nāgārjuna helps bring us to a nondualistic insight. According to the wisdom of the Middle Way, scientific progress is hampered by duality—in particular by the idea that the subject and object of consciousness (or perception) are separate. In the Kaccānagotta Sutta, we learn that most people are caught in ideas of being and nonbeing. Nirvāṇa is the truth of no birth, no death; no being, no nonbeing; no space, and no matter. Nirvāṇa can be realized when there is the insight of nonduality. Our ideas about conditioned co-arising (*pratītyasamutpāda*), inter-arising, reciprocity, interbeing, and interpenetration all point to the same thing. The notions of emptiness, mere designation, and the Middle Way mean the same thing.

The text of the Verses on the Middle Way is a walnut: good to eat, but with a tough shell. If we do not break this shell, we will not be able to enjoy the walnut's richness or its sweetness. With the aid of a nutcracker, you do not have to wait long to enjoy the rich and fragrant taste of the nut—you just put the nut between the pincers and press hard to quickly break the nut's shell. This commentary is a nutcracker that helps to crack the nut of these verses.

Nāgārjuna was born into a Brahmin family at the end of the second century CE. As an adult he studied and practiced Buddhism. He wrote in Classical Sanskrit rather than in Pali or in Buddhist Hybrid Sanskrit.

The Verses on the Middle Way expound and disseminate the ultimate truth (*paramārthasatya*) of Buddhism. Conventional or relative truth (*saṃvṛtisatya*) goes alongside ultimate truth. Although the conventional truth is not the ultimate truth, it can still point out to us the way of transformation and healing. As such, it is not in opposition to, nor does it contradict, the ultimate truth—in fact, conventional truth can help reveal the ultimate truth. Without the ultimate truth we would not have the means to guide us into the ultimate reality. As you read the Verses on the Middle Way, you will see that Nāgār-juna is sometimes critical of the teachings of Buddhist schools of his time, such as the Sarvāstivāda, Pudgala-vāda, or Sautrāntika. Despite this criticism, he does not condemn or contradict any of these schools, nor does he take the side of or defend them. His only intention is to reveal the ultimate truth as taught by the Buddha.

Everything we learn in these teachings is connected to the suffering, fear, and worries that we experience in our daily life. These teachings are not pointless theories. In bringing these teachings down to earth, we will be capable of seeing that they are rooted in our own lives—in our daily experience of happiness and suffering.

⚬⚬

I invite you to enjoy the taste of this sweet and delicious walnut.

TRANSLATOR'S NOTE: *Cracking the Walnut* is an edited translation of the commentaries, delivered in Vietnamese, offered during two three-month Rains' Retreats from 2001 to 2003 by Dhyāna Master Thích Nhất Hạnh on the following chapters of the Verses on the Middle Way:

1. Examination of Conditions (or Conditioned Arising) (Pratyayaparīkṣā) Chapter 1

2. Examination of Coming and Going (Gatāgataparīkṣā) Chapter 2

3. Examination of the Four Noble Truths (Āryasatyaparīkṣā) Chapter 24

4. Examination of Being and Nonbeing (Svabhāvaparīkṣā) Chapter 15

5. Examination of Fire and Fuel (Agnīndhanaparīkṣā) Chapter 10

6. Examination of Nirvāṇa (Nirvāṇaparīkṣā) Chapter 25

These chapters were chosen by Thích Nhất Hạnh because they best represent the spirit of the Verses on the Middle Way.

EXAMINATION OF CONDITIONS

All phenomena, the Buddha taught, arise due to causes and conditions—also known as "conditioned co-arising"—and this chapter looks deeply into this matter. We may already have a notion about conditioned co-arising, but our notion may be naïve and largely mistaken. These verses help us to free ourselves from these notions.

Unborn and undying,
neither permanent nor annihilated,
neither the same nor different,
neither coming nor going—
the Buddha thus proclaims conditioned co-arising
that puts an end to all speculation.
I bow down to him,
the supreme and excellent teacher.

不生亦不滅
不常亦不斷
不一亦不異
不來亦不出
能說是因緣
善滅諸戲論
我稽首禮佛
諸說中第一

anirodham anutpādam anucchedam aśāśvatam
anekārtham anānārtham anāgamam anirgamam
yaḥ pratītyasamutpādaṃ prapañcopaśamaṃ śivam
deśayām āsa saṃbuddhas taṃ vande vadatāṃ varam

These verses introduce the whole treatise and present the quintessence of its teachings. Nāgārjuna gives us, in the first four lines, what we call *the eight negations*. He does so with the aim of removing eight notions of what is not real: birth, death, permanence, annihilation, sameness, difference, coming, and going. We are unable to touch the truth because these eight notions are present in our mind. We believe that there is birth and death, permanence and annihilation, same and different, coming and going, and because of that, our view of reality becomes distorted. This is why the Buddha had to find skillful ways to remove these notions from our minds.

The eight negations express the teachings on emptiness (*śūnyatā*). Before the time of Nāgārjuna, emptiness had been taught by the Buddha Śākyamuni. Though these teachings were refined by the Prajñāpāramitā* writings, they had yet to be systematized. Nāgārjuna was the first person to do this. After him came Āryadeva and others, including Candrakīrti.

> *The Buddha thus proclaims conditioned co-arising*
> *that puts an end to all speculation.*

If we can offer these teachings on conditioned co-arising in terms of the eight negations, then we will be able to put a skillful end to all speculation.† Speculation refers to teachings and doctrines that do not lead us anywhere. Vain metaphysical speculation has no real benefit for our life.

> *I bow down to the Buddha,*
> *the supreme and excellent teacher.*

---

* The Prajñāpāramitā literature began to take shape in the south of India from the first century BCE onward for several hundred years. First was the Prajñāpāramitā in Eight Thousand Lines and then, over time, longer sutras such as the Prajñāpāramitā in Twenty Thousand Lines and the Prajñāpāramitā in One Hundred Thousand Lines were composed.

† The Chinese characters that we translate as "speculation" are 戲論, from the Sanskrit *prapañca*. 戲論 literally means "to enjoy theorizing."

Thanks to the original Sanskrit version, which gives us the more accurate meaning, we are able to translate this as: "I bow down to the Buddha—the best teacher—because he has proclaimed the teaching on causality and the eight negations; these teachings have the capacity to extinguish all useless speculation."*

1. *Phenomena are not born from themselves,*
   nor from others,
   nor both from themselves and others, nor without
      cause.
   Therefore we know they are unborn.

諸法不自生
亦不從他生
不共不無因
是故知無生

The topic of this chapter is what the East Asian Buddhist tradition calls *the four gates.*† When we talk about birth, we have to think about it in this or that way. Does something arise spontaneously from itself? Or do other

---

* It is not correct to translate the last line as "the best of all doctrines"—even though the Chinese characters could easily be understood in this way.

† We can provisionally call this the first verse. The preceding verse on the eight negations is considered the preface to the entire text of the Verses on the Middle Way, although it is included in the first chapter.

things give birth to it? Does it arise both from itself and from other things, or does it need no cause whatsoever in order to arise? From these questions come *the four gates* or *four cases*, which are:

1. *A phenomenon arises spontaneously from itself.*

2. *A phenomenon arises from something other than itself.*

3. *A phenomenon arises both spontaneously from itself and from something other than itself.*

4. *A phenomenon arises without any cause.*

Phenomena do not arise from themselves. This is what Nāgārjuna says regarding the first of the four cases.

Nor from others. It also cannot be the case that a phenomenon arises from something other than itself.*

Nor both from themselves and others, nor without cause. Phenomena cannot arise from themselves and at the same time from something else, nor can they arise without a cause.†

---

* In this verse the character 自, meaning "self" or "oneself," is opposed to the character 他, which means "other" or "other than the self."

† In this case the character 共, which means "together," represents two terms: 自生 (born by themselves) and 他生 (born from others).

Therefore we know they are unborn. Because of this we know that no-birth is the nature of all phenomena.

In these four verses Nāgārjuna proposes four different cases and then asks: Which case is true for the arising of phenomena? The answer is that *all four cases are unreasonable.* The following verses prove this and show further that the nature of all phenomena is no birth (*nirvāṇa*).

2. *Seed condition, condition of continuity,*
   object of cognition as condition and supportive
   condition:
   These four conditions give birth to all dharmas,
   and there is no fifth one.[*]

因緣次第緣
緣緣增上緣
四緣生諸法
更無第五緣

This verse is not difficult to understand; it presents the four conditions that are taken as being the reason for the arising of all phenomena. The teaching on the four

---

* In the Sanskrit version of the text, the order of the second and third verses of the Chinese translation is inverted. The Sanskrit version seems to be logically more correct, and therefore I propose that we invert these two verses to present them as they are found in the original Sanskrit text.

conditions was refined by the Sarvāstivāda school in northwestern India. By the fourth century CE this teaching was also explained in the Abhidharmakośa-śāstra and subsequently adopted by the Manifestation-only school (Vijñaptimātra).

When Nāgārjuna went to northern India to pursue his studies in Buddhism, he was exposed to the teachings of the Sarvāstivāda school, which was prospering. As a result, the teaching of the four conditions is mentioned in the Verses on the Middle Way. However, we do not see any mention of the six conditions. This may suggest that the teaching on the six conditions was developed later.*

1. Seed condition (hetu-pratyaya)

The seed condition is the first and foremost condition, just as the corn seed is the primary or chief cause of the corn plant. The Chinese character for "cause," 因, looks like four walls limiting what is inside of them, the character 大, which means "large": something large remains hidden by a small frame, but other conditions could allow this thing

---

* The four conditions are first attested in the Vijñānakāya from the first century CE. The Jñānaprasthāna, a later Sarvāstivāda text, additionally lists six causes: *kāraṇahetu*, the efficient cause; *sahabhūhetu*, the coexistent cause; *saṃprayuktahetu*, the associated cause; *sabhāgahetu*, the homogenous cause; *sarvatragahetu*, the universal cause; and *vipākahetu*, the ripening or retribution cause. cf. Buswell, Lopez, Princeton Dictionary of Buddhism, Princeton University Press, 2014.

to become visible. For example, a sunflower seed is extremely small, but within the limits of the seed a much larger sunflower plant is contained. In time, thanks to soil, water, and sunlight, the walls that constrain the sunflower will be taken away; it will have a chance to grow large. The seed condition—or chief cause, as it is often translated—is the seed-cause of a phenomenon. Unfortunately, neither of these English terms used to translate *hetu-pratyaya* captures the full meaning of the Sanskrit term.

2. Continuity condition (samanantara-pratyaya)

The Chinese term used for this condition is 次第緣. 次第 means "order" or "consequentiality." Something goes before and something goes after. If the thing that goes before is not there, how can we have that which goes after? In Sanskrit the term means "immediately contiguous." The literal translation is "thoroughly without an interval." The equivalent in Chinese for this is 等無間緣. The character 等 means "equal." 無間 means that there is no interruption. This second condition is the condition of continuity, of an uninterrupted chain. If one ring of the chain is broken, how can the chain continue? This is the continuity condition. In this way a past instant is a condition for the following instant. If the previous instant were not there, then the next one could not follow. The same is true for us: if we did not have parents, how could we be here? It is because of our parents that we have a chance to continue them and our ancestors. Our parents are a condition of continuity for us.

3. Object of cognition as condition (ālambana-pratyaya)

The Chinese characters for this condition can be simply 緣緣, but the complete form is 所緣緣. As long as there is a subject there must be an object. A perception must always have an object of perception. For hatred and love to arise there must be an object of the hate and of the love. The same is true for joy and for sadness. This is why the third condition for something to arise is the object of cognition.

4. Supportive condition (adhipati-pratyaya)

The supportive conditions are those elements that help the other three conditions to bear fruit, to bring about a result. If there weren't any supportive conditions, how could a grain of rice grow into a plant of rice? The grain of rice needs conditions like earth, fertilizer, rain, sun, and a farmer.

In these verses, Nāgārjuna is not trying to prove a point. He mentions these four conditions so that we can look deeply into them and see that the notions we have about them are still naïve.

It is possible that while reading the Verses on the Middle Way there will be one or two verses you do not understand. You can continue and read the next verses and then return to the one you have not understood. Over time you will understand the deep meaning.

3. *The self-nature of phenomena*
   is not found in the conditions.
   Since there is no self-nature,
   how could there be an other-nature?

如諸法自性
不在於緣中
以無自性故
他性亦復無

The self-nature of phenomena is not found in the conditions.

What do we mean by self-nature (*svabhāva*)? It is the real existence of a separate entity, standing on its own. When we recognize something as being real, we give it a self-nature. Your self-nature is what makes you different from another, who has other-nature (*parabhāva*). Can we find the self-nature of phenomena within their conditions? It seems that we can't. Can we find self-nature—whether it is for something that has arisen or is yet to manifest—in the conditions that have given birth to that thing or are about to give birth to it?

For example, we may look for the self-nature of a flame in a box of matches. In the box are matches made of wood and sulfur. Outside the box is oxygen. When we search inside the wood, sulfur, and oxygen can we find the self-nature of the flame? Whether the match has already been lit or not, we cannot find this self-nature. What we call the self-nature of something cannot be found in its conditions at all.

*Since there is no self-nature, how can there be an
other-nature?*

Self-nature and other-nature go together just as left and right, inside and outside go together. If there is no right there cannot be a left. Self and other are a pair of opposites. If you remove one of them, you remove the other.

When we talk about self-nature we mean that something is an entity, and we do not confuse that entity with a different one. For example, fire has the nature of fire. Since it has that nature, it cannot be confused with ice. Fire is hot and ice is cold. So, the self-nature of fire must be heat and the self-nature of ice must be cold. This is how most people understand self-nature. If something cannot maintain its self-nature, then it is no longer the same thing as before. This is why we believe that everyone and everything has a self-nature. But in this verse Nāgārjuna invites us to look a little deeper and to see that the self-nature of which we are speaking does not really exist. This is the first cannon shot of Nāgārjuna that begins to destroy our notions about self.

In Chinese Buddhism there arose two schools of thought that almost seem to oppose each other. On the one hand there was the Dharma-characteristic (法相) school, on the other hand the Dharma-nature (法性) school. The Dharma-characteristic school specialized in the outer characteristics of things and used analysis to see that one thing is different from another. It was represented by the Manifestation-only (Vijñaptimātratā) teachings.

The Manifestation Only school defined a *dharma* (phenomenon) as "something that can retain its nature— i.e., the principle which gives rise to our thought about that phenomenon." For example, the nature of ice is *hardness* and *coldness*; a piece of ice must retain those characteristics so that we may perceive it as something different from what is not ice. This is how the Manifestation-only school defines a dharma.

In Buddhism the word dharma has many meanings. In English usage, when Dharma is capitalized it stands for the teachings of the Buddha. When it is not capitalized (dharma), it means "phenomenon" or "thing." A flower, a cloud, and a pebble, for example, are all dharmas. Nowadays, Buddhist scholars translate the word dharma as *elements of existence* or *elements of being*, a formulation considered to be closer to the meaning of the Sanskrit word. We should remember, however, that a dharma is first of all an object of mind.

We have six sense organs: eyes, ears, nose, tongue, body, and mind. The objects of these six sense organs are what we call the six sense bases: form, sound, smell, taste, touch, and dharmas. Dharmas are the object of our mind. Ice is an object of our mind, and fire is also an object of our mind. Therefore, the best and most fundamental definition of dharmas in the Buddha's teachings is that they are *the objects of our mind.* To define them as elements of being, things, or phenomena is not the best because it could lead people to think that they exist independently from our cognition. We have to translate this term in such a way that we remember that dharmas are only an object of our mind and that they do not have a separate reality outside of our mind.

While the Dharma-characteristic school specialized in looking at the exterior appearance of the dharmas, the Dharma-nature school specialized in *understanding their nature.* This school wanted to break the shell in order to penetrate the core: it wanted to break through the outer appearance in order to penetrate the nature within. The nature here is 自性, which is sometimes translated as "own-being." Ice has the nature (自性) of ice and fire the nature of fire. The two of them cannot be confused. In verse 3 we read, *Since there is no self-nature, how could there be an other-nature?* According to the Dharma-nature school, that which we call self-nature is only an idea. When we look deeply into something, we see that it does not have a self-nature, and we conclude that there is no self-nature (*niḥsvabhāva*, 無自性).

The Dharma-characteristic school is not only concerned with the outer characteristics (*lakṣaṇa*). It also helps us to penetrate the true nature. This means that when we look deeply at phenomena, we are able to touch their ultimate reality. The phenomenal world is the world of signs (相), and this world is the object of study for the Dharma-characteristic school.

The object of study of the Dharma-nature school is the noumenal world or ontological basis. The aim of the Dharma-characteristic school is not simply to examine the characteristics of all things; it has the deeper aim of breaking through to the noumenal world. This is the meaning of the sentence "from the phenomena we penetrate the noumena" (從相入性). When I was twenty years old I wrote in the poem, "The Boat Returns to its Old Moorings":

> *Paddling in the direction of the water and the drifting*
> *clouds,*
> *from the world of phenomena the boat returns to the*
> *noumenal.**

---

* Thich Nhat Hanh from his poem "Thuyền về bến cũ" in the collection *Thơ từng ôm và mặt trời từng hạt*.

We apply this principle in our practice. The Dharma-nature school is often called *the empty of intrinsic nature* (*svabhāvaśūnya*) teachings. *Nature* goes together with *empty of nature*. The North American poet Gary Snyder brought out a collection of poems entitled *No Nature* in 1992. Few people understood what was meant by this title. People thought it meant there is no natural world, but Gary Snyder is a student of Buddhism and practices meditation.

The statement "the self-nature of phenomena is not found in the conditions" is essential. Looking at and around a box of matches we see that all the conditions are present for creating a flame, but we cannot find the self-nature of the flame in any or in all of those conditions.

To recap the four conditions:

The *seed condition* can be compared to a grain which, thanks to *supportive conditions* such as the cloud, the rain, the sun, and the earth, will sprout and become a plant. Without the *continuity condition* something cannot come about. If you take a grain that has just sprouted and put it in a drawer, then replant it three days later, it cannot continue to grow. The *object of cognition as a condition* belongs to the philosophy of perception. Everything that exists is an object of consciousness. If there is no object of consciousness, how can there be consciousness? The

object of cognition is a condition for the presence of consciousness. Only when there is consciousness can there
be the earth, the heavens, this, and that. All of these
things are the object of cognition as condition.

As we look into these four conditions, can we see the
effect produced from them? Can we see the flame? In the
match, in the matchbox, in the sulfur, and in the oxygen
do we find the heat of the flame? We do not. If we look
into the conditions that make the coldness of ice possible, can we find coldness in those conditions? Coldness
is the self-nature of ice and heat is the self-nature of fire.
We cannot find heat and cold in the four kinds of conditions that make heat and cold possible. This principle
is the lynchpin of the empty-of-intrinsic-nature teachings. Further evidence of this emptiness is found in the
examination of *supportive conditions* that help a seed to
grow and become a plant. The seed needs the earth, the
manure, the rain, the sun, and the farmer.

Nāgārjuna reasons to the point where no response
is possible. Having reached this impasse, we are given
a chance to look again, to look deeply, and to let go of
some certainty around our theories and points of view.
The method Nāgārjuna uses to teach in this way is called
dialectics. His particular type of dialectics is called "arguing to prove that you are absurd, that you are wrong"
(歸謬論證), which we refer to in Latin as *reductio ad*

absurdum. Throughout the Verses on the Middle Way Nāgārjuna uses reductio ad absurdum to put his opponents at a loss to respond, but he does not intend to disgrace them.

The path of the intellect and concepts is like a railway line. As long as the railway line continues, the train proceeds. If the railway line is removed, the train can no longer run; the train will have to find a different way to travel. It may have to find a way to take off, like an airplane.

When people are caught in words and notions, they are unable to touch the true nature of all that is. Once someone is caught like this, they cannot take the path of intuitive understanding; all they have is the path of the intellect. Using the intellect is to play with words and concepts, rather than to realize how things really are.

The experience of enlightenment is like that. It is a direct experience of reality, realized by an understanding called *understanding of all aspects* (*sarvākārajñatā*), or *nondiscriminative* or *nonconceptual wisdom* (*nirvikalpa-jñāna*). This wisdom is like an airplane flying up into the sky. Discriminative or conceptual knowledge holds fast to a two-dimensional plane—not able to take us very far. There are many philosophers and students of religion who are caught in the intellect. They engage in a kind of mental gymnastics that manifests itself in the realm of concepts and reasoning, but remain unable to fly up into the sky of intuition. Intuition or direct experience is nondiscriminative wisdom.

The intention of Nāgārjuna is to bring us to an impasse so that we see for ourselves that the intellect is not ultimately capable of taking us anywhere. When we see this, we have a chance to transform ourselves from a train to an airplane.

Since self-nature is empty, how could there be other-nature? Self-nature is *svabhāva;* it is the opposite of other-nature, which is *parabhāva.* There cannot be one without the other. Self-nature is our own nature, while other-nature is the self-nature of something else.

The Sarvāstivāda school (from the first century BCE), which was one of the Mainstream Schools of Buddhism in India, taught that "the self is empty, but dharmas exist." The name of this school, Sarvāstivāda, means "all things are." It maintained that all dharmas have a true existence in the past, present, and future. The school moved to Kashmir in its early days, where it continued to flourish for a thousand years. Kashmir's location on the Silk Road resulted in the teachings of the Sarvāstivāda being brought to China.

The Tamraśāṭīya school, a branch of the Vibhajya-vāda, which later came to be known as the Theravāda or Mahāvihāravāsin tradition, moved to the south of India and became established in Sri Lanka. The Vibhajya-vāda rejected the notion that *all exists.* When the Prajñā-pāramitā sutras began to appear in the first century BCE, they stated clearly that the Buddha taught the emptiness not only of the self (*ātman*), but of all dharmas; all dharmas are without self-nature. Nāgārjuna was one of the first people to systematize these teachings on emptiness, which are also known as *Śūnyatāvāda.*

The four lines of the third verse bear the mark of Nāgārjuna's technique of reductio ad absurdum. For example, we can imagine that there is a white screen in a hall, and that there is an eye looking at the screen. The eye senses that there is nothing on the screen. In the back of the hall there is a roll of film and a light bulb. The lightbulb shines through the film and projects the image of a person onto the screen. A sound system produces sound and music. The screen, the film, the electric light, and the sound system are all conditions that come together to create the image of someone singing a song on the screen. At that moment the eye sees a singer. The singer singing is what we call the *fruit* or the *result*; it is a manifestation, just like ice, a flame, a nun, or a novice monk is a manifestation. We cannot say that the image of the singer is not real. In the same way, we cannot say that ice or flames are not real. If we put our finger in the flame, we will get burned; if we put ice in our mouth, our tongue will go numb. We cannot say that these manifestations of ice and flame do not exist. They are objects capable of interacting with other objects around them. The same is true for the image of that singer—it is capable of interacting with other objects around it. That image can make us happy, or it can make us feel sad so that we sob. Anyone who has watched a film knows this. Many people cry in the cinema.

Let us look for the self-nature of the image of the singer on the screen. To think that the image is something that exists of itself is not correct, because the singer needs to have all the conditions we have mentioned to manifest. This is what the Śūnyatāvāda school calls *empty of a separate existence.*

This example helps us to see that although it seems there is nothing real on the screen, the image there still has an effect on people. After watching a movie some people might go as far as to commit suicide. Others might go and get drunk, and yet others might look for a prostitute to satisfy their sexual desire. We cannot say that this movie does not exist. It is truly there, and it has a strong effect on its surroundings, just like fire or ice.

Whether we are a young girl, a young man, or an old person, we are like that. We are created by the coming together of many different conditions; we do not have an independent self-nature. We are also a dharma, just like the singer on the screen, the piece of ice, or the flame. We have a clear effect on our world, and therefore a responsibility toward it; at the same time we do not have an independent existence, and thus we are said to be *empty of a separate nature.*

We believe that we are we, but in fact we are not we. Since we are formed of conditions, we have to see those conditions in order to remove the idea we have of ourselves.

In our—we have to use the word *our,* although it is not quite correct—mouths live many beings. They rely on us to live and sometimes we rely on them to live. Our health depends on the bacteria that live under our tongues. If we destroy all of these bacteria we are likely to get sick. Though there are bacteria in our mouths that make us sick, there are also those—especially the ones under our tongues—that keep us in good health. Therefore, a dentist once advised me not to scrape the tongue to remove the bacteria. The population of bacteria in our mouth is greater than the population of Germany and France put together. Also, in our intestines are countless bacteria and fungi, some of them essential for our health. If we were to destroy them all, we would fall sick. They are countless, but we cannot see them with the naked eye. Science in this way helps us to see something of the interdependent and nonself nature of the Buddhist teachings.

Inside every cell of our body there are tiny organelles called mitochondria. We believe that they belong to us, but actually they don't. They have a completely different genome and DNA from us, and they replicate by themselves; in doing so they produce a kind of energy called oxidative energy. If we did not have this type of energy, we would not be capable of lifting our feet, of tapping our fingers on the table, or of moving at all. We owe our capacity to do these things to these tiny organelles and to the energy they produce inside of our cells. They are not us, but they are also not not-us. We live in symbiosis with them. If they die, we die; if they live, we also live.

Beans are another example of the interdependent and nonself nature presented in the Buddhist teachings. On the roots of a bean plant is a bacteria called "rhizome bacteria." The beans and these bacteria live in symbiosis. If these bacteria are not there, the bean plant will not be able to develop or to produce flowers and beans. Likewise, if the bean plant is not there, these bacteria have no chance to live and grow.

We rely on each other in order to manifest. When you sing, the mitochondria are singing for you. When you think, do not imagine that *you* are thinking. It is they who think. They sing our song, they think our thoughts, and they walk our walk. Our whole spiritual and genetic heritage—the suffering, the happiness, the mistakes, and the insights of our ancestors—continue in every cell of our body. We have the Buddha, we have our teachers, and we have our father and mother in every cell of our body. When we walk, we should know that Thầy, the Buddha, our mother, and our father are walking too. Do not think: "I am the one who is walking." What are *you*, after all? You are quite empty, and you have to see this. Insight is the ability to see this.

A young novice monk was struggling to work on the computer. He had only been acquainted with computers for half a year, and he found working on one difficult. He practiced breathing short, then breathing long. At that moment, an elder brother with more computer experience came along and said, "Let me do it." The novice was so happy; his elder brother was a computer expert! Joyfully, the novice monk moved aside to let his brother sit in front of the computer. How miraculous were the fingers of the elder brother! He only had to press a few keys, move the mouse, and everything that the novice was looking for appeared. Once I told a student, "You should practice like that. Every time one of the afflictions or some difficulty arises, leave space for the Buddha. Invite the Buddha into that space so the Buddha can do what you need to do." This is a practice that I have applied successfully. Let the Buddha walk your walk; let the Buddha breathe your breath; let the Buddha sing your song, and everything will be ok. "Dear Buddha, please take this step for me. I will not make the next step; I'll just let you do it. Dear Buddha, please breathe for me. I will not take the next breath; I'll just let you do it. Dear Buddha, please smile for me." When we say this, we can quickly overcome the difficulty that we are struggling with. Why do we get stuck in our difficulties? Why do we stand our ground, even to our own detriment? Why don't we allow the Buddha to help us?

But who is the Buddha? The Buddha is also us; we keep occupying his or Thầy's place. If we are lucky, then Thầy will come and say, "Move over! Let me do it for you." At that moment we will be overjoyed. Since this practice is so easy, why do we not do it? When we look deeply into the teaching on conditioned co-arising and see the empty nature of all things, we shall become unstuck. The insight of emptiness can be applied in very practical ways.

We hurt from our hurt, we suffer our suffering, and we worry our worries. We rush around erratically as if we were walking on hot coals; we sit as if we were sitting on a hot stove. Why don't we make room for the Buddha to do it? The Buddha is inside of us, so give him a chance! Give Thầy a chance! Thầy and the Buddha are present in every cell of our body. We have the Buddha's feet, but we don't let the Buddha walk. We have the eyes of the Buddha, but we don't let the Buddha look. We keep standing our ground saying: "Dear Buddha, just step aside and let me take care of this. I can do it." And who am I? I am the one who is rushing around erratically, caught up in so many things.

These first verses might appear to be difficult to understand, but in fact they are quite easy; going deeply into them is difficult. They are like advanced mathematics: if we are capable of resolving the problem, the result will reveal something truly wonderful.

4. *Does the effect arise out of the conditions,*
   or does it arise out of a non-condition?
   Is the effect contained in the conditions,
   or is there no effect in the conditions?

果為從緣生
為從非緣生
是緣為有果
是緣為無果

This verse questions again the argument that *an effect arises out of the conditions,* and in doing so allows us to examine this assumption and to make it an object of contemplation.

This is the question: "Did you say that the effect arises from its conditions? Or did you say the effect comes from a non-condition?"

For example, when we say that the egg is born from the chicken, what we mean is that the chicken is the condition and the egg is the effect. But if you say the egg is born from the table, then is the table a condition or a non-condition? As far as outer appearances are concerned, we see that the hen is one of the conditions for the egg, while the table is not. The hen is a condition (緣), while the table is a non-condition (非緣).

The second question is: "Is the effect contained in the conditions, or is there no effect in the conditions?" Is the egg already contained in the hen, or not? The answer to both of these questions lies in the fifth verse:

5. *A seed condition that gives rise to an effect*
   is called a condition.
   When the effect has not yet arisen,
   why then don't we call it a non-condition?

因是法生果
是法名為緣
若是果未生
何不名非緣

The fifth verse is the first gunshot that Nāgārjuna fires to shatter the theory that the effect is already contained in the conditions. As stated above, there are four conditions, and the first condition is called "seed condition."

Here Nāgārjuna examines the first condition before continuing on to look at the other three conditions.

A seed condition that gives rise to an effect is called a condition. The chief cause is thought to be that which produces the effect. It is one of the four conditions that produces the effect. This is why we call it a cause.

When the effect has not yet arisen, why then don't we call it a non-condition? There are two things: one is the condition, and one is the effect. Only after the condition has given rise to the effect can we call a condition a condition. Therefore, before the condition has given rise to an effect, why don't we call it a non-condition? What, if the effect has not yet arisen, is the condition conditioning? For example, after a hen has laid an egg, we will say the hen has *caused* the egg to arise—the hen is the *condition* and the egg is the *effect*. Before the hen has laid the egg the hen, just like a table or anything else, is a "non-condition." Another example is seen in the fact that a woman only begins to be called a mother when she becomes pregnant with her first child; at this point, she has become the cause of the child, she is a *condition* that gives rise to the child, who, though still in the mother's womb, is an effect of the mother. Before that pregnancy, the woman could not be called a mother. In this example we see that the same person can at one time be a condition and at another time be a non-condition.

Only when the child manifests can the mother be called the condition—her existence has given rise to that of the child. What is it that makes her a condition as opposed to a non-condition?

We can talk of condition and effect because there is a relationship of causality between the two. Why don't we call the thing referred to as a condition a non-condition before it has given rise to an effect? This question confounds us because we believe too much in our own concept of causality. Our ideas regarding causes, conditions, and effects are still naïve and shallow. We are caught in certain dogmas without being aware of it. This question is meant to make us feel less sure of ourselves: Can the same thing which we call a condition after the effect has arisen be called a non-condition before it has given rise to an effect?

Looking at the hen we see its connection to the egg clearly, but looking at the table we see no apparent connection with the egg. Is it certain, though, that the table did not give rise to the egg? What could be the connection between the table and the egg? When we ask ourselves this question we begin to see that the table is made out of a tree and that if there were no trees, then neither the hen nor the egg could exist. This same insight will be taught by the Avataṃsaka Sutra a few centuries after

Nāgārjuna: there is not a single thing which is not related to everything else. The one contains the all. Often we are not able to see the sun or the clouds as the mother of the egg, and so we believe that the hen is its only mother. But if there were no clouds, or if the sun was not there, how could there be an egg? Our distinction between condition and non-condition is faulty and naïve. For now, it is enough for us to understand that this distinction is not correct; later, with time, we will understand more.

6. *To say that the effect, prior to arising,*
   exists or not within the conditions, has no meaning.
   If it does not exist, then what does the condition condition?
   And if it does exist, then why do we need a condition?

果先於緣中
有無俱不可
先無為誰緣
先有何用緣

It is illogical and incorrect to say either that the effect is already present in the conditions or not yet present in the conditions. Why?

If it (the effect) does not exist, then what does the condition condition? If the effect is not yet there, then what is that condition conditioning?

And if it does exist, then why do we need a condition? If the effect is already there, there is no need for a condition.

This verse is talking about no-birth. Here we begin to touch our notion of birth. We believe that we have been born, but in truth no-birth is our essence. If the egg is not found in the conditions, then it cannot be born from conditions. If the egg is not in the conditions, just as it is not there in the table, then how could it be born from the conditions? But if the egg is already there in the conditions, then it does not need to be born anymore. The egg only needs to be born when it is not there, but if it is already there, then there is no need for it to be born.

Are you afraid of Nāgārjuna? He is firing cannonballs to blow up our ideas about being and nonbeing, our ideas about birth and death. Nāgārjuna is like Oppenheimer, the man who directed the Manhattan Project. Oppenheimer's team developed nuclear bombs that made atoms collide and undergo fission to create a great explosion. With Nāgārjuna it is our concepts of birth and death, of after and before, of being and nonbeing, which collide and undergo fission. Nāgārjuna uses his art to make our concepts collide and explode. Reductio ad absurdum uses concepts, reasoning, and words to demolish these very things.

Conditions are only conditions when the effect needs them in order to be born. But if the effect is already contained in the conditions, then the conditions no longer need to play the role of conditions. If the effect is not present in the conditions, the conditions cannot be called "conditions." The sixth verse is telling us that it is unreasonable for the effect to be present in the conditions, just as it is unreasonable for the effect not to be present in the conditions.

7. *If the effect is already present before it arises,*
   or if it is not present before it arises,
   or if it is both present and not present before it arises,
   how can we say that it is conditioned?

若果非有生
亦復非無生
亦非有無生
何得言有緣

The seventh verse continues to discuss the seed condition.

Just like the fifth and sixth verses, the aim of the seventh verse is to destroy our notion of a seed condition. We call this *examining the seed condition to see that it cannot be established.* Contemplating in this way, we gradually see the nature of no-birth.

In this verse Nāgārjuna presents three different cases:

- *The first verse says that the effect is not present in its cause.*
- *The second says that the effect is present in its cause.*
- *The third verse says that the effect is both present and not present in its cause.*

In each of these cases, our notion of a seed condition turns out to be illogical. If the effect is not in the conditions, why do we call them conditions? If the effect is already contained in the conditions, then the conditions no longer need to play the role of conditions. The case in which the effect is both there and not there in the conditions is completely unreasonable.

If all three cases turn out to be unreasonable, the notion of causality is not correct. Nāgārjuna is not trying to argue a point or to show off his knowledge. He seeks a way to clarify a number of misunderstandings of the Buddha's teachings so that the true teachings of the Buddha can be apprehended.

About one hundred years after the Buddha's parinirvāṇa, the Sangha split into two different schools: the Sthaviravāda, which was the conservative school, and the Mahāsaṃghika, which comprised the majority, focused on adapting the Buddha's teachings. After this initial split at least eighteen different schools arose over a period of several hundred years. This is called the period of the Mainstream Schools of Buddhism.

One of these eighteen schools was the Sarvāstivāda school, which taught that everything exists (*sarva-asti*). The position of this school was: *the self is empty, but the dharmas really exist.* Such a philosophical standpoint is today called Realism. Not only phenomena are real, but time and space are also real, because they are the framework in which phenomena lie. Reality is just like a painting; it needs to have a frame. This is why the Sarvāstivāda school maintains that *the three times are real, and the nature of the dharmas is constant.* We find the opposite tendency later on in the Vijñānavāda school, which maintains that *everything arises in consciousness.*

The Sarvāstivāda school upheld that everything exists—except the self. At first glance it looks as if they remained loyal to the teachings of the Buddha. They upheld the three Dharma Seals: impermanence, nonself, and nirvāṇa. They accepted that everything is impermanent and remains just for an instant. Things were there in the past, they are there in the present, and they will be present in the future—they are not just illusions; they are real. Even though the past is no longer there, those things were there in the past and they will be there in the future.

The danger in this kind of thinking is that it can mislead people into believing that there is something permanent—a self-nature (*svabhāva*)—that lies beneath this process of change. Someone could think that although phenomena keep changing, underneath that process of change there is a permanent basis.

The Sarvāstivāda school belongs to the Mainstream Schools Buddhism, but it made a radical departure from the original teachings of the Buddha. To say that the Mainstream Schools of Buddhism are equivalent to original Buddhism is not correct. Original Buddhism was very pure. We need to be skillful in order not to depart from the Buddha's original meaning.

The Sarvastivādins said that if the present is there, then the past must be there too. The present is present in relation to what? If the past is not there, how could we have the present? If the future is not there, how can the present be? Just like left and right, if right is not there, how can we have left? This argument stands solidly on its own. It does not need to be based on the sutras and it does not need the Buddha to say that the past and the future are real. The Buddha just needs to say that the present exists; this is enough for us to conclude that the three times are all real.

During the time that the Sarvastivada school flourished in Kashmir they created a wealth of treatises and commentaries. The Abhidharma literature[*] of the Sarvāstivāda School is extensive and comprises commentaries called the Vibhāṣā. They seem endlessly long. The Sanskrit version of this text is no longer extant, except for a few fragments, but its Chinese translation has survived in the Chinese Tripitaka.[†]

The Vibhāṣā is a monumental philosophical work specializing in analysis. When Nāgārjuna went to the north of India he studied the philosophy of the Vibhāṣā. Thanks to this, his insight into the Middle Way deepened. He saw that he needed to use some method in order to destroy the philosophical views that had departed from the original teachings of the Buddha. This is the reason why he composed the Verses on the Middle Way. The purpose of these Verses on the Middle Way was "to destroy what is wrong and make manifest what is right,"[**] which means to destroy all incorrect points of view and reveal the authentic, original Buddhadharma.

Nāgārjuna studied famous Vibhāṣā commentaries and used examples to demonstrate that *there is a*

---

[*] The various Abhidharma works were a development and systematization of the Buddha's teachings by the mainstream Buddhist schools. —Eds.

[†] T. 1545, 1546, 1547.

[**] 破邪顯正 is an expression often used in Mahāyāna commentaries in Chinese. It is discussed in the Sanlun xuanyi, The Profound Meaning of the Three Treatises.

self-nature. First, Dharmatrāta used the example of gold and things made out of gold. A pair of earrings, a ring, and a bracelet made of gold, he said, are three distinct pieces of jewelry, but they all share something fundamental: *the gold.* In the same way, underlying apparent differences between the past, present, and future and whether we consider something to be present or absent is something fundamental to all three times. Looking deeply into the earrings, the ring, and the bracelet, we see that they have something in common that is always there. The same is true for the three times.

Another teacher of the Sarvāstivāda School named Ghoṣa used another interesting example. Imagine that a number of different people have the same duty—for example, that of being head cook. We see that brother Pháp Độ, brother Giác Trí, and brother Nguyện Hải are three different monks who all share the responsibility of being a cook in Plum Village. Despite their differences, when they enter the kitchen each has the same duty. This means that even though we see their differences, their responsibility is the same. Looking at these three people, we see that deep inside there is something they all share: their capacity to be head cook.

Vasumitra, author of the Samayabhedoparacanacakra, The Wheel of the Formations of the Divisions of the Doctrines (in other words, the tenets of the eighteen Buddhist

Schools), used the example of numbers like 1, 2, and 3. Each of these numbers can play many roles. The number 3, when combined with 0, becomes 30. Combined with two 0s it becomes 300, and when followed by three 0s it becomes 3,000. We can see that 30 is not the same as 300 and that 300 is not the same as 3,000, but in all three cases we find the idea of 3. Similarly, different things like past, present, future, form, sound, smell, taste, and touch are different, and yet beneath the differences they all share something: self-nature.

The fourth commentator, Buddhadeva, offered the example of a young girl. When she is born, she is called a daughter and plays the part of a daughter; when she grows up and marries, she is called a wife and plays the role of a wife; when she gives birth to a child, she is called a mother and plays the role of a mother. These three roles—daughter, wife, mother—are all distinct, but there is only one woman who plays these roles. What remains the same throughout these roles is called self-nature according to the Sarvāstivāda.

This viewpoint is dangerous because it brings Buddhism close to the Saṃkhyā and Vedānta viewpoint. It is no longer orthodox Buddhism as taught by the Buddha Śākyamuni. The viewpoint that *the nature of dharmas is constant*—that the self-nature of phenomena is always there as with the gold of different pieces of jewelry, the number 3, the responsibility of head cook, and the young girl who becomes a woman—concerned Nāgārjuna enough that he needed to use dialectics to destroy it.

⁂

Nāgārjuna had the great merit of using his extraordinary intelligence to destroy the viewpoints and the teachings that led people far away from the original meaning of the Buddha. During his lifetime and for generations afterwards, people considered Nāgārjuna a second Buddha who came to rescue the first Buddha by ensuring that Shakyamuni would not be misunderstood.

The Buddha taught that "My teachings are like a finger pointing at the moon; you should not confuse the finger for the moon." In doing so, he hoped that people would avoid becoming caught in his words. For example, the Buddha taught that "there is only the present moment" to help people avoid losing themselves in the future or in the past. When the abhidharmists of the Sarvāstivāda school held that *if the present exists, there must be the past—it is only because of the past that the present is here,* they took their argument too far. The Buddha did not want to prove that the present exists. He was not aiming to philosophize, but to help us *stop living in forgetfulness.* If we take this teaching and make it the foundation of a philosophical theory, we have lost the Buddha's intention.

8. *When the effect has not yet arisen*
   its cause cannot cease.
   How can a phenomenon that has ceased condition
      something?
   Therefore there is no continuity condition.

果若未生時
則不應有滅
滅法何能緣
故無次第緣

The aim of this verse is to destroy our view about the continuity condition. This is described as "examining the continuity condition to see it cannot be established." When an effect has not yet arisen, it cannot logically cease. That which came before ceases so that which comes after can arise. The grain of rice has to cease in order for the rice plant to arise. If the rice plant has not arisen, the rice grain has not ceased. The continuity condition refers to uninterrupted continuity. When the effect has not yet arisen the cause has not yet ceased; if it had ceased, it could not now be a condition for something else. Having ceased, it would no longer be present to condition something else.

Nāgārjuna reasons: when the effect has not yet arisen, the cause has not yet ceased. That which we call cessation cannot be—the continuity condition requires *uninterrupted arising and ceasing in the stream of reality*. Something that has ceased can no longer be called a condition, yet without its cessation, its continuation cannot arise. This proves that the continuity condition is simply an idea in our head and is not found in reality.

9. *As proclaimed by the buddhas,*
   the true and wonderful Dharmadhātu
   transcends subject and object of cognition,
   So how could there be an object of cognition as condition?

如諸佛所說
真實微妙法
於此無緣法
云何有緣緣

This verse, called "examining the object of cognition as cause to see it cannot be established" examines the third condition, called *object of cognition as condition*, to reveal its absurdity.

When translating "object of cognition as cause," the Chinese uses three characters (所緣緣). The character 緣 is used twice, and each time it has a different meaning. When combined with the character 所, 緣 means "the object of cognition." When it occurs on its own it simply means "condition." Sometimes these three characters are shortened to just two: 緣緣, as in verse 9 above.

Object of cognition as condition is a technical term in Buddhism. For example, if our hand is measuring a pencil, the hand is the subject of the measurement while the pencil is the object of the measurement. If the eye is looking at a flower, the eye is the subject that looks and the flower is the object looked at. Our mind is the subject and it looks for an object to be its condition. "Condition" here is the object that our cognition approaches and grasps as its object. Cognition contains both the object of cognition and the subject of cognition; they go together. The object of cognition as condition means that if there is no object of cognition, there cannot be a subject that cognizes.

As proclaimed by the buddhas,
the true and wonderful Dharmadhātu

This refers to the realm of the Dharma (Dharmadhātu), which is wonderful and true in the ultimate dimension. The buddhas have spoken about the Dharmadhātu which transcends the view that there is a separate subject and object.

Transcends subject and object of cognition,

In the wonderful realm of the Dharma, there is nothing we can call the grasper or the grasped. There is no subject and no object. For example, in a dream we could see ourselves holding a diploma, a beautiful person, or an important position. Actually there is nothing really there to hold. All these things are simply made up. This is true not only when we dream, but also when we consider ourselves to be awake. When we are awake, we still live as if we were in a dream. Consider the following example.

⚬⟡⚬

In China there is the story of a student who went for the imperial examination. He had devoted himself to his studies for ten years, dreaming of what would happen once he had passed the examination. When he failed the exam he was overwhelmed by despair. On the way back home, hungry and tired, on a mountain slope he saw a hermit cooking a pot of gruel. The hermit looked free and at ease.

The hermit spoke and asked the student, "Where are you going with such a sad look on your face?"

The student replied, "Master, I'm fed up! I don't want to live. My hopes have been destroyed. For ten years I devoted myself to my studies and now I have nothing left. How can I show my face at home?"

"Oh, so you failed your exam . . . "

"That's right."

"How about stopping here to rest for a while before you go on? You can lie down under that tree over there and rest your head on its roots. Take a nap and you will feel better. I am cooking some millet gruel, and when it is ready, I will wake you up so that you can eat some before continuing your journey."

⚜

The young student lay down. As soon as his head touched the root he fell fast asleep and started to dream. In his dream he passed the examination. The emperor sent for him and offered his own beloved daughter in marriage. The young student became a distinguished mandarin and was full of happiness, lacking nothing in fame or position. Then the frontier was threatened by invaders, and the emperor appointed him to go and quell the invasion. Somehow, the invaders flooded over the border despite his efforts. As a result, the emperor gave orders to cut off his head. Just when he was about to be beheaded, he woke up.

The hermit said, "I can tell you slept really well! The millet gruel is not yet ready, but it will be ready soon. Go and wash your face and then I will serve you a bowl."

What happened in the dream must have taken longer than ten years, but it was not long enough for the hermit's gruel to cook. Millet has a golden color; therefore, in Chinese literature the young student's dream is called "the golden millet dream." In his dream, the student's mind went looking for things to grasp. The objects it grasped were clear: an important degree, a wonderful wife, the emperor, an influential position at court, a guillotine, and a headsman. His mind reached out to find all these things and then grasped them. The subject goes to find an object condition for itself.

The object of cognition is a creation of cognition and not an independent reality. It is not a reality that lies outside. When we love someone, we always think that that person is a reality outside of ourselves, but the truth is that the image of the person we love is something we create ourselves. You marry each other, and only three years later do you begin to know the truth!

Transcends subject and object of cognition here means that there is no separation between—and therefore no independent existence of—the object of the grasping and the subject of the grasping. Grasping here means "appropriating." When we read this verse we should understand: "As the buddhas have taught: in the wonderful and true Dharma Realm, all dharmas transcend the notions of subject and object of cognition. So how can there be an object of cognition as condition?"

10. *If phenomena are without a self-nature*
    they do not have the mark of "being."
    For this reason we cannot say
    this is because that is.

諸法無自性
故無有有相
說有是事故
是事有不然

This verse examines the fourth kind of condition, called the *supportive condition*; these are the conditions that help the seed condition become an effect. For example, if the grain of corn is not supported by the soil, the water, and the sun, it will never become a plant of corn. Therefore the soil, the water, and the sun are all supportive conditions. This tenth verse is called *examining the supportive condition to see it cannot be established.*

If phenomena are without a self-nature. This means that no phenomenon has a separate self-nature, as we have seen earlier.

They do not have the mark of "being." In other words, if things have no own-being, they do not possess the mark of being. In Sanskrit the word for being is *sat* and the word for nonbeing is *asat.* In this verse we see that the essence of all phenomena is neither being nor nonbeing. We have a notion: "That thing exists," but we have to be careful because our idea of being is far from the truth. If we then say, "Ah, then it does not exist," that is also not correct. Only when there is *is* can there be *is not.* If *is* is not, how can there be *is not*? Is and is not are a pair of opposites that need each other. Phenomena, such as a pen or a flower, do not have a separate self-nature, they do not have a separate essence or reality. They do not have the characteristics of being and nonbeing. If we say that they exist, we are wrong, and if we say that they do not exist, we are also wrong. For this reason we cannot say, as the sutras do, "This is because that is." We cannot say, for example, "Left is because right is." In the third and fourth lines of verse 10, Nāgārjuna tells us that "This is because that is" is not evident. "This is because that is" is an essential phrase! In the Āgamas and Nikāyas the Buddha teaches this many times.

In this verse Nāgārjuna says that since things do not have a self-nature, they do not have the characteristic of *being*. Therefore, Nāgārjuna asserts, we cannot say "This is because that is." It seems as if he is disparaging the Buddha's most important teaching about conditioned co-arising! Although on the surface, yes, he seems to be contradicting the Buddha, he is in fact a soulmate of the Buddha who helps his own contemporaries to understand the Buddha's sentence more deeply. He is helping them not to be caught in the teachings. The Buddha did not want to validate the existence of all that is. He did not want to prove that all things exist or do not exist. He just wanted to show us: *There is a relationship of conditioned co-arising between things. This is like this because that is like that. This is because that is. This ceases because that ceases.* He just wanted to speak about the relational patterns between this and that. Everything is relational patterns.

Earlier we explored the example of a screen and a singer dancing on the screen as being the creation of the screen and the singer. There is a manifestation of the singer because of a relationship between singer and screen, but the screen and the singer do not have a self-nature. They are not separate self-entities.

The Buddha did not want to allow that "this" is real. He did use the words "this is," but he did not want to prove that all things have a self-nature, a real existence. The word "is" refers simply to a manifestation. This manifests because that manifests. In the example of the singer we have a camera, a screen, a light bulb, and a singer. We make the singer manifest on the screen and then we laugh and cry based on what the singer does. She really *manifests*, but the Buddha did not mean to say that she really *is*. If we don't read the sutras carefully, we will think that since the Buddha said *This is because that is* we have to hold on for dear life to the word "is." We have to see what the Buddha meant by *This is because that is* and not be caught in the words he used. Our spiritual ancestors often said, "If you explain the meaning of the Dharma relying on the sutras, you betray the buddhas of the three times." This means that if we depend on single words in the sutras to explain the meaning of the teachings, we are doing a real injustice to the buddhas of the past, present, and future.

It is the disciples of the Buddha who do the most harm to his teachings. Disciples of the Buddha are not necessarily his soulmates because many of them misunderstand him. He knew that this would happen and said, "I have not said anything that you say I said. In the last forty-five years I did not say a single thing!" This expresses the suffering of a spiritual teacher who has been greatly misunderstood. Whenever he said something, people would take hold of it and make all kinds of wrong deductions. In the end it seemed better to say nothing because saying something was so risky. *This is because that is; this arises because that arises; this is like this because that is like that*—these sentences simply mean what they say, but later generations interpreted them as proof that the Buddha taught that there *is* birth and death. Nāgārjuna was a continuation of and a real disciple of the Buddha. This is why many people say he is not a Mahayanist, but a teacher of original Buddhism. When he saw how the Buddha was greatly misunderstood he used the sharp sword of dialectics to cut through the ropes that were trying to tie the Buddha to this or that theory or doctrine.

The Sarvāstivāda teachings, which belong to the Mainstream Schools of Buddhism, had deviated from the teachings of original Buddhism by taking them in the direction of realism. This was risky; it came close to proposing that there is something like a true self that lies deep within phenomena: the concept of ātman (the soul or the self) found in the Vedānta. The Buddha had freed the Dharma from this idea, but then people tried to resuscitate it. Ātman was a basic and early teaching of Brahmanism, and the Buddha won a formidable battle against this concept to liberate people from the idea of a separate self. It was his disciples themselves who then pulled Buddhism back into the belief in a separate self. In the Sarvāstivāda school, the four great commentators of the Vibhāṣā used four examples to prove the underlying reality of things. Although they tried to keep the teaching of the three Dharma Seals—impermanence, no-self, and nirvāṇa—their realistic approach, articulated in the theory *the three times exist, the nature of things is constant,* had gone far from the teachings of the Buddha. It opened the way for the concept of something eternal that lies deep in the heart of things to infiltrate the Buddha's teachings. Whether that thing is called nirvāṇa or suchness, it comes close to being a separate self and therefore betrays the Buddha.

What some people call the Mahāyāna of Nāgārjuna is nothing more than an effort to make original Buddhism clear again. The Mainstream Schools of Buddhism had gone farther from the teachings of original Buddhism than did Mahāyāna Buddhism.

In the Alagadūppama Sutta (MN 22)* the Buddha said, "My teachings are like a raft for you to cross over to the other shore." You should not mistake the raft for the shore! Often people are caught in the Buddha's teachings; this is like holding on to the raft as if the raft itself were the shore of liberation.

The First Mindfulness Training of the Order of Interbeing*† tells us that we should not be caught in any doctrine or ideology—not even Buddhist ones. The Fourteen Mindfulness Trainings of the Order of Interbeing reflect deeply and faithfully the nondogmatic spirit of original Buddhism, which is not being caught in any idea, even if that idea was taught by the Buddha himself.

In the last line of the verse *This is because that is,* "this" is understood to be the effect and "that" refers to the conditions that brought about the effect. *That* is the supportive condition for *this.* This verse demonstrates that the supportive condition does not truly exist; it is empty of a separate self-nature. There is nothing that can

---

* Translated and commented on by the author in *Thundering Silence*, Parallax Press, 1993, 2008.

† The Fourteen Mindfulness Trainings of the Order of Interbeing are discussed in detail in *Interbeing*, Parallax Press, 1987, 2020.

be said to be, because nothing has a self-nature. That is why the phrase *this is because that is,* when understood literally, is not correct.

The introductory verses with which Nāgārjuna began this text express his deepest respect for the Buddha.

> *I bow down to him,*
> *the supreme and excellent teacher.*

Nowhere does he contradict the Buddha's teachings. We need to understand these verses in this spirit: Nāgārjuna wants to destroy the contemporary misunderstandings surrounding the Buddha's declaration that *this is because that is.*

11. *Looking into conditions, at length or in brief,*
    we are not able to see the effect.
    If it is not found in the conditions
    how can we say the effect arises from the conditions?

略廣因緣中
求果不可得
因緣中若無
云何從緣出

In the first line, 略 means "briefly" and 廣 means "extensively." We could translate the first two lines of this verse as, *Looking deeply into causes and conditions, either extensively or briefly, we cannot see the self-nature of an effect.* For example, when we look into a match we are not able to see the self-nature of the fire. The nature of the fire is heat, warmth, and the capacity to burn. Looking into what people call causes and conditions of an effect, we are not able to see the nature of that effect. We cannot see the characteristics (*lakṣaṇa*) of the effect in the causes and conditions, nor can we see the self-nature (*svabhāva*).

If the nature of the effect produced cannot be seen in its causes and conditions, why are we so bold as to say that it arises from those conditions?

12. *If you say that the effect is not in the conditions,*
    but that the effect arises from the conditions,
    then why does not that effect
    arise from what are not its conditions?

若謂緣無果
而從緣中出
是果何不從
非緣中而出

Here we are speaking of cause and effect. Causes give rise to effects. Looking into the causes, we can discern whether they will have a certain effect or not. The first possibility is that the effect is *in* those causes. The second possibility is that the effect is *not* in them. For example, looking into a hen (the cause) we see the egg and the chick (the effect). Thus, apparently the effects are already in the cause, but something that already *is* does not need to arise or be produced. To arise or be produced means that from nonbeing something comes into being. If something is already there, then why should it arise? This reasoning leads to the conclusion that things are unarisen: because the effect is already in the cause.

We may alternatively say that the effect is *not* in the cause. For example, the egg and the chick are not in a table, so how could we say that the table produces the egg? When we look into a cause and cannot see an effect, then it is obvious that this cause cannot give rise to that effect. How can a table give rise to an egg? In this case we come to the conclusion that the egg cannot arise. If the effect is not there in the conditions, then it cannot arise.

The substance of the twelfth verse is, "If we say that the effect is not in the conditions, then we cannot say that this effect arises from the conditions. If it can arise from a condition in which it is not present, then why does that effect not arise from a non-condition?" The term 非緣 (non-condition) means "something that is not a condition for the effect," just like the table is not a condition for the chick. A chick cannot possibly be born from a table; therefore, the table is a non-condition. A chick is born from a hen, so the hen is a condition for the chick, but before the chick is born *the chick is already present in the hen.* If we say the chick is *not* present in the hen then the hen would be a non-condition. If the chick is already there in the hen, *it does not need to be born.* We can conclude that there is no birth, no arising. Birth is just a notion that we create in our mind, it is not a reality. The effect is not in conditions, and also not in non-conditions; this is why conditions and non-conditions are no different from each other.

13. *If the effect comes from conditions,*
   those conditions do not have a self-nature.
   If, then, the effect comes from conditions that do not
      have a self-nature,
   how can it be said to come from those conditions?

若果從緣生
是緣無自性
從無自性生
何得從緣生

If the effect arises from conditions, those conditions must not have a self-nature; if they did, they would be unchanging and always remain themselves, incapable of giving rise to something else. If the effect, however, comes from something without a self-nature, then why do we say that it arises from conditions? We have to remember that the first chapter of the Verses on the Middle Way points a bayonet toward the concept of a self-nature. The idea of a self (*ātman*, the soul) that lies under all that changes but does not itself change had long been a part of Brahmanism, in the Vaiśeṣika and Saṃkhyā philosophies. When the Buddha was teaching, he made a revolutionary declaration: *what you call a soul or a self is not there.* He showed us the nature of phenomena, saying: t*here are only phenomena and behind those phenomena there is nothing immortal or unchanging—not even the unchanging ātman or Brahman.*

The Buddha only recognized the psychesoma (*nāmarūpa*), the coming together of the five skandhas: body, feelings, perceptions, mental formations, and consciousness (body being the soma or *rūpa* and the next four skandhas being the psyche or *nāma*). Looking into this composite we see that everything is changing; nothing can endure for any length of time. We see clearly that there is nothing solid and unchanging to be equated with the self or the soul of Brahmanism. Therefore, there is no self (*anātman*). All that we experience is impermanent and changing, like the five skandhas. Looking deeply into the skandhas we are unable to grasp at anything eternal or constant. These teachings are very practical, and when the Buddha manifested he set this important revolution in contemporary thought into motion.

Brahmanism holds that lying underneath the anāt-man (what Buddhists call the five skandhas) is the ātman. According to this teaching, by meditating on the individual self (*ātman*) one sees that it is one with the ultimate (*brahman*).

The Buddha used the teachings of impermanence and nonself to point a bayonet at the notions of *ātman* and *brahman*. Both of these notions involve the idea of a separate self and an immortal soul. Well-known Hindu texts were refined to respond to Buddhist teachings. Nowhere do the teachings of the Buddha accept a separate self, a self-nature, or an own-being. Brahmanic teachings reacted to this insight by arguing strongly in favor of a separate self. The Buddha's disciples, in turn, had to develop the Buddha's teachings as a response.

The Buddha's teachings powerfully influenced the historical development of Indian thought. The Buddha categorically denied the idea of ātman and brahman. His phenomenological way of looking perceived all things as impermanent and without a separate self. The upholders of Brahmanism reacted strongly to this and continued to react centuries after the Buddha had passed away. On this account the Mainstream Buddhist Schools had to develop their tenets to oppose the attack of Brahmanism.

During the lifetime of the Buddha and for hundreds of years afterward ideological and philosophical debate flourished in India. The Sarvāstivāda school developed and refined a profuse Abhidharma literature, mainly represented by the Vibhāṣā. The Vibhāṣā develops the notion of a self-nature and maintains that the three times are real, though the self is not. According to this theory, matter can be divided into small particles or atoms (*aṇu*) and time into instants (*kṣaṇa*, an extremely short period of milliseconds). The Sarvāstivādins split time and space into its most elementary particles and said that, though everything is changing, elements underlying these changes in time and space are real and made up of the self. According to the Vibhāṣā, the self is not real but the elements which make up the self do exist.

The Sarvāstivāda wanted to be faithful to the Buddha and his teachings, so they maintained that there was no self. Despite this, they claimed that the elements that give us the feeling that there is a self *are* real. The basic tenet of the Sarvāstivāda school is *there is no self but there are elements*. These elements are the *aṇu* of matter and the *kṣaṇa* of time. *These elements exist but the self does not*. In the theory that *there is no self but there are elements*, the Sarvāstivāda comes very close to a self-nature. This is not orthodox Buddhism, which is to say it is not faithful to what the Buddha taught. The Sarvāstivāda school was a branch of the conservative Sthaviravāda, but because it had to compete with Brahmanic theories it developed and refined theories of its own. Out of this need to contend with Brahmanism, the Sarvāstivāda arrived at a dangerous idea with the potential to deny the original teachings of the Buddha on no self.

Contemporary to the Sarvāstivāda school was another important Buddhist school: the Sautrāntika school. The particularity of the Sautrāntika school was that it held fast to and followed the words of the original sutras; it only based its arguments on these sutras and refused to rely on other documents and arguments, and they had no interest in composing new Abhidharma material like the Vibhāṣā. They simply adhered faithfully to the words of the sutras, as evidenced by their name, which means "relying on the sutras." A basic tenet of this school is "the past does not exist, the future does not exist, only the present exists." They had probably read the Bhaddekaratta Sutta (MN 131)* where the Buddha taught:

> *Do not pursue the past.*
> *Do not lose yourself in the future.*
> *The past no longer is.*
> *The future has not yet come.*
> *Looking deeply at life as it is*
> *in the very here and now,*
> *the practitioner dwells*
> *in stability and freedom.*

---

* Translated by the author as the Sutra on the Better Way to Live Alone in *Our Appointment with Life*, Parallax Press, 1990, 2010.

The Sautrāntikas had read this sutra or others like it, but did not have the insight that the three times inter-are. They maintained instead that only the present was real and that the past and the future are merely ideas. They claimed to be the school closest to the Buddha's teachings because the Buddha himself had said: "The past is already gone, the future has not yet arrived, there is only the present."

The Sarvāstivāda school, on the other hand, maintained that the past, present, and future were all real. The Sautrāntikas accepted the Sarvāstivāda's notions of aṇu and kṣaṇa. They also thought that something must connect a thing to what it becomes as part of the cycle of birth and death of phenomena. As a result, the Sautrāntikas arrived at the peculiar idea that there is a self, but that this self is found neither in the skandhas nor outside of them.* This idea was later taken up by many other Buddhist schools.

Where can we find the self? Is it in the five skandhas or outside of the five skandhas? Two viewpoints are common. One is that the self is found in the skandhas, the other that it is found outside of the skandhas. The Sautrāntika viewpoint is a third viewpoint, namely that the self that is found neither inside nor outside of the skandhas. This idea, which is challenging to understand,

---

* 非即非離蘊我.

was used to explain why there is a continuation between cause and result. They called this idea of a self *pudgala*. Pudgala means the person, but the Sautrāntikas used the word pudgala rather than ātman to mean the self.

The Sautrāntikas often quoted from the sutras: "Bhikkhus, there is a *person* whose appearance in the world is of great benefit for so many people."[*] The *person* in this sentence is the Buddha; thanks to the Buddha appearing in the world, countless people overcame their suffering. According to the Sautrāntikas, the sutra says "there is a person," so why would you say there isn't a person, a self? The person is a pudgala. The Tathāgata is a person. We do not have a self, but we have a person. The Sautrāntikas looked for a self that could explain continuation in the round of birth and death. This is completely unorthodox, as far as Buddhism is concerned.

The Sarvāstivāda, Sautrāntika, and other schools did not want to betray the Buddha. They wanted to be loyal to the teachings of impermanence and no self. However, the opponents of Buddhism (who maintained the existence of ātman and brahman) attacked them with such force that they had to come to a compromise and explain continuation from one life to the next with what would later become the teachings called Pudgalavāda. When Master

---

[*] AN 1.13 and EA 8.2.

Xuanzang came to India in the seventh century to bring Buddhist texts back to China, the prospering Pudgalavāda tradition comprised 70,000 monks. The idea of pudgala that arose in the Sautrāntika school was very important.

The difference between Buddhism and Brahmanism was becoming blurred. In the beginning Buddhism and Brahmanism were distinct, but as time went on the boundary between the two was eroded. Today, people often confuse Buddhism with Vedānta.

This is why the first chapter of the Verses on the Middle Way aims its bayonet at the idea of self-nature. Nāgārjuna did not aim at Brahmanic philosophies but at Buddhist ones: he saw that the Sarvāstivāda and Sautrāntika Schools had gone too far. He wanted to be faithful to the Buddha and to correct the mistakes being made in the Mainstream Schools of the time.

The first chapter of the Verses on the Middle Way criticizes the viewpoint of a self-nature. Only when you understand that, can you understand the following text: *If the effect comes from conditions, but looking into those conditions you see they are always changing and do not have a true substance, then those conditions do not have a self-nature. If, then, the effect comes from conditions that do not have a self-nature, how can it be said to come from those conditions?* Nāgārjuna thus lays the irrationality of this argument bare.

14. *There is no effect that arises from conditions,*
    nor an effect that arises from non-conditions.
    Since there is no effect,
    there are neither conditions nor non-conditions.

果不從緣生
不從非緣生
以果無有故
緣非緣亦無

This verse is the concluding verse of the chapter. It says that the effect does not arise from conditions nor from non-conditions and that, because the self-nature of the effect is not there, the self-nature of conditions or of non-conditions is also not there. This brings us to the concept of nonbeing. Since the effect has no characteristic of real existence, the conditions and non-conditions have no real existence either.

We have to understand this verse in light of verse 13. The effect does not arise from conditions or from non-conditions because the nature of the effect is not something real. Therefore, what are called conditions or non-conditions cannot be real either.

2

EXAMINATION OF
COMING AND GOING

1. *That which has already gone is not going;*
   that which has not yet gone is not going.
   Besides already-gone and not-yet-gone,
   the present going cannot be known.

已去無有去
未去亦無去
離已去未去
去時亦無去

In this, as in the last chapter, Nāgārjuna brings our attention to certain Sarvāstivāda and Sautrāntika theories on
time and on self-nature.

When somebody has died we say that the person is
gone, and when someone is born we say that the baby
has arrived. Arriving means that from not being we

become something, while going means that from being we become nothing.

When we go looking for what we call "going" we cannot find it in the past, in the future, or even in the present. In English, when someone dies we also say they have "passed away," which means that from here they go over there.

The main thesis of this verse is that the idea of *going* is simply an idea in our mind. In reality there is no such thing as going.

If we look for the act of going in the past, we cannot see it. Since the act of going belongs to the past, we cannot possibly see it now. In the present we cannot see the existence of a subject that goes or a place that it has gone to.

Someone who has gone is not going somewhere, nor is someone who has not yet gone going. When we say that someone is going, or has not yet gone, this means that they are still alive! How could going or dying be found while someone is still alive? In the end, going is not found in any of the three times. The next verse is the antithesis of this proposition.

2. *When the act of going is taking place,*
    there is going;
   There is no having-gone nor not-yet-gone at the time
       of going,
   but there is going at the time of going.

動處則有去
此中有去時
非已去未去
是故去時去

This is the higher mathematics of Nāgārjuna. This verse represents the standpoint of the interlocutor: the going actually exists. We do not see the act of going in the past, and cannot yet see it happening in the future, but in the present we *do* see it happening. If we now reread the previous verse, we might ask, "Why would you say there is no going?"

動處 means literally where the going is happening. In the place where the going is happening, how can you say there is no going? 去時 means literally "time of going." The present moment of going does not refer to something that has gone or to something that is about to go. According to the interlocutor, this proves that at the present moment of going we can see the going. The interlocutor wants to prove that there actually is a going and a time of going. They recognize that the going is not found in what is already gone or in what has not yet gone, but they also stress that when the act of going is taking place, there *is* going. They say it is incorrect to deny the existence of going because at the time of going, there is going; this proves that there is such a thing as going. This is a way we all reason, and Nāgārjuna responds to this objection in the following verse.

3. *How could the fact of going be there*
   during the time of going?
   If there is no fact of going
   how can there be a time of going?

云何於去時
而當有去法
若離於去法
去時不可得

If there is no fact of going, there is no time of going. Only if there is going can there be a time of going.

We all object to Nāgārjuna and say that while the action of going is happening there is going. How could there not be? The action of going proves that there is a time of going in the present moment, which means that there is an action of going and a time of going; going has a framework—the time of going.

How do we understand the word "go"? To go in this case means to go out of sight: having been something, to become nothing. There is going and arriving, but where do you come from? In your mind you think that at birth, you automatically become something from nothing. You have a concept of coming into existence or of coming into being. Previously something did not exist, and then, automatically, it started to exist. "Arriving" means this: it was not before, but now it is. And what is "going"? Going means going out of existence.

In the teachings of the Buddha, nirvāṇa is non-arriving and non-going. As far as our daily life is concerned, we perceive arriving and going. This is the conventional truth. Looking deeply, however, we see no arriving and no going. This is the ultimate truth. Nāgārjuna's purpose was to throw open the hatch of conventional reality so that we can see into the depths of ultimate reality. The Diamond Sutra says that wherever there is a sign (an object of perception) there is deception. We are caught in and deceived by the sign *arriving* and then *going*. Nāgārjuna says: "Dear friend, don't be deceived! Let me tear apart the veil of notions." He uses dialectics in order to show us that what we call "arriving" does not truly exist and that what we call "going" does not truly exist either.

There are many ways that lead us to the truth. The Vijñānavāda school examined the characteristics of phenomena, while the Dharma-nature tradition examined the underlying essence. Nāgārjuna used the method of dialectics.

In the second verse Nāgārjuna presents to us objections of people who reflect our own misunderstanding. Just like them, we also understand that when we haven't yet gone, there is no going, and that when we have gone, we also cannot see the going but that, clearly, at the time of going, the going is really there. How could we say otherwise?

Nāgārjuna continues: "How, at the present moment of going, could there be a going?" How could it be possible that at the time of going we can see the truth of going? Before a woman has gone, she is still alive. When she passes, we say she has gone. But while she is on her deathbed, she is not going anywhere; she is still alive. The time of going in the present moment is an idea and so is the going. Before we go we do not see going, and after we have gone we do not see going. Even at the time of going we do not see it!

The practice of meditation requires us to look deeply. There are things that a superficial look will not reveal. When we speak of "going," we mean there is both a goer, who performs the action of going, and the action itself, which is the going. If there isn't a goer, how can there be going? We are getting in touch with a basic Buddhist teaching: there is *neither an actor nor an acting*. Going is an action. The subject who goes and the act of going are based on the premise that there is a present time of going. For the whole time of the action there is presumed to be an actor and an act.

In Plum Village we usually learn that the past has already gone, the future has not yet come, and there is only the present moment. We come close to following the doctrine of Nāgārjuna's opponents when we say that there is no past and no future, that there is only the present and that we have to live the present moment deeply. However, when we say this we are aware that we are speaking in terms of conventional truth and not of the ultimate truth. According to the conventional truth *we* are eating and *we* are going to bed; we use personal pronouns like you, we, and I to distinguish one person from another. But if we tear apart the net of conventional truth, we are able to see the ultimate truth.* The language of the second verse employs the conventional truth. Nāgārjuna does not deny conventional truth, but he wants to tear it apart to reveal the ultimate truth.

The theories of the Sarvāstivāda School represent analysis at its peak. These theories say that reality is simply atoms (aṇu) and instants (kṣaṇa) in an attempt to prove the teaching of no self. According to this theory there is nothing eternal, enduring, or unchanging. When faced with the problem of how these atoms and instants relate to each other to give the impression of a continuous

---

* In the chapter "Examination of the Four Noble Truths" Nāgārjuna demonstrates how there are these two kinds of truth; the conventional and the ultimate.

life force, the Sarvāstivāda school resorts to a theory of self-nature (*svabhāva*).

Consider again the example of the woman. When she is young she is called a girl, later she becomes a wife, a mother, and in the end even a grandmother. Therefore, although the girl, the wife, the mother, and the grandmother are four different roles, there is something underneath that connects them—the self-nature. This teaching is dangerous and can devalue the Buddhist teachings. The idea of a self-nature can lead people to conclude that a self underlies all the things we consider nonself.

Nāgārjuna was perturbed by this and so in the first chapter of the Verses on the Middle Way he aimed his bayonet at a self-nature. When we say someone goes, there is clearly an entity that does not change, at least for the time that the going is happening. Once we establish a subject, we establish a self.

If we are in touch deeply with the present moment, we see that it contains the past moment and the future moment. We see that the past has not gone anywhere at all! It is still complete, right there in the present moment, and it has the form of the present moment. Our happiness and suffering from the past are in the present moment. If we are in touch deeply with the present moment, we are also in touch with the happiness and the suffering of the past. If a past wound has not yet healed, it is still there.

Some unkind words spoken to our mother are still there unless we have taken the time to transform them and to begin anew.

If we touch the present moment deeply, we can also be in touch with the future. In Plum Village we learn that to worry about the future is useless—the way to ensure a beautiful future is to take good care of the present moment. Taking care of the present is the only way we can build a future. Although the future has not yet come, we can already be in touch with it. Everything we do for the present, we do for the future. To be in touch with the present is to be in touch with the past and the future. This is the view of interbeing. We do not simply say, "The past has already gone, the future is not yet there, there is only the present moment." Our present moment cannot exist independently from the past and the future. Even though we say that the past has already gone and the future is not yet here, the truth is that our practice reveals that the past and the future are found in the present moment. This insight of the Avataṃsaka Sutra—that the one contains the all—is followed closely in Plum Village; it helps us not get caught in the notions of permanence or a self.

When we hear the Buddha say that the past is no longer there and the future has not yet come, we have to understand his words intelligently. If we think that the Buddha negates the past and the future and only recognizes the present, we have not understood. Past, present, and future are all ideas. The correct understanding is that the past contains the present and the future; the present contains the past and the future.

The American philosopher William James, in his work *The Principles of Psychology,** discussed the notion of the present moment. He wrote that the present is not a knife-edge with no duration. The present always has its own duration. We sit on that duration of time as on a saddle looking at the past and the future.[†]

Nāgārjuna's opponents argued that there is a person who is going during the time of going, even if that time is no longer than ten or twenty milliseconds. However, according to the teachings on impermanence, the person who was going in the previous instant is not the same as the person who is going in the following instant. Thus in contemplating the time of going we see that there isn't really a person going. If there is a person who is going, then there is a self, but if there is not a person who is going, how can there be the act of going?

---

* William James, *The Principles of Psychology* (New York: H. Holt and Company, 1905), Chapter 15 on the Perception of Time.

† "In short the practically cognized present is no knife-edge but a saddle-back, with a certain breadth of its own, on which we sit perched, and from which we look in two directions of time. The unit of our perception of time is a duration with a bow and a stern. . . . " William James, *Principles of Psychology*.

In 1968 I came up with a poem called "The Great Lion's Roar" while I was in the British Museum. This poem came from my insight and not from fanciful imagining. The poem begins like this:

> *Clouds float, white clouds float;*
> *the sweetbriar blooms.*
> *Floating is the clouds;*
> *blooming is the flower.*

If there were not the cloud, how could there be the floating? And if there were no flower, how could there be blooming? How could we understand this stanza without knowing that it arose from meditation? The poem continues:

> *One sweetbriar blossom opens.*
> *White clouds float in clusters.*
> *Without clouds there is no floating;*
> *without flowers there is no blooming.*
> *Clouds are the floating.*
> *Flowers are the blooming.*

If there is no subject, there is no action, but if we acknowledge there is a subject, we also acknowledge a self. In reality that acknowledgement is not correct, because everything changes at every moment. If finding the subject is not possible, how can there be an action?

How could the fact of going be there during the time of going? This means: How, at the time of going, can you find the action of going? *If there is no fact of going, how can there be a time of going?* If, as it seems, there is no act of going, how can there be a time of going?

When we look at an unlit match we cannot see the flame. When we strike the match we see a flame and we say, "The flame has arrived!" If the flame exists, it has come from somewhere into existence. We ask: "Where did the flame come from?" It arrives as a real entity from a place of nonexistence. "It arrives" here means from nothing it becomes something. Arriving means coming into existence. In the action of arriving there must be a subject which arrives, but where do we find this subject? Who are you? Why have you come here? Who am I? What brought me here? That is our gong an.* Someone comes, but who is that someone? It is like the gong an in the Chan school: "Who is reciting the Buddha's name?" Those who practice this gong an should know that Nāgārjuna also practiced like this; he can help us practice it successfully.

---

* Gong an refers to a saying or a story recorded from meditation masters of the past. It is a subject of reflection to be used as a skillful means to help us realize awakening. See Thich Nhat Hanh, *The Admonitions and Encouraging Words of Master Guishan*, pp 125 ff., Parallax Press, 2022.

The flame is gone! Do we feel some regret or miss the flame? Where did the flame go? Did it really go? Was there a time of its going? And how long did it take to go? We are restless people, busy making a living, building our houses, looking for work, and taking care of our children. Do we have time to look deeply into concerns like this that are so essential to our lives? We are alive, but we do not know who we are. The flame comes as if it were a self. It is still there, but we know that tomorrow, or in the next moment, it will not be there anymore.

Now the flame has gone. Before it went, we did not see its going. Now that it has gone, we do not see its going. When it went, we did not see a time of going, not even if that time was only a millisecond. Why? Because there is no subject that goes, and thus there is no action of going.

The Manifestation-only school found a way to reveal what Nāgārjuna shows using dialectics. Manifestation-only means there is only manifestation—there is no arising or coming into being; there is no destruction, there is only hiding. There is no coming and no going. The Manifestation-only way of looking is a different way of looking that can help us understand this. We ask, "Where is the flame?" "Who are you? You will come, but where will you come from?" We say, "You will be born and then you will die." This is how we see things. In truth, if we look carefully we see that nothing is born and nothing dies, nothing arrives or goes away. When certain conditions come together, you manifest; when conditions are no longer sufficient, you hide. The Manifestation-only way of looking helps us to see this. If you look deeply according to the Manifestation-only school teachings you will also see the nature of no-coming and no-going in everything.

When an acquaintance or a loved one hides we do not weep, because we know that it is not a departure. It is not that they have become nothing after being something. They have not gone out of existence. When they are manifesting we do not say they have come into existence, and when they die we do not say they go out of existence. We only say that somebody has gone out of existence because we grasped onto the idea that they were really existing while they were manifesting. When they go into hiding we cling to the idea that they no longer exist.

No coming and no going is the practice of freedom—of nirvāṇa. There are people who translate the word nirvāṇa into English as freedom. Freedom is freedom from ideas; it is not being in the grip of ideas of being and nonbeing, of coming and going. Nāgārjuna has his way of helping us to find freedom and likewise Asaṅga, a founder of the Manifestation-only school, has his way of helping us to find freedom. I also have my own ways of helping you to find freedom; for example by writing calligraphy that reads: "You are not a creation, you are a manifestation."

The term manifestation can help us to overcome our ideas of birth and death and our ideas of coming and going, but if we are not cautious we can still become caught and think *there is someone* who is manifesting. We have to see manifestation in the light of impermanence and nonself to dwell in the insight of the Buddha.

Let's try practicing by contemplating a flame. Normally we see the flame in terms of signs—that is, based on its usual appearance. Are you able to see the signless nature of the flame? Can you see the flame in the sulfur, in the wood, and in the oxygen? We know that without oxygen the flame would not be able to manifest. We need to be able to see the flame apart from its usual appearance. The same is true for the Buddha. We need to be able to see him in a signless way. The Buddha taught:

> *If you see me in form,*
> *or search for me in sound,*
> *you are practicing the wrong path,*
> *and cannot see the Tathāgata.**

---

* Vajracchedikāprajñāpāramitā, the Diamond Sutra.

This is to say that the people who want to see the Buddha by looking at his outer form or find him by listening to his voice are going on a mistaken path and will not see him. The verse tells us to look for the Buddha with the eyes of signlessness. We have been looking with the eyes of signlessness for the flame; once we can see the flame in this way, then we can also see the Buddha and ourselves. We find the flame, the Buddha, and ourselves by looking deeply to see that the flame cannot be contained in the mental boxes called *coming* or *going, still there* or *no longer there, being* or *nonbeing*. Only when we see this are we able to see the nature, or *suchness*, of the flame. Once we have seen the flame in this way we will also be able to see the Buddha, our beloved, and our enemy in the same way. Our mind will then be completely empty, no longer in the grips of any idea or notion. We will be able to say, "My dear little flame, I have seen you! Your nature is neither being nor nonbeing, neither birth nor death. When conditions come together we see you. When we see you we do not have ideas that you exist or do not exist. When you manifest, we perceive that you are not being and at the same time you are not nonbeing, so when you cease to manifest what reason is there for us to cry? We see very clearly that your reality does not come or go, and we are no longer caught in the ideas of coming and going." This is a great freedom!

To practice the Buddha's teachings is a great happiness; it gives us a good chance of being in touch with the freedom we call nirvāṇa. Nirvāṇa lies in the present moment. The flame abides in nirvāṇa. We long for or miss the flame because we are not there with it in nirvāṇa.

4. *It is a mistake to say that there is going*
   during the time of going.
   Without going, how could the time of going
   go by itself?

若言去時去
是人則有咎
離去有去時
去時獨去故

The time of going here represents the actor who is doing the action. There must be a subject who goes in order for the going to take place, but we cannot see any subject going! Instead of a subject that goes, the opponent in verse 2 says that the going takes place only with the time of going. Thus we would have to conclude that it is the time of going which goes, and not the subject of the action which goes. By illustrating this absurdity, Nāgārjuna drives his opponent into a place where they have nothing more to say.

There are three ideas: the idea of something that goes (the subject of the verb), the idea of going (the verb), and the idea of the time of going. During the time of going we have the impression that these three things exist. Looking with the light of impermanence and nonself, we see that there is no one going. If there is no one going, how can there be going? How can there be what we assume is a time of going? Is there any good reason for saying that the time of going goes on its own?

⁂

Now we will practice looking with the light of manifestation, non-manifestation, and conditioned co-arising. When we look at the flame carefully, we see that it does not really arrive. In the idea of arriving there must be something arriving, and if we say that there is something arriving it means that it already existed before arriving. If it already existed, it does not need to come into being. We learned this in the last chapter: *If the effect is already present in the conditions, it does not need to arise anymore.* In this chapter, Nāgārjuna is not using the word "arise" but rather the word "arrive."'

If there is arriving, there must be something arriving! If there isn't a subject of the verb, how can there be the verb? If there isn't a cloud, how can there be floating? And if there isn't a flower, how can there be blooming?

unreasonableness of what they are saying and to let go of their view.

5. *If there is going in the time of going,*
   then there are two goings:
   the first is the time of going,
   and the second is the act of going.

若去時有去
則有二種去
一謂為去時
二謂去時去

If in the present moment of going, the reality of that going is happening, we create two kinds of going: *the going* and the *the going that is going*. However, there is nothing or no one going. If they have gone they would no longer be there, yet we see that they are still alive and present. Are we looking at the one who goes with the eyes of impermanence and nonself, or with the eyes of permanence and self? If we look at them with the eyes of impermanence and nonself, we discover the ideas we have been caught in and grasping at. We discover our ignorance.

In our daily life, while washing dishes, cleaning vegetables, or gardening, we should know how to use this time to look at ourselves, other people, the trees, and the plants in such a way that we see the true nature of all things. In doing so we gradually untie the ropes that bind us. This is our daily practice. It is the cream of Buddhism: seeing that all mental formations (such as fear, sadness, and complexes of superiority and inferiority) arise from ideas of being, nonbeing, coming, going, self, and other.

For example, in the countryside of Vietnam if you were a poor person, you might walk past the gate of a rich person and envy their heaps of straw, hencoop, and granary full of rice and say, "Good heavens! What a blessing it would be to have a hencoop like that! But the greatest blessing would be that granary full of grain. With a heap of straw like that I could cook my meals for an entire year." You are caught in and long for these things. Yet you are not aware that inside the rich person's house are custom-made, ornate wooden cabinets, rare calligraphies, expensive paintings, and valuable gems.

The same is true for the Buddha's teachings. When we come to the practice we see a couple of Dharma doors that help us to feel relaxed and well. We like these practices very much and we master them in our daily life. Most of us are satisfied just to know how to breathe, survive, and smile, but we are not interested in going into the depths of Buddhism—into the rich person's house—to discover its most precious treasures. This cream of the

Dharma is our true inheritance; with it, we can attain fearlessness, nirvāṇa, and insight capable of snapping all of the ropes that bind us. That is the greatest aspiration of a practitioner. To be caught in our monastery, in our organization, in our particular group of friends—the shared joys, sadness, and dreams—is a real waste.

Therefore, to learn to transform our anger so that we can survive, smile, say a few kind words to another person, and be just a little less angry is good, but it is not our deepest aspiration. Our deepest aspiration is complete freedom. Therefore, we have to devote our lives to the practice with true determination. That is the heroic resolve we need to commit to in order to realize freedom.

6. *If there are two goings,*
   there must be two subjects who go.
   Without a subject who goes,
   how can we establish the fact of going?

若有二去法
則有二去者
以離於去者
去法不可得

7. *If there is no subject who goes,*
   the act of going will be impossible.

When there is not an act of going,
how can there be someone who goes?

若離於去者
去法不可得
以無去法故
何得有去者

8. *The goer does not go;*
   the non-goer does not go.
   Apart from goer and non-goer,
   there is no third possibility.

去者則不去
不去者不去
離去不去者
無第三去者

When the Buddha walked together with his attendant, the monk Ānanda, he used conventional language, as we do: "Ānanda, do you want to climb that mountain with me?" Here the Buddha used the words *you, me,* and *climb* or *not climb*. Though the Buddha uses conventional language like this in the sutras, we need to know when he is using conventional language and when he is talking in terms of the ultimate truth. The Sautrāntika school used to quote the following: "There is a person whose appearance on earth benefits so many living beings. Who is this person? The Buddha." In this quote we see distinctly that there is *a person*, there is *the appearance* of that person, and there are *benefits* for others. Based on this sentence the teachers of the Sautrāntika school affirmed that there is a person and that there is the arriving of that person (their appearance on earth). This is language that all of us can easily accept.

When an enlightened person says these words, they are not caught in them. They look on the words as conventional designations. When we use someone's name it is to point to a certain reality; the name is a conventional designation used for convenience, just like the words "person," "appearance," "benefit," and "living beings." These terms are things we have mutually agreed upon and are convenient to use.

If we go deeply into the heart of reality, we will see clearly that the person whose name we use—whether it be the Buddha or Śāriputra—transcends this name. The name is merely a convenience that gives us a narrow and relative notion of reality. When we go deeper, we see that the reality of a thing is not contained in its conventional designation.

In our daily speech we say that something arrives or goes, that something is you, is me, is them, is born or dies. When we go deeper into the heart of reality we see that those conventional designations no longer speak the truth. For example, someone may say, "I hate my father and my mother because they have made me suffer my whole life." That hatred and suffering arise from being caught in a perception that father, mother, and myself are separate realities. When we are caught in conventional designations, our suffering and anger flare up. When we look deeply we see that we are in our father and our father is in us. When we see this we go beyond conventional designations and get in touch with a deeper dimension of reality. Quite naturally, our sadness and anger will vanish.

The aim of our practice is to go from the plane of phenomena to the plane of suchness, from the plane of conventional designation to the plane of the Middle Way. The Middle Way transcends conventional designations. When someone sees that they are the continuation of their father and that their father is intact in every cell of their body, the idea of not wanting to have anything to do with him will not arise. We cannot possibly be an independent reality separate from our father. Therefore, anger and hatred towards our father cannot continue, and gradually the situation is transformed.

A wave is only afraid of continuing or ceasing, of being high or low, of going up or going down if it does not know that it is water. Once the wave knows that it has always been water it is not afraid to go up, not afraid to go down. It no longer fears taking this or that form. The important thing is to transcend conventional designations and touch a deeper dimension—nirvāṇa. Nirvāṇa is a reality that transcends every idea: I, you, going up, going down, arriving, going, one, and many.

Nāgārjuna has his way of helping us transcend conventional designations. His dialectics show us that our speech—based on conventional designation—is deceptive. He invites us to inspect conventional designations to see that they are full of contradictions. Seeing these contradictions, we transcend conventional designation and see deeply into reality. As long as we are caught in ideas of I and you, this wave and that wave, and so forth, we have anxiety and fear. When we can transcend I and you, our suffering and anxiety naturally come to an end. We see that we are everything; the wave sees that it is also water.

⚬

Now let us imagine—and this is just imagination, because it does not occur in reality—that there is a border between what is and what is not, between being and nonbeing. Someone is standing on the side of being and gradually they approach the side of nonbeing; once they cross the border, they no longer are. They go from being to nonbeing. We could also imagine the inverse: starting from the opposite side of nonbeing someone goes toward being. This is the idea we all have of birth and death (arriving and going).

Let's imagine again that this person is gradually crossing the border between being and nonbeing. This is the *time* of departing from being and of arriving at nonbeing or of departing from nonbeing and arriving at being. We can think of this process being divided into four stages:

- *In the first stage we see the person wholly on the side of being.*
- *In the second stage they have become ⅔ being and ⅓ nonbeing.*
- *In the third stage they are only ⅓ being and ⅔ nonbeing.*
- *At the fourth stage they are wholly nonbeing.*

In the first three stages the person is still living, but gradually they are dying. This is the time of gradual going. At the time of going there must be a person going, a time of going, and an action of going. Nāgārjuna invites us to examine this. In the first stage the person who goes is still completely there. They can speak, make their last will, and say their last prayer. After this they begin to decompose, and when the decomposition is complete we say that they have gone out of existence. If having arrived on the other side they were still alive, they would not have become nothing. Therefore we have to reexamine our way of thinking, which is deceptive.

Imagine a monastic who wants to go back to lay life. In the beginning they have not gone back, then they have gone back a little, then a little more, and then they go back completely. Those of us who are monastics can ask ourselves: "Where am I?" You may think that you have not gone back to lay life because you still wear the monastic robe and you are called "sister" or "brother." This, however, is not certain. Look again, because you may have begun to go back without being aware of it. Your mind of love and your sense of purpose in the monastic life may have begun to wither. You may be going back to lay life without knowing it. Nothing happens all at once, it happens gradually. The death of a monastic takes place slowly. You think someone is on this side of the border, but in fact they have gone across to the other side. So we have to examine the matter of *arriving* and *going* carefully.

A practitioner of the spiritual path, just like any other phenomenon, is like a candle or a match. When a flame arises it needs to be nourished by fuel, for example by wood and oxygen. The conditions that nourish the flame depend on the amount of wood and the presence of oxygen, both of which keep the flame burning. Once the matchstick comes to an end, the flame can be kept alive by more wood or another match. The life of a practitioner, just like a flame, needs to be nourished by the nutriments necessary for practice. These nutriments are the mind of love and the aspiration to practice in order to transform oneself and to help others. If you are not nourished, you are on the way to death as a practitioner. You are already going back to the life of no practice, and you do not need to wait until you leave the sangha to go back to that life.

As far as our body, feelings, perceptions, mental formations, and consciousness are concerned, we experience constant change, loss, and death. The cells of our body are dying in every moment. Our feelings and perceptions also change and die at every moment of our daily life. Birth is also happening at every moment. There is input and output at every moment. We do not need to wait for death to happen at a certain moment. Birth gradually gives way to death. Birth and death are taking place at every moment of our daily life. Life and death support each other.

If you say there is going, it means there is going at every moment. If you say there is arriving, it means there is arriving at every moment. When you breathe out, your out-breath is a departure from the inside to the outside of your body. When you breathe in, your in-breath brings outside elements into you. Your in-breath could be the out-breath of someone else. There is no doubt that someone else's breath is in your breath. Look and you will see. When there are two hundred people sitting in a hall, they are all breathing. Without a doubt the out-breath of one person will become the in-breath of someone else. You breathe in through your nose and the air is in contact with your flesh. The air goes back and forth between people all the time, making a close connection between us.

Our ever-changing body, feelings, perceptions, and mental formations—including our joy and our sorrow— are also closely connected to each other. Clusters converging and diverging at every moment show us that arriving and going happen at every moment. When we look carefully, we do not see a goer that can be recognized as an identical and unchanging reality.

We imagine that we go through space and time and that the one who is going is always the same. In truth it is not like this because impermanence takes place at every instant. We cannot find a real, unchanging person who goes. The one who goes *is* the going, and the one who goes at this moment is not the one who goes in the next moment.

If we imagine that the one who goes remains intact while going, we are wrong. We are caught in the idea of *someone* who goes, in the idea of *going*, and in the idea of *a time* in the present when there is going. We are caught in conventional designations. The line of demarcation between being and nonbeing is being crossed at every moment—even while someone is seen to be on the side of being. Thus we are able to remove the line of demarcation that we have imagined to exist. We can see that the thing which we think is not there actually exists in the present moment. Being and nonbeing, arriving and going, always go together, like a form and its shadow.

As far as the opposites of arriving and going are concerned, when we say *arrive* we think that from nothing something comes into existence. As far as the flame is concerned, if we say that it comes from nothing, we are wrong. We imagine that there is a side called *nothing* and that from there *something* arrives at the side called being. This is a perversion of the truth. If we are caught in the signs of the flame, caught in the color red, the heat, and the burning, then we have not yet seen the flame. Our view is caught in the signs. The Buddha said: "If someone attempts to see me by means of my physical form, they have not yet seen me."

The flame could also say: "If you want to recognize me by my physical form, color, or sound, then you will not recognize me!" We ourselves are not different from the flame. When other people have an idea about us, we can say to them, "Dear friend, do not think that I am the image you have of me in your mind. It's not like that!" The flame says the same. Maybe it is smiling at us.

Not only the Buddha or the flame, but all of us—all things in the world—can say the same: *Do not recognize me by means of signs, because it will make you suffer.* When conditions are sufficient for something to manifest, do not say that it exists. Before it has manifested do not say that it does not exist. In truth there is no arriving and no going.

While the flame is manifesting it is nourished by wood, oxygen, and other supporting conditions. When a contradictory condition arises, the flame ceases to manifest. It does not go from being into nonbeing. The flame did not go anywhere. We ask, "Dear flame, where have you gone?" and the flame says, "I have gone nowhere, just as I have come from nowhere." That is the authentic voice of the flame. Consider the final line of my poem,"*

You are not a creation. You are a manifestation.

This line is an expression of the teachings on the Middle Way. The three notions of the goer, the time of going, and the action of going are not real. They depend on each other in order to be. They are simply conventional

---

* See Thich Nhat Hanh, *Call Me By My True Names*, Parallax Press, 1999, 2022.

designations. If we are deceived by them, we will suffer and continue to suffer. These teachings are not philosophy. They are a Dharma teaching to help us see the true face of reality to overcome our suffering.

Nāgārjuna says that goer, going, and time of going are just notions. Each notion is a conventional designation: words that we agree with each other to use, but which have no absolute, independent value. When we use these conventional designations we have to use them in such a way that we do not become caught in them. We are free if we dwell in the insight of the Middle Way when we use conventional designations. In the chapter on "Examination of the Four Noble Truths" there is a famous verse:

> I call empty
> things that arise from conditions.
> They are conventional designations
> and they are the Middle Way.[*]

Everything that manifests on the basis of conditions is empty, conventional designation, and the Middle Way. The Middle Way transcends all pairs of opposites: being and nonbeing, arriving and going, one and many, birth and death. Therefore, the Middle Way is the nature of nirvāṇa—in other words, the reality that

---

[*] Verse 18, Chapter 24 of this text, the Mūlamadhyamakakārikā.

transcends pairs of opposites. The nature of phenomena can be described by the terms conditioned arising (*pratītyasamutpāda*), emptiness (*śūnyatā*), conventional designations (*prajñaptir upādāya*) and the Middle Way (*madhyama-pratipad*).

Conditioned co-arising is the essence of all phenomena. When we can see deeply into the interdependent nature of phenomena we see that all phenomena are empty: there is nothing firm, eternal, and unchanging.

The word "empty" (in Chinese 空, in Sanskrit *śūnya*) can be misunderstood as "not existing." The English adjective "empty" does not imply that something is not there. The trunk of a banana tree is made up of many different layers. If we peel them away one by one, we will see that in the end there is nothing inside. The same is true for an onion. We might peel off all the layers, but we will never arrive at its core. This is how we understand the word emptiness. It simply means that inside there is no solid core, no firm entity that does not change. Things are just a reflection—a synthesis of different causes—and are empty of a solid reality. Emptiness is not being, nor is it nothingness; emptiness is hollow of all reality.

Conventional designations are like that. They are there, we receive them and we have a perception of them, but when we look carefully we see that they are empty. This is because they are interdependent. They are like the film projected on the screen. The images are there—they are not nonexistent—but when examined closely, we see there is nothing firm; if the electricity is cut, they vanish. The banana tree, the onion, our body, and five skandhas are also like that, and so they are called empty, which also means they are conventional designations. I, you, appearing, vanishing, arriving, going, climbing the mountain, or not climbing the mountain, all of these words are conventional designations. If we know that the ideas of birth, death, being, nonbeing, continuing, and ceasing are all conventional designations, then we are free. To be free is to dwell in nirvāṇa and in the Middle Way. The Middle Way is nirvāṇa. It is the reality that transcends the ideas of continuing, ceasing, being, nonbeing, real, and not real.

Let us contemplate an elder brother of our sangha, Thầy Giác Thanh. We say he has gone. When we were made aware of what people called "the passing of Thầy Giác Thanh," we were all deeply moved. It was a bell of mindfulness for me and my disciples. It was a chance for us to look deeply. All of us, to a greater or lesser extent, were able to touch the no-arriving, no-going nature of Thầy Giác Thanh. Some of us touched this deeply, some more superficially, but we all touched it. We practice this kind of looking deeply too rarely. We wait until there is a great bell of mindfulness—like what we call a death—to look deeply. Instead, we have to practice signlessness at every moment, in our daily life, in terms of our own body and in terms of other signs around us.

For example, for how many years more do you think that I will be with you? This question is a mindfulness bell, giving us a chance to look deeply. Am I still there, or not? Am I going, or am I not? These questions help us to avoid being caught in signs and conventional designations. If we are caught, we will suffer. We ask the same questions about ourselves, the people we love, and those we hate. All of them are conventional designations. We need to see the nature of conditioned co-arising in ourselves and between ourselves and others; when we do, our suffering, despair, regrets, and anger will automatically disappear. What saves us from suffering is not a superhuman being, but our insight into the Middle Way.

We have all been to a funeral home and witnessed a corpse lying in the coffin or at a cremation. We have heard the heart-rending cries and laments for a close relative who has departed. We may fall into deep despair and want to die along with our loved one because we believe so strongly that there is being and nonbeing, life and death, continuing and not continuing, going and not-going. In these situations, however, if we are able to tear apart the veil of concepts—the covering of conventional designation—and get in touch with a deeper dimension, we will not cry or grieve in this way. If we look deeply in the years and months before the departure of our beloved, at the moment they go into hiding we will not suffer so much.

Someone does not need to wait until they have gone into hiding to manifest in a new form. You do not need to wait two or three years after I have gone into hiding and then go and look for a young child who is somewhat like me and who can stand in my place, as in the Tibetan tradition. If you look deeply, you see that going into hiding and manifesting anew takes place at every instant; this is true for us all, not only for me. At every moment we go into hiding and manifest in new forms. We need to see our new manifestations in us and around us. If we are imprisoned by the outer form—our body or our five skandhas—and think that they are ours and are unchanging while that which lies outside of them is not ours, then we are caught in signs and conventional designations.

⊰⊱

There are two types of truth spoken of by the Buddha and mentioned by Nāgārjuna. The first type is "worldly truth" (*loka-saṃvṛti-satya*). *Loka* means the world. This is the kind of truth that we have come to an agreement about together. This truth is the birth certificate that has to be made when someone is born, and the death certificate when someone dies. We have established a convention with each other that the baby who *was not*, now *is*, and so we have to certify the date when the baby *began to be*. Similarly, the old man who used to be has now ceased to be, and so we have to certify the time of his death. This is what is meant by worldly truth. We have to recognize this worldly truth, but if we live only in worldly truth we will experience an infinite amount of suffering. Therefore, while we are still alive, we should practice so as to be in touch with the second, deeper kind of truth, which is the "ultimate truth" (*paramārtha-satya*).

Nāgārjuna did not intend to deny the conventional truth. He only wanted to say, "You should not live with the conventional truth alone. You should transcend it and practice to be in touch with the ultimate truth." All these verses are to help us look deeply at the conventional truth so that we can be in touch with the ultimate truth that lies deep in the heart of things. The way to be in touch with the ultimate truth is very clear: when we look deeply into the interdependent nature of things, we realize that they all are empty. When we see that all conceptualized and named phenomena are simply conventional designations we can dwell in the reality of no birth and no death, of no being and no nonbeing. This is called the Middle Way.

The world suffers a great deal because people are caught in ideas that are based on only the first type of truth (worldly truth). We have to open up a way for the world to be in touch with the ultimate truth, so that we can all suffer less. How can we help the wave be in touch with the water? The wave does not need to go far; without going anywhere it can be in touch with the water. When the wave knows it is water all of its fear, sadness, and jealousy ceases.

When we look carefully we discover that the time of going either is or is not taking place at every instant. When we see the impermanent nature of all things we transcend the notion of a time of going. The time of going is not a stage that we shall reach one day. It is happening at every moment of our daily lives. When we see this clearly our ideas about going simply disappear, along with ideas of a person who goes. We quoted above the following lines from a poem I wrote:

> *The cloud is floating,*
> *the white cloud is floating*

We saw that the cloud *is* the floating, *is* the drifting. If a cloud does not float or drift it is not a cloud, it is rain. If we remove floating and drifting from a cloud, it is no longer a cloud. Therefore, we cannot differentiate the cloud and the floating as two separate realities. In Confucian philosophy it is said that *the king kings, the subject subjects, the father fathers, the son sons.* This means that the king has to be a king. A nun has to nun—if she doesn't, she cannot be a nun. The subject has to subject. If a father does not father, he cannot be called a father, and the son to be called a son, has to son. In the sentence *the king kings,* the second word is the verb. This is called *the rectification of names,* 正名, by Confucian scholars (*a king can only rightly be called a king if he kings),* but the name that has been rectified is also a conventional designation.

Every noun can be a verb. In English "mother" can be a verb as well as a noun, as in the sentence "Please don't mother me!" The action of mothering cannot be separated from the actor, the mother. In English we can also say "the house houses many people." House was originally a noun, which then became a verb. In the poem we have: *The cloud floats; the cloud is the floating. The flower blooms; the flower is the blooming.*

We imagine a person, and then we say that this person makes use of the action "going" and we call the person "the one who is going." The danger in this is that we think that the one who is going is *separate* from the action of going. The one who is going and the action of going depend on each other to manifest. This is clarified in verses nine to eleven. Verse five reads:

If there is going in the time of going

Here we have not yet seen the reality of going. Being in the act of going means that there is also a sense of *remaining*—we are still there in the act of going. This way of looking results in two ideas: the idea of the going (remaining in the going), and the idea of the going of this going! Verse six says:

> *without a subject who goes,*
> *how can we establish the fact of going?*

When the one who is going is still there, how can there be the reality of going? The person is obviously there (on the side of being); if they have gone, how can they be there? *Is going* also means *has not yet gone*. When we say, they have gone (from this life), we mean they are already dead and they do not need to go any more. We must reexamine our unreasonable idea of *is going*.

Verses seven to eleven elucidate the fact that *the one who is going cannot go*. As long as they are present, they are not going. See verse eight:

> *The goer does not go,*
> *the non-goer does not go.*
> *Apart from goer and non-goer,*
> *there is no third possibility.*

The realities of going and not going cannot be established, and neither can we establish a third possibility apart from these.

9. *How can we conceive*
   of the goer going?
   Without the act of going,
   how could there be a goer?

若言去者去
云何有此義
若離於去法
去者不可得

You cannot conceive of a goer without the action of going. Therefore, to talk about a goer going—as if the goer were something separate from the going—does not make sense. A father can only rightly be called a father if he fathers. A flower can only rightly be called a flower if it flowers.

10. *If you say that there is a goer going*
    there would be two kinds of going:
    the going of the goer
    and the going of the act of going.

若去者有去
則有二種去
一謂去者去
二謂去法去

For example, imagine someone is eating: there is a person, and there is the action of eating. At the time of eating, the person eating and the action of eating happen simultaneously. Before the person began to eat, were they someone eating? If there is no one eating, how can there be the eating? If there is no action of eating, how can there be someone eating?

The important thing here is to examine the actor and the action. As long as there is the idea that the actor can exist independently from the action there is a fundamental mistake and we are caught in the idea of a self. Slowly, as we go deeper into these teachings, we shall begin to see this in detail.

Let's take the example of a meter-long measuring tape. We roll it up and put it in a bag. The tape in its bag exists independently of the length and breadth of the room it is in. When we take the measuring tape out and begin to measure, there is an action of measuring. While the tape is still in its bag we cannot say it is measuring. We cannot call it a measuring tape because it is not measuring. We could use it to tie something up or to do something else with, but at that point there is no act of measuring.

If we conceive of a goer independent of the act of going, we make a mistake. When the goer is identified with the act of going, the goer *is no longer an independent reality*. If you say that the goer goes, then there are two goings: the going of the goer and the going of the going. The goer is going, and the going itself is also going. Two goings happen.

11. *If you say that the goer goes*
    that would be a contradiction:
    there would be a goer apart from the going
    that the goer undertakes.

若謂去者去
是人則有咎
離去有去者
說去者有去

If you say that the goer goes, you are making a mistake. Only if there is an independent goer who goes with no relation to the action of going, can you say that the goer goes.

❧

The three following verses will speak about whether the action of going begins. Everything has a beginning (in Chinese, 發). According to the Sarvāstivāda, every phenomenon has four signs: beginning or arising (*jāti*), abiding (*sthiti*), decaying (*jarā*), and ending (*anitya*).

Future monastics anxiously waiting to know whether they will be accepted by the sangha and become part of the monastic family are an example of a beginning. Four days before the Lunar New Year* is the proposed date of their birth. On that day, they will manifest a sign traditionally called *round head, square robe*. The aspiring monastics are waiting for that sign. If they are deceived by the sign, they will continue to wait with anticipation—anxious and afraid—and will easily become caught in joy or sadness. But if they look carefully, they will see that even though things manifest in this or that way, their true nature is that of no-arising.

When we have a box of matches, we do not yet see a flame, As soon as we strike a match, we see a flame arise. That is the sign "beginning" or "arising." If we have insight, we only need to look at the matchbox to see a flame in it. We can see the flame hiding in the conditions that give rise to it. We can see the flame without needing to see the sign "arising." We talk about "manifesting" rather than "arising."

If you are wondering, anxious, or sad because you don't know whether something will arise or not, it is

---

* This was the date of the novice ordination in Plum Village in 2002.

because you do not know how to look deeply into conditions. If conditions are sufficient, you have nothing more to worry about—sooner or later that thing will arise. You can already see whether it will arise or not. You have to see the no-arising nature of the thing you long for.

When we look at the matchbox we can already see the flame clearly. All the conditions necessary for the flame are present inside and outside of the matchbox. Inside the matchbox there is the sulfur and the wood; outside there is the air and our fingers—all important elements for the flame to manifest. Therefore, we should not be caught in the sign "arising." Likewise, we should not be caught in the sign "going" or "ending" the equivalent of "death" or "going out of existence" in the four signs of arising, abiding, decaying, and ending.

For example, when our grandfather is dying we may ask ourselves, "Has grandfather gone yet?" "He has gone" in this case means he has died. Death is a sign that we take as the opposite of the sign birth. The idea of death is closely linked to the idea of birth. We have to look deeply into the nature of birth and death so as not to be deceived by the signs.

Besides the signs "birth" and "death" there is the sign "abiding." To abide means to stay on. There is the person who stays on and the person who goes; the one who has gone is no more, while the one who stays on still exists.

From the phenomenological point of view, the sign abiding is opposed to the signs of arising (birth) and ending (death). The newly-arisen is a tiny baby or an embryo after conception. Between the stage of arising and the stage of ending there is a longer-lasting stage called abiding. In this stage we have the impression that something stays on and remains itself, but in fact it is also changing at every moment; we cannot see this because of ignorance. It is only at the moment someone begins to lose their teeth that we begin to see the sign of "decaying." "My goodness! There is that beautiful picture I took when I was twenty, why do I now look so decrepit?" We have to practice looking deeply so that when we contemplate the four signs we are not trapped by them and do not become worried and depressed. Only then are we liberated.

The following verse investigates the matter of beginning (發). The action of being born can last for a time— any action whatsoever has a beginning and an ending. The sign "birth" has a beginning and an ending, just as the sign "death" has a beginning and an ending—that is, the time of being born and the time of dying. Nāgārjuna, by inviting us to contemplate the starting point, helps us to see more clearly what we mean when we speak of the time of birth and death.

12. *The starting point is not in what has gone,*
    nor is it in what will go,
    nor is it in the present going.
    So when does the starting point happen?

已去中無發
未去中無發
去時中無發
何處當有發

In all three times of going—past, future, and present—we cannot find a starting point for the going. Take, for instance, a novice monastic. We say that their novitiate will begin at the time of the ordination ceremony—for example, the morning of January 26. Examining this closely, we see that the ordinees have already begun to be novices. In the same way, though people assign a date to their birth, they actually began before that date. As far as the novice is concerned, the conditions that will allow them to ordain on a particular day have been there since the beginning of time. Who can find the beginning? We say that we ordained and shaved our head on the 26th of January, but that is only an outer sign. When we look deeply we see that we have been ordained since the beginning of time. The merit of our parents and ancestors has a great deal to do with our journey to become a monk or a nun. The beginning is already found in the conditions, and so to say that we began on a certain day or in a certain place is not correct.

13. *When going you do not begin to go,*
    nor do you begin to go when you have already gone.
    If the beginning is not found in these two cases
    how can you begin to go before you have gone?

未發無去時
亦無有已去
是二應有發
未去何有發

Before the going starts, how can there be the time of going? And while the going is taking place, there is no starting to go. Neither when you have gone nor while going is happening can you find the starting point. In these two things (having gone and going) you cannot find the starting point. So how can you find the starting point in something that has not yet gone?

14. *When going you do not begin to go,*
    nor do you begin to go when you have already gone.
    If the beginning is not found in these two cases,
    how can you begin to go before you have gone?

無去無未去
亦復無去時
一切無有發
何故而分別

In the three times—the going (the present), the gone (the past), and the not yet gone (the future)—we cannot find the beginning of the act of going, which would be *the sign of the coming into existence of that act*. If we cannot find it, why do we have this notion of beginning—the sign of coming into existence—in our heads at all? If in the three times we do not find what we call a beginning, then how can we give rise to the idea of the three times being separate (*vikalpyate*)? How can we give rise to ideas of the three times at all?

When we contemplate the four signs of arising, abiding, decaying, and ending, we are in touch with the realities of no-self and of impermanence. When we look deeply into the truth of no-self and impermanence in what is happening at each moment of our arising, abiding, decaying, and ending, we discover that the one who arises, abides, decays, and ends is a constantly changing entity. What (or who) arises? What (or who) endures? What (or who) decays? What (or who) ends? Once we have discovered the true nature of the actor in this play, all these questions will be answered, and we will be free from the notions concerning these four signs.

If we look at a flame, we see that all the conditions are sufficient for the flame to arise and to continue. The continuation of the flame is assured by the fuel. If the flame does not continue, we say that it ends. In fact the flame does not end (i.e., become nothing) and does not arise (from nothing). It relies on conditions to manifest. When the flame has manifested, we witness what is called the manifestation of the flame. Is that flame the actor? Is it, as the actor, a reality separate from the action?

We say that the flame has been lit, but if it is not lit it is not a flame! When the one who goes is not going, they cannot be called a goer. We cannot conceive of a flame that is not lit. We have to see its self-nature before it becomes a lit flame, which means we have to see its presence in the conditions that help it manifest.

We can put a candle on the table and let it burn for two or three hours. Because of a deluded perception we think that the flame has begun to manifest at the time we lit it and that it then continues as the same flame, not a different one. However, if we remember the moment the match helped the flame to manifest we will see that as we lit the candle, it seemed there was a second flame. There was the flame of the match and, now, the flame of the candle. After we light the candle we put out the match flame. We can ask ourselves, are the two flames the same flame or two different flames? The flame of the match was transmitted to the candle flame, but are those two flames the same or different? We cannot say that they are completely the same, nor can we say that they are entirely different. It is easy to see that the flame is not one, because there was a moment when it manifested as two—but we cannot be certain that there are now two separate flames.

The true nature of things—that is their nirvāṇa nature—is not sameness or difference. We can see the not-same-not-different nature of the flame by observing that the flame, having manifested on the match, now manifests on the candle. However, people who did not see the match flame and only now see the candle flame will say, even after watching the candle flame for an hour, that there is only one flame. They can only see the sameness of the flame; they cannot see the difference. If they were to look carefully, they would see that the wax and the oxygen are different at every instant. In the light of impermanence we see that nothing can last for two milliseconds and still be considered to be the same thing. When we see impermanence we see nonself.

Saying "the flame is lit" is like saying "the goer goes." The goer is not an unchanging reality. In our mind that person, the goer, is always that person; in fact, the goer is a reality that is constantly changing. The nature of the flame is, like the goer, neither the same nor different.

The goer referred to in the verses is a person we think of as an unchanging reality. We have not understood the nature of the goer or of the action of going. The teaching of not the same or different helps us understand the teaching of no birth and no death. When we say birth, there must be something that is born. When we say death, there must be something that dies. Therefore we have to establish a subject or an agent to do the described action. There is the action of coming and going, and so there has to be a comer and a goer. Looking deeply into the nature of the comer and the goer we see the nature of emptiness, because the comer and the goer are a collection of conditions. The same is true of the flame; it is not a separate entity. It is not a subject waiting to perform the action of being lit or not being lit. We should look into the starting point of the flame to see that it is not coming into being out of nothing, and to see that at the moment it goes into hiding it does not go from being into nothingness.

In New York there were the twin towers of the World Trade Center. Before they were blown up and collapsed they were a familiar scene for the people who walked past them every day. After the collapse, something was missing for New Yorkers when they walked past that place. When did the twin towers come into existence such that now we say they have gone out of existence? We see that there is arrival and departure, and that in that arrival and departure we experience pleasure, joy, and suffering. We cannot see the nature of arrival and departure because we cannot see clearly the arriver and the goer. When we can see the original face of arriving and going we are no longer caught in the signs or appearance of arrival and departure.

In this chapter Nāgārjuna teaches about going but we learn about both arriving and going. If we understand the nature of going (ending), we also understand the nature of arriving (arising), abiding, and decaying. Impermanence and no-self are the basic teachings of the Buddha. The meditation practice of impermanence and no-self is the basic Buddhist meditation. Insight into impermanence and no-self helps us become free of signs of arising, abiding, decaying, and ending. When we are free of these signs we can be in touch with the ultimate reality, or nirvāṇa.

In the first chapter of the Verses on the Middle Way the author uses no-birth to teach us to see the nature of being. In the second chapter, the topic is not-gone (not-arrived, not-gone). One question people often have and sometimes put into words, is: "What happens when I die?" Whether we express it or not, we all have this question. What will become of me when I die? In this question there are three things we can meditate on. There is the word "I," which is the person who goes, there is the word "die," which refers to the action of going, and there is the word "when," which refers to the time of going. When we contemplate these three words in the light of impermanence and no-self, we realize what Nāgārjuna is teaching. Some people answer this question—and I see that it is a good answer—by saying that when you die, you don't die. That is the truth. When we can comprehend the nature of the one who goes and of the action of going, it is clear that there is no death or departure from this life. There is only transformation and going into hiding.

Say you are looking at a sheet of paper in terms of the signs arising, abiding, decaying, and ending. The moment when it arose in the form of a sheet of paper is called arising. After that it will abide for some time, which is called abiding. When you tear it up and it no longer has the form of a sheet of paper, it is decaying, and when you burn it, it is ending. It can have these four signs. When you look carefully at a sheet of paper, what do you see? You see trees in a forest. You see the trees, using your eyes of meditation. If there were no trees, how could there be paper? Without looking deeply you cannot see this, but someone who looks deeply can see the trees—even if they do not think of themselves as a meditation practitioner. Looking at the paper you must see the cloud in it. If you have not yet seen the cloud in it, you have not truly seen the sheet of paper. Without clouds there would be no rain, and without rain trees cannot grow. From a scientific point of view, you can be certain that the cloud is present in the sheet of paper. Looking at the paper, you must see the sun. Without the sun how can trees grow?

When you look at a sheet of paper you need to see signs other than the sign "paper." Only Dharma eyes can see these other signs. Our ordinary eyes do not see them. All of us have Dharma eyes. In our daily life we use our eyes of flesh and blood, but the Buddha and Thầy have transmitted the Dharma eyes to us. In our daily life we should know how to use our Dharma eyes to see the signless nature of a sheet of paper. Let us not be caught in the sign "paper," and instead see all the non-paper signs in the paper. These include the forest, clouds, the sun, soil, etc. We have to see a myriad of non-paper signs in order to see the paper correctly. If we see the sign paper as something separate from the non-paper signs, we have not seen the true nature of the paper. When we burn a piece of paper, we are also burning the forest and the cloud. The fire is just another condition, which we can call an opposing condition or supporting condition depending on how we look at it. If the piece of paper wants to be a cloud, the flame will be a supporting condition, because once it is burned it will be a cloud. If the piece of paper wants to continue as a piece of paper, the fire is an opposing condition.

We say that the piece of paper has gone, but we should ask: Where did it go? The truth is, the piece of paper has let go of the sign paper; it has gone into hiding. It is no longer manifesting as the sign paper, but it has begun to manifest as other signs. If we look deeply, we shall be able to recognize them.

While the paper is burning, we see that there is the sign "heat." Before it burned we did not think that the paper had the heat sign, but in the paper there is the heat sign because paper is a fuel. The heat from the piece of paper, even though it is a miniscule amount, goes into the hand of the one who lights it, into others, and into this universe. Now the piece of paper is in the universe, in space, time, and in the one who lit it. To say that the paper has gone from being into nothingness is completely wrong.

The piece of paper also manifests the new sign of smoke. The smoke rises and, though our eyes no longer see the paper, one of the paper's new signs is smoke. The smoke sign becomes part of a cloud. One day, when a drop of rain falls on your head, you and the piece of paper will be reunited. The ashes are also a new manifestation of the paper.

Manifestation can always be seen in the light of impermanence and no-self. It is wholly incorrect for a meditator to say that something that exists becomes nothing. From a scientific point of view it is also incorrect. Nothing can go from being into nonbeing, just as nothing can come from nonbeing into being. If we recognize this truth, we recognize that there is no birth and no death. When we recognize no birth and no death, we recognize no arriving and no going. The Buddha teaches: *when conditions are sufficient, something manifests; it does not come from anywhere. When conditions are no longer favorable, it ceases to manifest, but it does not go anywhere.* If you say that something goes at a certain time or to a certain place, you are caught in ideas such as being and nonbeing, birth and death, coming and going.

When we are asked "What happens when you die?" we could say "Nothing happens! When you die, you don't die at all." Often people are afraid that when they die they will become nothing—that there will be nothing of them left—but in life there is only change and manifestation. There is no being or nonbeing. For example, when we heat cold water, after one or two minutes the cold water will not be cold water anymore, but this does not mean that the water no longer exists. The temperature of the water rises gradually, and at the boiling point the water becomes steam. If water is not water, it is steam, clouds, or snow. It goes in a cycle like this. If we look deeply to see this continuity of manifestation, we shall see that the water, just like a Buddha, has the nature of no-birth and no-death.

Therefore the question "What happens when we die?" can only be answered when we look deeply into three things: the goer, the act of going, and the time of going. If we do not look deeply, we might wrongly say: "He will be reborn in the realm of the gods! He will no longer need to be in this world." That is just hypothesis and speculation. In order to answer the question of "what happens when we die" we have to reexamine our notions regarding the one who goes, the act of going, and the time of going. As we reexamine them, we shall see that the teachings on no birth and no death and on no coming and no going are connected to the teaching on no same and no different. The teaching on no same and no different helps us to understand no coming and no going and no birth and no death.

Generally, when we look at a flame we think it is simply a flame. We do not know that this flame is formed by a million flames coming one after the other. Rather than the one flame that we imagine, the nature of all these flames is that they are neither the same nor different. When we see the goer in this light, we are no longer caught in our idea of someone who is going. When we are not caught in the idea of someone who is going, we are also not caught in the idea of going and the idea of a time of going. All our sadness and fear vanish and we become free when we realize that birth and death are not a reality but just an idea. According to conventional truth there seems to be birth and death, but when we are able to tear apart the net of conventional truth and go deep into the reality of the ultimate truth we touch the nature of no birth and no death, no arriving and no going. At that point we are free from the sadness and fear of loss that come with ideas of arriving and going, arising and ending, remaining and loss.

How can we apply this teaching in our daily life? There are countless ways. Take, for example, someone who hates and harbors a grudge against their father or their mother. They are not able to experience ease and happiness in their life as others do because they always hold on to their grudge. How can you help them to remove their anger? When someone hates their mother, they do not want to think about her. They want to dissociate themselves from her because she wounded them and made them suffer. Other people may have sweet mothers, but because their own mother is unkind, ungrateful, and cruel they do not love and respect her.

They are distressed and cling to their distress for their whole life, finding no way out of the situation. They nurture resentment; they are angry, and their mother is the object of their anger. They do not want to identify themselves with the object of their anger and they declare, "I'm not my mother." Many young people who have suffered because of their mother will declare: "I hate her! I don't want to have anything to do with her!"

In the light of Nāgārjuna's way of looking deeply you see clearly that you and your mother, although you are not the same, are also not different. The nature of your mother and the nature of yourself are not the same, not different—in other words, you are the continuation of your mother. You cannot take your mother out of yourself. It is just like the candle flame. It could think its mother—that is, the match flame—is an entirely different flame from itself. That is incorrect. The nature of the flame is not the same and not different. If there were no match flame, there could be no candle flame. The candle flame is the very continuation of the match flame. Children are all the continuation of their mother. If you are angry with your mother and you do not want to have anything to do with her, it is utterly irrational and naïve. A daughter who is angry with and hates her mother does not know that she carries within herself the entirety of her mother, including her mother's imperfections. If she does not practice, in the future she will behave just as her mother did and in doing so will make her children and others suffer. This is the simple truth! It happens because of ignorance; if someone can look deeply, they will realize understanding and love.

Toward the end of the twentieth century in Europe, the elm tree met a catastrophe. A microfungus carried by elm bark beetles entered just under the bark of the trees and made its home there. To protect itself the tree produced a gum, but this gum blocked the xylem tissue and killed the tree. Elm trees in England and France were almost completely wiped out. Such was the misfortune of the elm trees. In the garden of my hermitage there used to be a beautiful elm tree, but it died of this disease. Before we had the time to fell it, the tree rotted and crashed down, killing other small elm trees that were thriving in its shade. Looking into this you can see that the elm tree did not want this to happen. It did not want to be infested by the microfungi, to die and crash down, or to crush the small elm trees in the garden, but that is what happened! Maybe something like that happened to your mother. She was born and raised in an unfavorable environment with the fungi of greed, attachment, and despair. In short, the environment which nurtured her was not a good one. The many negative seeds in her had a chance to manifest, while the positive seeds had no chance. As her child you know that, from a scientific point of view, you have received your mother's seeds—both the positive and the negative ones. If you were put in the unfavorable environment your mother grew up in, you would have grown up like your mother. If in the past she had been placed in a favorable environment, the negative seeds would not have manifested and she would not have made you suffer. It is a question of environment.

Two factors influence our lives: the environment (nurture) and nature. You may be luckier than your mother; perhaps you have found a safe environment full of understanding and love and have had the chance to practice. In this environment your mother's negative seeds will not have a chance to manifest, and you will not treat your children as she treated you. At the same time, you have been able to manifest the good seeds that your mother did not have the chance to develop in her lifetime, thanks to your positive environment. You have become a sweet person who can manifest love. When you see things in this way all of the resentment for your mother will vanish and your love for her will overflow. It is this love that transforms all your anger and hatred. You see clearly that you and your mother are not the same, but are also not different.

You think that you were born on that day, in that month and year, in that particular place, but in truth you were already in your mother before your birth. Birth is just an outer sign. Though a valid birth certificate may exist, what it certifies is just the sign of birth. After that you go through abiding, decaying, and ending, but these are all just signs. Your essence has never been born. You have always been present in your mother.

Look at a baby lemon tree. Although you cannot see lemon flowers and lemons, they are already there in the tree. The signs of the flowers and the lemons have not yet manifested, but with the eyes of the person who planted the tree—or with the eyes of someone who looks deeply—you know that the lemon tree will offer you flowers and lemons. You are the same.

Maybe as far as outer characteristics are concerned you do not yet have children, but your children are already there inside you. Outwardly you do not yet have disciples, but your disciples are already there, waiting to manifest. You have to see the no-birth nature of your children and disciples so that when they arise you will see that they are not a separate reality, but your own continuation.

As a son or daughter, you can see that you and your mother are both unborn and that you are not a reality isolated from her. You are the continuation of your mother, with all her positive and negative seeds. Her own negative seeds manifested while her positive seeds never had a chance to because she did not have a good environment. You no longer think that there is nothing good about your mother. You love your mother because you see that her good qualities did not have a chance to manifest. In this way you develop respect for her. In your mother there is a bodhisattva, there is a buddha, but the wholesome seeds that would allow the bodhisattva or the buddha to manifest were not watered in her life. This realization inspires you to live your own life so that the buddha nature arises. If you can help the bodhisattva and buddha nature in yourself to manifest, you are helping them manifest in your mother. This is the true way to love and respect your mother—just one example of how we can apply Nāgārjuna's teachings.

The elm does not want to die and crush her children. Your mother did not want to suffer, to betray you, and to make you suffer. She did that because she was not lucky enough to have a good environment. Once her children see this, they will sympathize with her, transform their anger, and love her more. It is the people who suffer, the people who did not have a chance—who deserve your love the most. You have to practice to love. Love is not something just to enjoy, but a practice. The more you make love your practice, the more your understanding grows. The more you look deeply in the way Nāgārjuna teaches, the more your love grows. All that we have learned here about no birth and no death, about no arriving and no going, about not the same and not different, is deeply related to our happiness and to our suffering in daily life.

You have to be very careful when you hate someone. When you do not have a practice and do not look deeply, you will behave exactly as the person you hate. This is a real risk. Practicing and looking deeply you will see how the other continues in you. If you have thoughts of suicide, you should know that these thoughts have been transmitted to you by the people you continue. It could be your mother or your father. If you were to take your life, you would be doing as they had done; you would have failed to transform this genetic inheritance. Mindful of this fact, you know that these seeds of suicidal thoughts have not yet been transformed. What you need to do is to practice to transform them. If thoughts of running away from home or running away from the sangha come up in you, you know that they do not come from nowhere. These thoughts in the form of seeds have been transmitted to you from many generations of ancestors. Your part is to recognize and transform them.

Let us remind ourselves of the eleventh verse:

If you say that the goer goes
that would be a contradiction:
there would be a goer apart from the going
that the goer undertakes.

In the phrase *the goer goes* there is a contradiction that we do not see. When we say *the goer goes*, it is as if the *goer* is a reality that exists independently of the action of going and as if the going exists independently of the one who goes. This is irrational, but because we are used to thinking in this way it appears logical. For this reason Nāgārjuna needs to help us see the irrationality of our way of thinking. I like to think about what would have happened if Nāgārjuna had had a conversation with Wittgenstein. Wittgenstein, like Nāgārjuna, exposes for us our illogical ways of using words and thinking. The things we say are all wrong; we do not know what we are saying.

We believe that there is a person going who is separate from the action of going, and this is why we say *the goer goes*. This is ridiculous. Consider again the examples previously given: the cloud drifts, the flower blooms, the king kings, the citizen citizens, the father fathers, and the child childs. The reason why the king exists as a king is that he kings. If the king did not act as a king, how could he be a king? The reason why the subject exists as a subject is that they serve and obey the king. Otherwise they cannot be called subjects. This is the Confucian "rectification of names" (正名): using the proper name to call something by its true name. How could you call someone who was not acting as a king, a king?

To illustrate this point, let us analyze the phrase, "I know the wind is blowing." If the wind is not blowing, how can you call it wind? Is there a wind that does not blow? Of course not! Without blowing, there is no wind. It is ridiculous to say the wind blows, yet we all say it. The verb blow is redundant because wind implies blowing. We do not need the word "blow."

In the phrase "I know," there is the subject I and the verb know. I know means I perceive or I am mindful of that fact. Perceiving or perception is one of the five universal mental formations (*sarvatraga caitasika*). This kind of mental formation happens all the time. The five universal mental formations are: contact, attention, feeling, perception, and volition. The manifestation of a mental formation includes the manifestation of a subject of that mental formation and an object of that mental formation. Everyone has the mental formation perception happening in them at every moment. The perception of wind is the awareness of wind. Wind is the object of perception. All you need is for perception to manifest and there will be the subject of perception and the object of perception. You do not need an "I" that stands outside of the perception in order for perception to arise. You do not need a perceiver, you only need the perceiving. It is as if the actor is already present in the action, which means that the subject that perceives and the perceived object are in the perception. According to the Verses on the Middle Way, the idea of an I that exists independently of the knowing is incorrect. So we could say: "know the wind blows"—where "the wind blows" is the object of perception. But "the wind blows" is still too much. *Wind* is quite enough. Then we have the wind as the object and knowing as the subject. What is known? The wind is known. However, "know wind" is still too many words. Wind is the object of perception, so it is enough if we keep the object; why do we have to say "know"? In the beginning we said, I know the wind is blowing. We have removed, one by one, all the unnecessary words and are left with just the word wind. When we hear the wind blowing, we just say, wind. That would be enough, do you see?

This is Nāgārjuna analyzing language to show us that our language and the way we think takes us far from reality. In "wind" there is consciousness, since wind is the object of consciousness. Actually, there is just the manifestation of consciousness. When we use the word wind with insight, we know that this word is a manifestation based on conditioned arising, which means there are countless conditions that come together to make the wind manifest. The wind is not an independent, permanent, and self-existent reality. The wind is a conventional designation, born of conditions. Its self-nature is empty. The wind is a reality that cannot be described with concepts like being and nonbeing, coming and going, same and different. Again, recall the famous verse in the Verses on the Middle Way:

> *I call empty*
> *things that arise from conditions.*
> *They are conventional designations*
> *and they are the Middle Way.*

In this verse there are four terms: arising from conditions, emptiness, conventional designation, and the Middle Way. Everything arises because of conditions, and we see that the true nature of everything is emptiness. Things are nothing more than names that have been established by convention. Looking deeply into them, we see they belong to the Middle Way: their nature is not being, nonbeing, coming, going, abiding, or being destroyed.

When we listen to the wind and see conditioned co-arising (*pratītyasamutpāda*), emptiness (*śūnyatā*), conventional designation (*prajñapti*), and the Middle Way (*madhyamā pratipad*), at that moment we realize the path of practice. We should be able to see these four qualities in everything we name.

The Chinese meditation master Zhiyi founded the famous Tiantai school based on this verse. Although this school practices meditation, it is not called one of the meditation (*Chan*) schools. Its practice is to contemplate the original nature of all things, namely emptiness (空), conventional designation (假), and the Middle Way (中). All the treatises of this school go back to this verse, and the school's adherents practice contemplating these three characteristics. However, if we do not also take conditioned co-arising as the basis, then we shall certainly not have a clear insight into these three contemplations. Conditioned co-arising is the basis for the three contemplations on emptiness, conventional designation, and the Middle Way.

The Tiantai school was transmitted to Vietnam. When I was a young novice, I learned and practiced certain Tiantai teachings. In my first year at the Buddhist institute in Huế I studied the Tiantai book *The Practice of Śamatha and Vipaśyanā for Young Beginners*, which is also called *The Smaller Book on Śamatha and Vipaśyanā* (侗懵 止觀) Since we now have other, better teachings, I have not taught this book in Plum Village. In the past, after studying *The Smaller Book on Śamatha and Vipaśyanā*, people studied *The Larger Book on Śamatha and Vipaśyanā* (摩訶止觀). In my class there were fifty novices who all learned *The Smaller Book* together. Later in my life as a monk, I discovered teachings that are better, and I wish to transmit to you these more appropriate Dharma doors. However, if you want to learn about what happened in the past and how your teacher studied, you would need to read *The Smaller Book on Śamatha and Vipaśyanā*.

⁂

If you say "I know the wind is blowing" it is excessively wordy and could give rise to a misleading perception of reality. Instead you can just say "Wind!" Wind can express the wonderful nature of reality, and help you avoid getting caught in the idea "I," the idea "object of my perception" (i.e. the wind is blowing), or the idea "you"— the one listening to our declaration. If you know how to contemplate the wind in light of emptiness, signlessness, and aimlessness, you can see the true nature of things. You are enlightened and overcome attachment and suffering.

If "the goer goes" is a contradiction, "the wind blows" is also a contradiction and quite strange! You create a goer apart from the going and a wind apart from the blowing—a wind that blows when it wants to blow and does not blow at other times. If the wind, however, does not blow, then it is no longer wind!

Verses 12–14 examine the starting of an action. Going must have a starting point and so must arriving. If we look for the beginning of the starting point, things become even more complicated and lead to endless recursion—the starting point must have a place where it has not yet begun. In these three verses, Nāgārjuna shows us, therefore, that the starting point is just an idea.

The next verse is about abiding. To abide means to stand still or stop in a place. It is the second of the four signs (arising, abiding, decaying, and ending) proposed by the Sarvāstivāda. We need to transcend all four.

15. *The goer does not abide anywhere.*
    The non-goer does not abide anywhere either.
    Apart from goer and non-goer
    how could anything abide?

去者則不住
不去者不住
離去不去者
何有第三住

This is Nāgārjuna's way. The goer is the person who goes. Someone who is going does not abide anywhere. The goer is different from the one who abides. It is obviously wrong to say that the goer is the abider. Admitting that the goer is not the abider, we also see that the non-goer does not abide anywhere. The non-goer is not the same as "the one who does not go," and this is why I translate the second line as: "the non-goer does not abide." Beside goer and non-goer, how could there be some third element that could play the role of abiding?

When we look deeply into the words go and abide, we see that our notions about going and abiding are incorrect. For example, if you are now sitting in the meditation hall, your five skandhas are different from the way they were before you came into the hall. You have sent forth thoughts and actions. You have breathed out carbon dioxide and toxins from your body, and your skin cells have died and fallen onto the lawn on your way here. There is not a single moment in your life when going is not happening in some way or another. According to the insight of impermanence and no-self, you are going in each moment, arriving in each moment, and abiding in each moment. The Buddha has said that we are reborn in each in-breath and out-breath. Looking deeply at yourself do you see going, abiding, or arriving? You could say that you are going, abiding, and arriving all at once. Master Guishan, in his Admonitions and Encouraging Words,* says:

> *One breath is the length of a lifetime. Why sit in idleness, allowing life to drift away, wasting time in a way that you will only regret?*

A new lifetime begins during one in- and out-breath, so do not be lazy! Why do you allow time to drift away without training yourself more, practicing walking

---

* See *The Admonitions and Encouraging Words of Master Guishan*, Thich Nhat Hanh, Parallax Press, 2022.

meditation, and dedicating yourself to the practice of mindfulness?

In the Sutra of Forty Two Chapters, the Buddha asks the monks:

"How long is a human lifespan?"
A monk replies:
"World-Honored one, one hundred years."
The Buddha smiles. Another monk answers:
"A few decades."
The Buddha smiles again. Another monk says:
"One day."
The Buddha smiles yet again. Another monk says:
"The lifespan of a human is just one breath."
The Buddha smiles and says:
"You are right. The lifespan of a human is just one breath."

A new life begins with every breath. Life, death, and saṃsāra (arriving, going, and abiding) are all happening in each moment. Looking deeply, we see there is ultimately no arriving, no going, and no abiding.

Your loved one has not gone anywhere. With no going, there is no arriving. Without going and arriving, the matter of abiding is a non-issue. You have to transcend your ideas of going, arriving, and abiding to see your loved one's and your own true nature. Nāgārjuna is trying to say that there is no starting point and no abiding. The ideas of someone who abides and someone who goes—along with our grief and feelings of loss—are wholly based on notions. Seeing this you realize what is called the Middle Way. You are able to touch the ultimate dimension and to see that the true nature of the wind and of your loved one neither arrives nor goes.

16. *It would be absurd to say*
    that it is the goer that abides.
    If the act of going is not
    how can a goer be possible?

去者若當住
云何有此義
若當離於去
去者不可得

We say that the goer is abiding. How can someone who is going abide? It is absurd. How can this make sense at all? How can we be both going and abiding at the same time?

Let us look deeply and ask the question again. Who among us is not going? We are all going towards what we think is old age and death—the cemetery. In this way of thinking, everyone is going. Our goal is the burial ground or the crematorium. In the historical dimension, according to conventional truth, we are all heading in one direction; this direction is *not* our ideal, but the crematorium.

Who among us does not abide? We are all present, laughing and talking. But if we are abiding, how can we be going? If we are going, how can we say we are abiding? Our ways of thinking do not make sense.

If the act of going is not
how can a goer be possible?

We need to contemplate: apart from the action of going, how can there be a goer? Nāgārjuna has an unusual way to help us reflect on this. He uses dialectics to help us see the absurdity of our way of thinking. Normally we act based on our illogical way of thinking, and because of this we make many mistakes. If our thinking is not right thinking, our action is not right action. Right action is only possible with right thinking and right view. Right view in the ultimate sense is the view of emptiness, conventional designation, and the Middle Way. When we have a deep understanding of these three contemplations, our thinking is right thinking. With right thinking, which is not caught in the ideas of going or abiding, not yet gone or already gone, being or nonbeing, we act as a buddha or a bodhisattva. This is called right action.

Without this right view we do not think according to emptiness, conventional designation, and the Middle Way. Our actions are misguided and bring about suffering and fear. They are not right action.

17. *Someone who has gone or has not yet gone does not abide.*
   Someone who is going also does not abide.
   Similarly someone who is going, has gone, or has not yet gone
   does not arise, decay, or end.

去未去無住
去時亦無住
所有行止法
皆同於去義

We've already learned these four signs according to the Sarvāstivāda: arising, abiding, decaying, and ending. We cannot find abiding in that which has already gone or in that which has not yet gone. Nor can we find that which is going. What Nāgārjuna says about abiding can be used to examine arising, decaying, and ending. What

Nāgārjuna says about any one of these can be understood for the other three. Here is a poem that I wrote at the beginning of 1964:[*]

> *Just like a stream that goes back to meet the great ocean tomorrow, when you leave, remember to sing a song for the new season.*
> *The sound of the song will resound, giving me enough strength to go on another stretch of my journey.*

This reflects a worry that we all have. We are anxious and fear that when our loved one leaves us we will be alone. *Just like a stream, returning to the great ocean* means that sooner or later you will have to go; I will be alone. For example, someone may say: one day Thầy will have to go, and I will feel lost. *Tomorrow, when you leave, remember to sing a song for the new season.* When you leave me all alone, remember to offer me some sort of legacy. With that legacy I shall be able to continue another stretch of my journey. We all demand this of the person we love, whether it is our spiritual teacher or someone else we take refuge in. We demand this because we are attached.

The sound of the song will resound, giving me enough strength to go on another stretch of my journey. "Poor me!

---

[*] "One Arrow, Two Illusions" in *Call Me By My True Names*, Parallax Press 1999, 2022.

I need you. I still need you. You have to leave something behind for me! If you don't, when you leave I will die, I will be lost and all alone." This is a human need. Here is the response of our loved one:

> At the place of departure there is the moon, the clouds,
> water, and wind.
> And at the place of arrival, yellow flowers and the
> violet bamboo will be there to greet me.
> Since you are a leaf, a flower, you have me from
> beginningless time
> and the blue of the immense sky in your eyes will
> always be there.
> But because you can't see this, out of love, you keep
> talking about my departure.
> I will not leave
> or I will leave but never go anywhere.

This is the insight into no-coming and no-going. We see distinctly that there is no one going, there is no time of going, and there is nowhere to go. The poet speaks gently and skillfully in order to remove the obstacles of his disciples, his younger brothers and sisters.

I will not leave is a bold declaration. *I will never die. I will never leave you, I will never leave my disciples, my brothers and sisters!* It should be enough just to say this, but since the disciple or the younger sibling is still so attached, we need to say more. *I shall not leave because I am of the nature not to depart.* If you look deeply, you will see this, and once you have seen it you will have nothing to worry about.

> *I will not leave*
> > *or I will leave but never go anywhere.*

This sentence means that I am not going anywhere. If there is no place to go to, then how can there be going?

> *At the place of departure there is the moon, the clouds, water, and wind.*
> *And at the place of arrival, yellow flowers and the violet bamboo will be there to greet me.*

If you say that I am going, you should see that at the place of my departure there is the moon, the clouds, the water, and the wind—all miracles. At the place of my arrival there are yellow flowers and violet bamboo. Wherever I go I am in the ultimate dimension, which means that I have not left. The moon, the clouds, the wind, and the water are not different from the yellow flowers and the violet bamboo. They are all manifestations of the Dharmakāya.

One of the beautiful names we give the Buddha is *Tathāgata*, which means "the one who comes from and returns to suchness." Is there a place which is not suchness? With this insight we see that Tathāgata does not arrive and does not depart. This is not only the nature of the Tathāgata, but also the nature of the flower, the cloud, and the wind. We have to see that nature in order to realize the path of practice. Poetry has a special ability to use images to demonstrate the truth. Whereas Nāgārjuna uses dialectics, the poet uses poetic images.

> *Since you are a leaf, a flower, you have me from*
> > *beginningless time*

If you are able to see that you are also a leaf and a flower, you will see that you have always had and will always have the person you love.

> *And the blue of the immense sky in your eyes will*
> > *always be there*
> *But because you can't see this, out of love, you keep*
> > *talking about my departure.*

When we look at the blue sky, it becomes the object of our perception. The blue sky can be seen in our eyes. Sometimes the clouds do not allow us to see the blue sky, and we believe it is no longer there; it is always there. The Vietnamese poet Trụ Vũ wrote:

> *It is because your eyes see the blue sky*
> *that they reflect the color of the sky*
> *It is because your eyes see the great ocean*
> *that they reach as far as it does*

When we love the Buddha and meditate on him, our mind reflects the Buddha. Subject and object become one; the object that is missed and the one who misses it are not two. The blue sky is always there for us, but because we do not see it we are anxious and regretful. Our ignorance is the cloud that covers up and obstructs our view of the blue sky. If we can see the blue sky in our eyes, we shall always have it. Our fear comes because sometimes we see it is and sometimes we see it is not. We believe that in the future the blue sky will be no more and we suffer. When my loved one dies what will become of me? We put ourselves in a state of anxiety and ask: How can I survive if you are not there?

We can sit with our children or our younger siblings and slowly find a way to remove their fears. My poem continues,

> *This morning*
> *after the moon and stars had slept*
> *the universe let refreshing tears fall.*
> *As clear as crystal,*
> *the late night dew gently rose.*
> *Do cry, and your soul will be more beautiful.*
> *Your tears will make the soul's wasteland*
> *a fresh country garden.*

> *Their freshness will penetrate the earth, caring for each*
>   *tender shoot and bud.*
> *In the past, I would sit and watch you cry.*
> *I let myself cry too, so that someone would comfort me.*

If you want to cry, please cry; you will feel better, because there is still anxiety and fear in your heart. There is a great deal of compassion in these lines. They are the words of a mother who hugs her child and says, "If you need to, cry."

> *The universe let refreshing tears fall.*

If the universe can cry, you have the right to cry. Do not be ashamed.

In the West people say that men should not cry. Why not? To be able to cry when we are witnessed and comforted by the person we love is a great happiness. In our heart we have some anxiety and fear that we are unable to express. If there is someone we love sitting next to us, like our teacher, our brother, or our sister, and we can express our emotions with our tears, we should do so. The author of this poem is exceedingly compassionate! He does not say, *Do not cry! There's no death, no coming and going. That's just foolishness.* He says, *You can cry, it doesn't matter. In the past, I was just like you, I cried so that someone could comfort me.* When we see others who cry are comforted, we also want to cry so that we too may be comforted. That is human nature. We can start by crying, but slowly we have to grow up.

> *Oh nature!*
> *Mother with green hair, green-blue earth and sky*
> *your smile fills the world with butterflies, birds, flowers*
> > *and leaves.*
> *As a leaf, as a flower, I have been yours from*
> > *beginningless time*
> *and in your narrow perception my true self has never*
> > *manifested in the realm of birth and death.*
> *Do you remember when mother first brought me back*
> > *to life*
> *and thanks to the five wonderful skandhas, you saw*
> > *my image appear?*
> *Tomorrow when that image disappears*
> *please smile*
> *and calmly look for me again*
> *beyond the voice and form that was born and died*
> *to see that I am still real*
> *I never left*
> *and I never arrived*
> *beyond time, beyond perception,*
> *beyond the existence of host and guest.*

Oh nature!
Mother with green hair, green-blue earth and sky.

We must return to nature. If we are able to entrust our suffering and distress to nature, we will suffer much less. A French poet, Alphonse de Lamartine, in a moment of deep suffering, wrote a similar poem:

Mais la nature est là qui t'invite et qui t'aime ;
plonge-toi dans son sein qu'elle t'ouvre toujours.
Quand tout change pour toi, la nature est la même,
et le même soleil se lève sur tes jours.

The poet says: But nature is still there, inviting, embracing, loving, gracious. Enter the embrace of nature. The embrace of nature is always ready to receive you. While everything is changing, impermanent, coming, going, love, hate, success, failure; nature is always nature, your mother. You have to return to her so that she can embrace your worries, your grief, and distress. The warm sun rises every day and brightens your days.

Mother with green hair, green-blue earth and sky

Here I call nature a mother with green hair.

your smile fills the world with butterflies, birds, flowers,
and leaves

Nature's smile is the manifestation of butterflies, birds, and flowers, and we can welcome them to soothe our suffering and distress.

> *and in your narrow perception my true self has never*
> *manifested in the realm of birth and death*

I am something that transcends the ideas of birth and death. It is because your perception of me is still narrow that you cannot see the no-birth, no-death nature of my true self, and its because of this that you are anxious and cry.

> *Do you remember when mother first brought me back*
> *to life*
> *and thanks to the five wonderful skandhas, you saw*
> *my image appear?*

Mother here is nature, is the universe, is conditioned co-arising—all the things that come together to make me manifest. With your narrow perception you saw me in the five skandhas. Normally the five skandhas are the five skandhas of grasping (*upādānaskandha*); when the five skandhas are free from attachment, they are infinitely wonderful. The Buddha has five skandhas and so do we, but we are attached to the skandhas—they become a prison. The five skandhas of the buddhas are the realm of the Dharmakāya. *My image* refers to the signs which make me manifest.

tomorrow when that image disappears

Do you remember that day? The image you saw was a sign—the object of your perception. You thought that when that sign manifested I began to exist and that when it went into hiding I no longer existed. This refers to the things that have gone, like the image of our beloved whom we think does not exist anymore.

please smile
and calmly look for me again

You should look for me outside the five skandhas to which you are attached. I believe you are attached to those five skandhas because you are not able to see me at other times and in other places. You should look for me with a smile, but where should you search?

look for me beyond the form and sound that arose and
disappeared
to see I am still real,
I never left
and I never arrived
beyond time, beyond perception,
beyond the existence of host and guest.

Look for me in a way that does not see me in signs that manifested and to which you were attached. Recognize my presence in time, in consciousness (perception), and in the relationship between subject (host) and object (guest). See that I am a reality not subject to birth, death, abiding, or going. This is the only way to overcome anxiety, yearning, and fear.

Find me and you have a chance to find yourself.

When you see the true nature of your beloved, you see your own true nature.

> *You discover pristine features*
> *showing you your nature of no birth and no death.*
> *You will see*
> *nothing goes, nothing is lost.*
> *And with one arrow, you fell two flags of illusion.*

This is truly wonderful! Not only the Buddha has the nature of no birth, no death, and an unlimited lifespan, you do too. You have the nature of no birth and no death; your lifespan is not limited. Seeing that the leaf is not born, does not die, does not arrive, and does not go, you see the same is true of yourself. It is truly wonderful.

The arrow is the arrow of looking deeply. The object of our meditation could be the Buddha, our teacher, or our beloved. When we see their true nature, we see our own true nature that does not arrive, does not go, does not exist or not-exist. The *two flags of illusion* are the goer and the abider, birth and death, being and nonbeing; each member of these pairs relies on the other to manifest. The highest aim of a practitioner is to nock the arrow, stretch the bowstring, and release it to fell two flags of illusion at once—to arrive at the Middle Way and to overcome pairs of opposites like birth and death, being and nonbeing, remaining and perishing, same and different, going and abiding.

> *Suchness will appear wonderfully in the midst of birth*
> *and death.*
> *I am smiling peacefully in the present moment*
> *and that smile blooms forever in the song of the eternal*
> *spring.*
> *In that smile you will see that you will always be there*
> *because you never really manifested in the illusion of*
> *existence.*

The ultimate dimension will show itself in the historical dimension. Without running away from the historical you can recognize the ultimate. Your true nature, just like mine, is no birth and no death, and it transcends the illusory notions *I have existed* or *I am existing*. We are not an illusory appearance in the world of birth and death, but are wonderfully present in the ultimate dimension of no birth and no death, no coming and no going. You just need to look at my smile and you will see the eternal spring. This spring is not replaced by the summer or the winter because it is the spring of the ultimate dimension. This is *the incomparable spring* referred to by king Trần Nhân Tông of the Bamboo Forest meditation school of Vietnam in a verse he inscribed on the wall of a temple in North Vietnam in 1308.* Here is the last section of my poem:

> *Tomorrow you will see the smile you saw today,*
> *right to the end of the path of illusion.*
> *Nothing has gone, nothing is lost*
> *and nothing will go, nothing will be lost.*
> *Today the stream and the birds encourage you:*
> *Keep being the flower that sings.*

If you can recognize the smile of today, then tomorrow, at the moment you are enlightened, you will see that smile; it will not be lost. The smile of the Buddha, of your teacher, of your elder brother and sister will not disappear in the future. The smile of Thầy Giác Thanh, the elder brother we think we have lost, is sublime. Do not think that it has been lost. The moment we wake up

---

* This poem has not yet been translated into English, but can be found in Thầy's history of Vietnamese Buddhism, *Việt Nam Phật Giáo Sử Luận*.

and transcend the ideas of going and abiding, that smile will automatically be with us forever. The best thing we can do is to be *a flower and sing*. That is our practice.

In my poem "Butterflies over the Field of Mustard Flowers," there are the lines:

Be the flower that stands quietly by the hedge.
Be the smile, be one part of the wonderful world of
appearances.

With our practice, we do not need to go anywhere; we have nothing to worry about, once we can dwell peacefully in the nature of the Middle Way—nirvāṇa. The best thing we can do is to smile.

In my poem "Looking for Each Other" there are these lines:

The moon of freedom has returned to me,
everything I thought I had lost.

We believe that we have already lost our youth, our love, our father and mother. The truth is that nothing has passed away or been lost. Everything is there, intact in the wonderful reality of the ultimate dimension.

Today the stream and the birds encourage you:
Keep being the flower that sings.

In these lines the elder brother is saying: the best you can do in the present moment is to listen to what the stream and the birds say: keep being a flower and sing. You should be present like the flower that sings a song, the flower of the poet Quách Thoại.*

In my poem "April" that flower is mentioned again:

The flower has never stopped singing. . . .
Everything joins in the everlasting song
of the wonderful world of appearances.

When I was young I wrote a poem entitled, "Let Us Pray for Darkness, O Sparkling Stars":

If tomorrow you are listening
then listen to my words
as you would to the murmur of the brook
or the birdsong;
as you would look on the green weeping willow, the
    pink roses,
the yellow chrysanthemum, the green bamboo,
the white clouds, and the bright moon.

---

* "Standing so peaceful by the hedge, / You are smiling your wonderful smile. / Silently looking at you I am caught by surprise / Because I hear your voice singing / The song of eternity / Full of awe I bow down before you."—an English translation of Quách Thoại's poem, which the author refers to here.

You have to practice listening to me as if you were listening to a murmuring brook or a bird singing, as if you were looking at a green willow, a rose, a yellow chrysanthemum, or green bamboo. Only then are you really listening!

Keep being the flower that sings.

This is the final encouragement. Do not be anxious. Enjoy fully the wonders of the Dharma body and offer your smile to humanity, to the universe, and to all species.

18. *It is absurd to say that*
    the goer is the act of going.
    It is also absurd to say that
    the goer is not the act of going.

去法即去者
是事則不然
去法異去者
是事亦不然

The act of going could be translated as the reality of going, or the business of going. If you say that the act of going is the one who goes, it does not make sense. If we say that the act of going is not the one who goes or is independent of the one who goes, it also does not make sense. The act of going and the one who goes are very closely connected; they are so closely connected that although you cannot say that the one is the other, you also cannot say that the one is not the other. If you remember the principle of "neither the same nor different" you will understand this right away. If there were not something that goes, how could there be the action of going, and if there were not the action of going, how could there be something that goes? They are not two separate realities, but they are also not the same. *The same* means: "A is B." *Different* means: "A is not B." This verse can only be understood in the light of "neither the same nor different."

19. *You cannot say the act of going*
    is the goer.
    If so, the author of the action and the action
    are the same thing.

若謂於去法
即為是去者
作者及作業
是事則為一

This verse presents the first proposition of verse 18: *the act of going is the goer*. If you say that the act of going is the goer, the one who does the action and the action are the same; A is B. Instead of mentioning A and B we only need to mention A. For example, instead of saying "the wind is blowing" you just say "wind" It is absurd to say the wind blows because it makes the wind (subject of the verb) and the blowing (the verb) two separate realities. If you talk about eating, there must be someone eating for there to be the act of eating. If no one is eating, then the eating cannot take place. It is absurd to say that the person eating is the eating, but it is also absurd to say that the eater exists separately from the act of eating. If we say that the actor is the action, then we are saying that actor and action are the same thing.

20. *If you say that the act of going*
    is different from the one who goes,
    then apart from the goer there is the act of going
    and there is a goer apart from the act of going.

若謂於去法
有異於去者
離去者有去
離去有去者

This verse presents the second proposition of verse 18: *the goer is not the act of going.* A is not B. The act of going is something completely independent from the one who goes. If you say that the act of going is entirely different from the one who goes, the act of going exists independently of the one who goes. If you say that the blowing has nothing to do with the wind, that would result in having a wind apart from the blowing and a blowing apart from the wind. This is absurd. The teaching "neither the same nor different" is a key. If you take this key and insert it in the keyholes of the verses 18–21 in this chapter then you will be able to open them.

21. *Whether you say that the goer*
    and the act of going
    are the same or two different entities
    your argument cannot stand.

去去者是二
若一異法成
二門俱不成
云何當有成

22. *Because of the going you recognize the goer.*
    How does the goer use the act of going?
    Before the act of going, the goer was not going
    therefore there is no goer who uses the act of going.

因去知去者
不能用是去
先無有去法
故無去者去

Because of the going you recognize the goer. This means that since the act of going is there, we can recognize the person who is going. When there is eating taking place we can recognize the person who is eating. When there is blowing, we can recognize the presence of the wind.

How does the goer use the act of going? Verses 21 to 24 discuss the concept "use." For example, a carpenter uses a saw. The carpenter is the subject that uses the saw and the saw is the object which is used. In this verse the goer uses the going, and the going is the object being used. The one who goes uses the act of going. Such a concept of "use" is absurd. It looks as if A is a separate reality from B. Only thanks to the act of going can we recognize a person who is going. However the goer does not *use* the act of going. Why?

> *Before the act of going, the goer was not going*
> *therefore there is no goer who uses the act of going.*

Before someone starts to eat, we cannot call them an eater. The same is true for a goer. The goer does not go; they do not use the act of going. How can there be a goer before the act of going takes place? Therefore it is not correct to say that the actor uses the act.

23. *You recognize a goer because there is going.*
   The goer cannot use another kind of going.

For one goer
there cannot be two kinds of going.

因去知去者
不能用異去
於一去者中
不得二去故

When there is going, you recognize someone who goes. If the goer does not use this going, how could they use a different kind of going? In verse 22 we have seen that the goer cannot use the going. Some people might think that although the goer cannot use this particular going, they could use some other kind of going.

We have already accepted that the goer cannot use the going. If we say, however, that there is another type of going, the goer still could not use it. For one goer there cannot be two kinds of going.

24. *If you insist there is a real goer*
they could not use the three times of going.
If you insist there is no real goer
they also could not use the three times of going.

決定有去者
不能用三去
不決定去者
亦不用三去

If you insist that there is a reality called "goer," then this goer could not use any past, present, or future act of going. If on the contrary you insist there is no real person who goes, that unreal person still cannot make use of going in the past, present, or future. If there is no one who goes, then why do you talk about going? If we say there is someone who goes, that person cannot use going in any of the three times—all the more so if there is no one who goes. How can we have going without a something or someone who goes?

25. *Whether the going is or is not,*
    the goer does not go.
    Therefore there is no goer going,
    and no destination.

去法定不定
去者不用三
是故去去者
所去處皆無

Whether the act of going really is or is not, the one who goes cannot use the past, present, or future of going. The goer, the going, and the three times of going are not real. They are only constructs of our mind. The destination is the place gone to and also the place arrived at. When we read this verse we may dismiss it as metaphysics, but it is the essential work of a meditator.

The Japanese Zen master Sengai Gibon (仙厓 義梵, 1751–1837) left a stunning calligraphy, in which he wrote an enormous character 死 (death) and below, in a column, wrote the characters which mean: "Whoever sees its reality I call a hero." Death is the chief subject for a practitioner of meditation. Someone who can uncover the true face of death is liberated from sorrow, regret, and fear. In the Chan (禅) school it is said that resolving the matter of birth and death is the most important thing. Whether you have your own temple and whether you are appointed to this or that position is not important. Whether your fellow practitioner loves or hates you, whether your teacher loves you more or less than others is not important. For a practitioner, the business of life and death is what matters most of all. Resolving the matter of life and death is the purpose and the aim of a practitioner. A practitioner of meditation has to stretch the bowstring and aim at this bull's-eye—the matter of your own or your loved ones' life and death. The day we conducted the funeral rites for Thầy Giác Thanh, one of our sisters read a farewell address that included the words: "Thầy Giác Thanh, I know that over these past months and days you have been meditating carefully and very deeply on the true nature of death."

If you have a deep insight into death, it will liberate you. In this chapter about arriving and going, you learn to look at death in order to see life more clearly. Life and death are not separate, but they are not the same. Out of ignorance you use concepts to draw a line: on one side of the line you put life and on the other side, death. For you, life and death are two distinct realms. You think you are on a journey that starts on one side of the line and gradually approaches it to cross into the realm of death—like when the sun sets on the ocean. It is like looking at the horizon and the surface of the ocean as the sun sets; you say the sun is dead after it goes down gradually and is embraced by the ocean. In the words of the Vietnamese poet Thế Lữ (1907–1989),

We wait for the last sliver of the sun to die

You mentally construct three ideas: The "I" who goes, "the act of my going" (death), and "the realm of death" I am going to. If you are able to aim your bow to fell these three flags of illusion all at once, you will be liberated. This chapter of the Verses on the Middle Way can help you do this. You use deduction and dialectics to see the absurdity underlying your ideas. We can understand "going" here to mean "dying," as in French: *Il est déjà parti* can mean he has died or he has gone to the afterlife. We have an idea that on one side of the line he is not dead at all, and that when he goes over to the other side he no longer exists. The ideas of still there/no longer there, being/nonbeing, are related to the idea of going/not yet gone.

People are busy their whole lives searching for fame and status. They are not free to do what is most important, what is worth doing, and what is most necessary. What is it that a practitioner should be doing? They should be looking into the great work of birth and death. If they are able to do this, they will have the smile of freedom, great love, generosity, and inclusiveness. Everything else will be manageable. Their daily tasks will present few difficulties and not be overwhelmingly important, because they will have laid down the greatest burden.

In the Verses on the Middle Way Nāgārjuna does not mention any Mahāyāna sutras. He does not speak in praise of the bodhisattva ideal. From start to finish we see that Nāgārjuna only praises the Buddha, the Dharma, and the Śrāvakasangha (the "hearer disciples," the original sangha of the Buddha.) At the time of composing the Verses on the Middle Way he was not yet a Mahayanist—though later on he is said to have composed the work preserved in Chinese as the Dazhidu Lun,* which was based on the Mahāyāna Prajñāpāramitā teachings as well as other works with a Mahāyāna flavor.

---

* There is no Sanskrit original of this work.

When I was young I thought that Nāgārjuna must have composed the Verses on the Middle Way at the end of his life because the teachings in it are so profound. Later on, I discovered that he must have composed this work first, and probably at that time had not yet read any Mahāyāna sutras. This is why he does not praise the Mahāyāna and the bodhisattva ideal, and why he does not cite any Mahāyāna sutra. The only sutra that he cites directly in this text is the Discourse to Kātyāyana— although we see indirect reference to other sutras of original Buddhism, like the Anurādha Discourse.* The Verses on the Middle Way can therefore be said to be very pure Buddhism.

In Nāgārjuna's time, the expansion of different trends of thought thrived in India. The Sarvāstivāda and the Sautrāntika Mainstream Buddhist schools used their knowledge to develop teachings that would uphold the Buddhist way and resist the attacks of the current trends of non-Buddhist thought. Nāgārjuna saw that these Buddhist schools had gone too far, and feared this would metamorphose original Buddhism. He undertook the composition of the Verses on the Middle Way to illuminate the essence of original Buddhism and to prevent the

---

* See Discourse on the Middle Way and Anurādha Discourse in *Chanting from the Heart, Volume 1*, Parallax Press, 2013, 2023.

teachings of Śākyamuni Buddha from being shaded with hues of meaning that the Buddha never intended—such as self-nature or concepts of a self (*pudgala*). Nāgārjuna went back to some of the basic sutras taught by the Buddha in order to demolish trends of thought that could metamorphose original Buddhism.

The Three Dharma Seals—impermanence, no-self, and nirvāṇa—are keys to unlock the door to the truth. Nāgārjuna was always loyal to the Three Dharma Seals, which are also mentioned in the Dazhidu Lun. In the Pali suttas the three seals are impermanence, no-self, and suffering rather than impermanence, no-self, and nirvāṇa. If you use no-self as a key, there is no lock you will not be able to open.

When you look at an azalea flower, a number of images come to mind. You bring out the images that are already in your store consciousness and, for recognition to take place, you compare them with what you are looking at. You recognize that this is an azalea, and in your mind there already is the word azalea. The azalea is the object of your perception; it is a sign that we can call "A." On the level of normal thought and perception, an azalea flower is just an azalea flower. It cannot be an azalea leaf, an azalea bush, a lotus flower, the sun, the wind, or a cloud. All it can be is an azalea flower. This type of perception is based on the principle of identity.

Based on this principle, most governments have established an identity card of some sort. Everyone's identity card is different. Mr. or Ms. Worry cannot be Mr. or Ms. Fear; they must be completely different. Everyone has their separate identity. We all accept this conventional truth—a truth we have agreed upon together. Someone who is a father cannot be identified as the son, and the one who is the son cannot be identified as the father. For pragmatic reasons we all accept the conventional truth of who is the father and who is the son.

Although you accept these conventions, if you have intelligence and can look deeper, you do not suffer from them. Looking deeply at the son you see the father, and looking deeply at the father you see the son. Thanks to this deeper view you discover the second kind of truth, which we call ultimate truth. When you master the ultimate truth, you overcome suffering. If you only live in the world of conventional truth, you will still suffer.

If, when you look at an azalea flower, you see it only as an azalea flower, you are doing what everyone does. If when you look at the azalea flower, you do not only identify it as an azalea flower but also see the wind, the rain, the seed, and the gardener, you have a deeper view—that of no self and of conditioned co-arising.

The best way of looking at the son is to see his father, his mother, his ancestors, his grandparents, his education, and society. You have to transcend the principle of identity and realize the principle of conditioned co-arising. A can remain A from the conventional perspective, but by looking deeply you see that A is no longer just A but *all the conditions that have led to the manifestation of A.* Looking at the flame you see the match, the oxygen, and other elements that make the flame possible, and that is the deeper view that leads to ultimate truth.

This does not mean that you deny the conventional truth. It does not mean that when you look at an azalea flower and see the sun, the earth, the cloud, the seed, and the gardener, the flower is no longer an azalea flower. It is still an azalea flower, but with understanding and enlightenment you are no longer imprisoned or ensnared by the appearance of the flower.

The equation is like this: A which is not A is truly A. In the Chan school it is said: *Before I began to practice I saw the river as a river and the mountains as mountains. While on the path of practice I saw rivers were not rivers and mountains were not mountains. After I realized the practice I saw the river was still the river and the mountains were still the mountains.* Now you can understand that this means: *once you are enlightened, that river and those mountains can no longer imprison you and make you suffer.* You have seen their source and origin—no birth and no death, no being and no nonbeing—and you have great freedom.

If you are the child, you have to know that you are the child, but looking deeply at the reality of yourself as a child you see you are also your father, your mother, and your ancestors. Seeing this you have a deep understanding of yourself. Although you are still the child, you are free.

The Diamond Sutra, one of the earliest sutras of the Prajñāpāramitā school, repeats this equation often:

> *"What do you think, Subhūti? Does a Bodhisattva adorn a Buddha land?"*
>
> *"No, World-honored One! Why? To adorn a Buddha land is not to adorn a Buddha land, and that is why it is called adorning a Buddha land."*

This is the equation: A is not A and therefore A is called A.

> *"Subhūti, the Buddha does not consider the ordinary person to be an ordinary person, and that is why he calls them an ordinary person."*
>
> *"A bodhisattva who thinks of themself as a bodhisattva is not a true bodhisattva. Only a bodhisattva who is not a bodhisattva, can be a true bodhisattva."*

There are two letter A's in the equation. If you have not yet seen its nature of conditioned co-arising, when you look at the first A in the equation it ties you up, overpowers you, and makes you suffer; but when you look into it and see it is made of non-A elements, you realize its signless nature. Although you still recognize it, it can no longer bind you, dominate you, and make you suffer.

The Buddha taught the Three Doors of Liberation: emptiness, signlessness, and aimlessness. Signlessness means not to be caught in signs or appearances. Liberation is freedom—to untie the knots. What are the knots that bind us? Grief, regret, and fear are knots. We are bound by them because we are caught in signs—the signs of being or nonbeing, coming or going. You nock your arrow and shoot it, felling the sign to reveal the true nature that transcends signs. When all signs have been felled, you are liberated. This is the meditation on signlessness.

The second chapter of the Verses on the Middle Way is a meditation on the sign "going." Once you have felled the sign "going," you fell the sign "abiding." With one arrow you fell two flags of illusion. As you go about your daily activities in the conventional world, you need to recognize signs for what they are, but this is not enough. If you live all the time at the level of signs, they will deceive you and you will suffer. You have to learn how to live in the reality of signlessness. To do this you have to meditate and to look deeply. Once you have realized the insight of signlessness, you continue to live with others in the same environment, but as a free person. You can stroll at ease in the realm of birth and death because you can perceive the signless nature of yourself, others, and the world, while those who are still caught in signs are drowning.

Signs are deceptive. If you do not want to be deceived and suffer, you must transcend them. The Diamond Sutra says: *where there is a sign, there is a deception.* This is why signlessness is one of the Three Doors of Liberation.

Nāgārjuna's way is to show us the empty nature of all phenomena, so that we can realize the insight of sign-lessness. When you contemplate signs like cloud, mist, rain, or snow, you see how they continue each other. The clouds become rain or snow, rain changes into ice, snow becomes water again. All these signs are impermanent; they are always in a process of change. We talk about someone arriving or going, but if we are caught in such signs, we suffer. When you look deeply into these signs so that you are not deceived by them, you can be happy. It's as simple as that. This is why we have a door of liber-ation called signlessness. If while practicing meditation you do not have a chance to look deeply at phenomena and the people around you with the eyes of signlessness, you are wasting your time.

3

EXAMINATION OF
THE FOUR NOBLE TRUTHS

The first six verses of this chapter are the voice of certain Buddhist schools that opposed the idea of the emptiness of phenomena as a teaching of the Buddha. From the seventh verse on Nāgārjuna replies to their objections.

1. *If everything is empty,*
   unborn and undying,
   the teaching on the Four Noble Truths
   cannot exist.

若一切皆空
無生亦無滅
如是則無有
四聖諦之法

2. *Without the Four Noble Truths,*
   seeing suffering, cutting off its causes,
   attaining extinction, and practicing the path,
   could not take place.

以無四諦故
見苦與斷集
證滅及修道
如是事皆無

Suffering or ill-being is the first of the Four Noble Truths. The roots, or the causes of ill-being, is the second Noble Truth; the cessation of ill-being is the third; and the path leading to the cessation of ill-being is the fourth. *Seeing suffering* means to witness suffering; *cutting off its causes* means to put an end to the causes of suffering; *attaining extinction* means to attain transformation or to overcome suffering; and *practicing the path* means to follow the path. Obviously, these four things cannot exist if the Four Noble Truths do not exist. If the truth of suffering does not exist, then we cannot see or witness it; if the truth of the causes of suffering does not exist, then we cannot put an end to those causes; if the truth of the extinction of suffering does not exist, then we cannot achieve that extinction; and if the truth of the path that leads to the extinction of suffering does not exist, then we cannot practice that path.

3. *Since all these things don't exist,*
   the four fruits also don't exist.
   And if the four fruits don't exist
   then the four kinds of orientation also don't exist.

以是事無故
則無四道果
無有四果故
得向者亦無

In the Buddha's teachings we speak of four fruits: the fruit of "stream entry," the fruit of a "once returner," the fruit of a "non-returner," and the fruit of an "arhat." The fruit is the result and product of our practice: ultimately enlightenment.

If the four fruits do not exist, then the four kinds of orientation do not exist either. In the Buddha's teachings we speak of four pairs and eight kinds of holy people. The first pair is composed of those who are oriented towards the path of stream entry together with those who have already achieved the fruit of stream entry. The people who have already entered the stream of practice, and already have the essence of holiness, are called stream enterers (*śrotāpanna*). But holiness is not only found in the people who have already entered the stream. There are people who haven't achieved this fruit yet, but who are on the way to achieving it, and these people are also considered holy. This is the fruit of "those oriented towards stream entry" (*srotāpannaphalapratipannaka*).

In the holy sangha there are people who sit stably and comfortably in the stream, and this stream will certainly bring them out to the sea. But there are also people who are oriented toward the stream. Here in Plum Village if we want to take a high speed TGV train, we have to go to the town of Libourne or to Bordeaux. The truth is that right from the moment we leave Plum Village to go to Libourne, we are already going in the direction of the TGV. The moment we actually board the train and sit down, we achieve the fruit of the TGV. This is what we call the first pair: the orientation towards and the fruit of stream entry.

The second pair is the orientation towards and the fruit of the once returner; the third the orientation towards and the fruit of the non-returner; and the fourth the orientation towards and the fruit of the arhat. Those who attain the four pairs of fruits comprise the eight kinds of holy people. Holy people means that in these practitioners there is holiness. We should not have the complex that in us there are only the seeds of profanity—desire, hatred, ignorance, complexes, doubt, and wrong views. In addition to these mental formations, we also have holiness. Every time we breathe in with mindfulness and know what is happening in the present—be it anger, sadness, or joy—we have holiness. It is wonderful that where there is mindfulness there is holiness.

Why do we have a community of practitioners living together in Plum Village? It is to nourish holiness. That is the business of a practitioner, to give rise to and to nourish holiness so that the race of holy people will not become extinct. Our practice is to help the race of holy people prosper and endure.

We are the descendants of holy people. As a descendant of the holy ones, we have to cultivate and nourish the seed of holiness inside of us with our steps, our breathing, our smile, and our deep looking. When the community has holiness, it can be called a holy sangha. The holy sangha is like the ocean, containing many wondrous creatures.* The wondrous creatures of this ocean are these eight pairs: those oriented towards the four fruits, and those who have realized the four fruits.

---

* The Buddha says that just as the ocean is the abode of many wonderful creatures, so the Dharma is the abode of the four kinds and eight pairs of holy people. (AN 8.19 and MA 45).

4. *If the eight kinds of holy people do not exist,*
   then the Sangha jewel does not exist.
   If there are no Four Noble Truths,
   then there is no Dharma jewel either.

若無八賢聖
則無有僧寶
以無四諦故
亦無有法寶

5. *If the Dharma and the Sangha jewels don't exist,*
   then there is no Buddha Jewel.
   Therefore the teaching on emptiness
   undermines the Three Jewels.

以無法僧寶
亦無有佛寶
如是說空者
是則破三寶

If there were no Dharma Jewel and Sangha Jewel, there would be no Buddha Jewel. From the beginning to the end, the opponent's reasoning is keen!

The teaching of emptiness undermines the Three Jewels. This attack didn't come, as you might think, from non-Buddhists, but from Buddhists who did not understand the teaching on emptiness.

6. *The teaching of emptiness undermines the teaching of*
    causality
    as well as that of merit and demerit.
    It also undermines
    worldly conventions.

空法壞因果
亦壞於罪福
亦復悉毀壞
一切世俗法

The teaching of emptiness undermines the teaching of
causality

Some Buddhists condemned Nāgārjuna for teaching an emptiness that denied the teaching of cause and effect. This verse refers to the following criticism: *If you (Nāgārjuna) say the Noble Truths are empty, it will corrupt morality, because, thanks to their belief in the law of causality, people do not dare to do wrong for fear of courting bad karma.*

as well as that of merit and demerit.

Your (Nāgārjuna's) teaching on emptiness also undermines the concept of merit and demerit. Listening to your teaching, people will say: Go on, do it! There will be no demerit because everything is empty. Here Kumārajīva translates the Sanskrit dharma and adharma as merit (福) and demerit (罪). Dharma means in accord with the principles of the spiritual path, while adharma is to deviate from these principles.

It also undermines
worldly conventions.

Buddhism has its code of conduct and the ordinary world also has its laws—conventional ethics concerning what is right and wrong. The opponent argues that the teaching on emptiness can destroy and damage all codes of conduct and is thus perilous.

These first six verses of the chapter contain the questions and the accusations of Nāgārjuna's opponents. The teaching on emptiness is subtle and deep—not many people are able to understand it. Many people panic when they hear about emptiness. They think that the teaching on emptiness denies all they have learned and studied so far—not only about Buddhism, but also about conventional ideas of right and wrong in the world. Nāgārjuna replies to their objections in the seventh and succeeding verses.

7. *You really do not understand*
   emptiness and the reasons for teaching emptiness.
   You do not understand the meaning of emptiness
   and so are troubled by it.

汝今實不能
知空空因緣
及知於空義
是故自生惱

You (the opponent) are not able to understand emptiness and why it is taught. Since you cannot understand the real reason for emptiness you are afraid of it, you discredit it, and you bring distress and harm upon yourself.

8. *The buddhas rely on the two truths*
   in order to teach the Dharma to beings.
   One truth is the worldly truth,
   the other is the ultimate truth.

諸佛依二諦
為眾生說法
一以世俗諦
二第一義諦

The Chinese character for truth 諦 has two parts: on the left the character 言 means speech, on the right the character 帝 means king. Since the emperor was considered to be the Son of Heaven, what he said was considered to be the truth and no one would dare to contradict it.

The first is the conventional or worldly truth (*saṃvṛti-satya*), and the second is the ultimate truth (*paramārtha-satya*). The ultimate truth is also called the absolute truth in Chinese. The conventional truth is mundane (*laukika*) and the ultimate truth supramundane (*lokottara*).

9. *If someone is not able*
   to distinguish one truth from the other,
   they will not be able to understand
   the deep meaning of the Dharma.

若人不能知
分別於二諦
則於深佛法
不知真實義

There are two kinds of Buddhism: superficial Buddhism and deep Buddhism. People who stay on the surface of the Buddha's teachings cannot understand the teachings of deep Buddhism. When someone asks a question, you can usually tell whether they are practicing the superficial kind of Buddhism. If they are, they will not understand if you reply in terms of deep Buddhism. It is interesting that in the second century CE Nāgārjuna already used the word "deep" (*gambhīra*) to describe the truth of the Buddha's teachings and we still talk about the deep teachings of the Buddha today.

10. *Without relying on conventional truth,*
   you cannot realize ultimate truth.
   Without realizing ultimate truth,
   you will not attain nirvāṇa.

若不依俗諦
不得第一義
不得第一義
則不得涅槃

To master the ultimate truth, someone has to learn about conventional truth. The fact that there is conventional truth and ultimate truth does not mean that you choose one and discard the other. Both truths are necessary. If you do not begin by looking deeply into the conventional truth, you will not be able to realize the ultimate truth. Therefore, Nāgārjuna says, "I am not undermining anything. I am simply going deeper into the truth. By going deeper into the conventional truth, you will be able to see the ultimate truth."

Without relying on conventional truth,
You cannot realize ultimate truth.

This means that the conventional truth is critical. There are good and bad, right and wrong, merit and demerit, causes and conditions. However, you should not be caught in them. You have to go deeper so that from the conventional truth you can attain the ultimate truth—a much greater fruit of the practice.

This verse shows clearly that Nāgārjuna is not out to fight, but to guide people to the truth. By relying on conventional truth, you are able to see ultimate truth. The point here is that you should not discard the conventional truth, but instead should use it in a skillful way.

> *Without realizing the ultimate truth,*
> *you will not attain nirvāṇa.*

The conventional truth does not have the power to allow you to realize nirvāṇa. It can help you suffer less, but if you want to attain nirvāṇa, you have to attain the ultimate truth.

11. *Without a right understanding of emptiness*
    a dull-witted person does harm to themselves,
    like someone who does not know how
    and grasps a poisonous snake the wrong way.

不能正觀空
鈍根則自害
如不善咒術
不善捉毒蛇

Without the capacity to practice looking deeply into emptiness in the right way, those of meager intelligence harm themselves by their lack of understanding and the confusion in their minds.

like someone who does not know how
and grasps a poisonous snake the wrong way.

You need special training to be able to catch a snake—without it, you will not know how to catch the snake skillfully.

12. *The World-Honored One knew that this teaching,*
    so deep and subtle,
    would be out of the reach of those of meager
       intelligence,
    so he did not want to teach it to them.

世尊知是法
甚深微妙相
非鈍根所及
是故不欲說

The Buddha knew that the teachings on emptiness were subtle, profound, and wonderful, and that they would be beyond the reach of people of meager intelligence. He did not want to teach it to them—not because he was unwilling to give the teaching, but because if such people heard it they would not understand it, and he did not want to give rise to misunderstanding.

13. *You say that I am caught in emptiness,*
    and so have made many errors.
    But the things you call errors
    have nothing to do with emptiness.

汝謂我著空
而為我生過
汝今所說過
於空則無有

You say that I am caught in the idea of emptiness and that is why I have made many errors. The things you call errors do not exist in emptiness.

14. *Because emptiness is possible,*
    everything is possible.
    If emptiness were not possible,
    nothing would be possible.

以有空義故
一切法得成
若無空義者
一切則不成

This verse is renowned. It shook the world in the second century CE and has continued to do so until this day. On the day I first read it I felt a deep happiness. Since all things are by nature empty, they can be there. Emptiness is the foundation of all that is. All things can manifest and be possible thanks to emptiness.

The word emptiness (*śūnyatā*) means empty of something. Sometimes people misunderstand and think that it means nonexistence. Say you have a cup with some tea in it, and next to it you have an empty cup. Whether there is tea in it or not, there is still a cup. Without the cup, you could not have tea or no tea in it. If there is no tea in the cup, it does not mean the cup is not there. The cup that is empty of tea has other things in it; it is full of air. Empty means empty of something. Even if the cup is empty of tea, it is full of air.

What are all things empty of? They are empty of a separate self. Empty means empty of an own-being, a separate self, a self-nature. All phenomena can only manifest because they do not have a self-nature. If they had a self-nature, they would not be impermanent, and therefore would not be born and die.

Say you plant a seed of corn. If it had a self-nature, it would always remain a seed, because self-nature remains itself and cannot be destroyed. However, the seed of corn does not remain itself; it can be destroyed, and because of this it can sprout and become a corn plant. Due to the absence of a self-nature, the seed of corn has a chance to manifest. A self-nature is an unchanging essence. It is always the same and it cannot become something else. If we say that all phenomena have self-nature, then no phenomenon would be able to manifest. It is because phenomena do not have a self-nature that they can manifest.

> Because emptiness is possible,
> everything is possible.

If a child were to have a self-nature, they would never be able to become an adult. The corn plant, the adult, and everything else are without a self-nature. It is thanks to emptiness that all things can exist. However, people do not understand emptiness, and when they hear about it they are afraid.

If now you are suffering—drifting and sinking in your life—you will want to be liberated and to find peace and joy. How could you possibly realize this desire if you had a self-nature? If you had a self-nature, you would suffer and be confused forever. Since suffering and confusion do not have a self-nature, they can become enlightenment, happiness, and peace. Instead of being troubled because nothing has a self-nature you will say, "It's fortunate that there is no self-nature; this truth makes everything possible." This is a very positive way of looking.

If your headache had a self-nature, then you would have it your whole life. Since it does not have a self-nature, it will come to an end. We can say, "Long live impermanence! Long live emptiness! Thanks to impermanence and emptiness, everything is possible." This is a wonderful sentence. It turns upside down all the complaints about impermanence and emptiness.

People are terrified of the idea of emptiness because they identify emptiness with the idea of nonbeing. People in the West especially are afraid when they hear the word emptiness, because they do not understand what it is.

The Sanskrit *yujyate* (Chinese 成) can be translated into English as "possible." Therefore, the first two verses tell us that "thanks to emptiness everything is possible." Nagarjuna's proclamation is loud and clear; it is wonderful, and profound.

When we understand this teaching, we begin to be in touch with the ultimate dimension, the ultimate truth (*paramārtha satya*), and with nirvāṇa—which is to say, with the reality of no birth and no death, of no being and no nonbeing.

15. *The mistakes you make,*
    you attribute to me,
    just like someone who rides a horse
    forgets the horse he is riding.

汝今自有過
而以迴向我
如人乘馬者
自忘於所乘

It is you (in this case, the opponent) who create misunderstandings, not someone else. Still, you bring these misunderstandings and lay them at my door, saying that I am the one who creates them.

You are riding a horse, but you forget you are riding a horse. This is an amusing example. You are riding the horse, and yet you say someone has taken your horse. It is like forgetting you put the car keys in your pocket and blaming someone else for taking them.

16. *If you see that all things*
    must have a self-nature,
    then you also maintain
    that they have no causes and conditions.

若汝見諸法
決定有性者
即為見諸法
無因亦無緣

If you see that all phenomena have to have a self-nature, since the self-nature must already be there, they will not need causes and conditions to arise.

17. *You deny cause and effect,*
    action, the actor, and what is made.
    You also deny
    the arising and ceasing of all things.

即為破因果
作作者作法
亦復壞一切
萬物之生滅

If you think or say that all phenomena have a self-nature you deny the law of causality, deny the action, the one performing the action, and the result. For example, the seed of corn has the ability to create. It creates the sprout and the initial corn plant. The seed is the one who creates. Its action is creating, and the sprout or the plant of corn are what is created. You, who say that there is a self-nature, deny the law of causality, the act of creating, the one who creates, and the object that is created. It also means that you refute and negate the arising and the ceasing of all phenomena.

If you see that all phenomena must have a self-nature, they will not need to be caused and conditioned. You refute the idea of cause and result, of creating, of the one that creates, and of what is created. At the same time, you also refute the idea of the arising and ceasing of all things. Nāgārjuna deflects back to his opponent all the accusations they raise. The opponent says, "If you teach emptiness, you refute all the teachings." Nāgārjuna replies, "If you say that emptiness does not exist, you say that there is a self-nature; in this way you—not I—refute all the teachings."

The next verse (verse 18), which we looked at earlier, is also well known in the Buddhist world; it is the foundation for the teachings and practice of an important Chinese Buddhist school, known as Tiantai. Master Zhiyi, (538–597) of this school, took this verse and created a Dharma door called the Threefold Contemplation (三觀): the contemplation on emptiness, conventional designation, and the Middle Way. The teachings of the Tiantai school are also practiced in Vietnam; when I was a novice, I practiced according to this school. Although we belonged to the Chan school, we used the teachings of the Tiantai school. Tiantai practitioners practice meditation, but the school is not called a Chan school.

As I mentioned, when I was sixteen and seventeen I studied the Tiantai textbook on meditation practice entitled, *The Practice of Śamatha and Vipaśyanā for Young Beginners* or *The Smaller Book on Śamatha and Vipaśyanā*. This book teaches how to harmonize the breath, the body, and the mind and how to meditate. In *The Smaller Book on Śamatha and Vipaśyanā* there is no mention of the contemplations on emptiness, conventional designation, and the Middle Way. Only later on in the book entitled *The Larger Book on Śamatha and Vipaśyanā* did we learn about these three contemplations. For now, all we need to know is that the Three Contemplations of the Tiantai School come from the following verse of the Verses on the Middle Way.

18. *I call empty*
    things that arise from conditions.
    They are conventional designations
    and they are the Middle Way.

众因缘生法
我說 即是空
亦為是假名
亦是中道義

This is Nāgārjuna's proclamation: *all things arise from conditions and I proclaim that they are all empty.* How is it possible to proclaim that everything is empty? It is because they arise from causes and conditions. They are empty because they arise from conditions.

They are also conventional designations (*prajñapti*), which we examined earlier in Chapter 2 on arriving and going. *Prajñapti* is the name we give something—we agree together to use that name for practical purposes. For example, the Euro coin on its own does not have a value. We come to an agreement to give it a certain value. If we did not have that agreement, the coin would just be a piece of metal. Its whole value is due to a convention invented by the human brain; that is why we can use it. Since the Euro coin is a conventional designation, it has a value, and you can exchange it for a few kilos of rice.

The Middle Way (*madhyamapratipad*) is the way that transcends all pairs of notions like being and nonbeing, coming and going, birth and death. The essence of all phenomena transcends these opposing concepts. It is neither coming nor going, neither being born nor dying, neither being nor nonbeing, neither the same nor different. That is the nature of nirvāṇa, and it is called the Middle Way. The reason all things are empty, conventional designations, and the Middle Way is because their nature is conditioned co-arising.

This chapter on the Four Noble Truths is important because it shows how the theory is applied in real life, whereas the first two chapters, "The Examination of Conditions" and "The Examination of Coming and Going," illustrate the fundamentals of Nāgārjuna's theory.

In this chapter we read the three most famous of the Verses on the Middle Way. The first is the tenth verse, which mentions the two truths: the conventional truth and the ultimate truth. When we bring the light of the two truths to shine upon the Buddhist teachings, we see that the teachings that seem to be most contradictory are not in conflict at all. If we do not do this, we will think that the Buddha at one time says one thing and at another time says the opposite. Those who are caught in the ultimate truth cannot see the conventional truth, and those who are caught in the conventional truth cannot see the ultimate truth. The teaching on the two truths (*saṃvṛti* and *paramārtha*) is therefore a light that helps us see that the two truths, which seem to present two different views, in fact depend on each other. Without one of them. there would not be the other.

The second important verse is the fourteenth:

> *Because emptiness is possible,*
> *everything is possible*

And the third important verse is the eighteenth:

> *I call empty*
> *things that arise from conditions.*
> *They are conventional designations*
> *and they are the Middle Way.*

The insights in these verses are like precious gifts of nourishing food. When we read them, we feel the kind of satisfaction that comes from being in touch with wonderful teachings. To have the time and opportunity to be in touch with teachings like this and to be able to meditate on them in our daily life is a great happiness for a practitioner. In the world people are very busy. They do not have time to breathe, so how could they have a chance to be in touch with these profound teachings and apply them in their daily lives? As a practitioner you should give rise to gratitude for these teachings; in that way your happiness can be really great and unending.

4

EXAMINATION OF
BEING AND NONBEING

1. *The existence of something's self-nature*
   is not evident in its conditions.
   A self-nature that arises from conditions
   is something that is made.

眾緣中有性
是事則不然
性從眾緣出
即名為作法

The self-nature (*svabhāva*) means "the intrinsic
essence" or "the reality" of something. We think that
there must be a self-nature that makes Brother Minh

Niệm Brother Minh Niệm, and not Brother Pháp Niệm. This self-nature makes it possible for us to distinguish Brother Minh Niệm from Brother Pháp Niệm. Nāgārjuna is asking us whether this self-nature can be found in conditions. If you want to find the self-nature of a flower, what is it that helps you not to confuse it with a table or a cloud? When you look into a flower you see the conditions (*pratyaya*) that have brought it about—the seed, the earth in which it germinates, the rain, and the sun that give the warmth and the moisture required for growth.

> *The existence of something's self-nature*
> *is not evident in its conditions.*

Is the self-nature of something in the conditions that give rise to it? Can we find the self-nature of Brother Minh Niệm in the conditions that have made him possible—his parents, his ancestors, the Buddhist institute, his temple, his daily food? The answer must be no. Is there something apart from those conditions in which we can find his self-nature? Again, the answer must be no. Apart from the conditions which give rise to them we cannot find the self-nature of a person or a flower.

> *The existence of something's self-nature*
> *is not evident in its conditions.*

In summary, the first assertion is: It is false to say there is the self-nature of something lying in the conditions that make it possible.

> *A self-nature that arises from conditions*
> *is something that is made.*

The second assertion is: *Something that is made (kṛtaka, 作法)* is something that was not there in the beginning and had to be made.

In the commentaries on logic and dialectics (因明論, hetuvidyaśāstra*) it is said that sound is impermanent because it is something made. According to our mind-made definition of self-nature, it is something permanent, eternal, with no beginning and no end. Something that is made cannot have a self-nature; it cannot turn into something from nothing or from something turn into nothing. It has to maintain its intrinsic essence. Things that are made—like a flower, a table, or a sound—cannot have self-nature.

We all believe that we have a self, our self-nature. No one can brush up against our ego, because if they do we will be hurt. If we know that there is no ego, no self-nature, we will not feel hurt anymore. By meditating

---

* Dignāga - Pramāṇasamuccaya.

to see there is no self-nature, we suffer less, our pride is not hurt, and we no longer want to pack up and leave our colleagues, our family and friends, or our community. Someone who wants to leave their community still believes they have a self-nature. We are like a flower, and the flower is something which is made. *Something that is made* means that it has the nature of being conditioned or made; since it has been made, it does not have a self-nature.

In summary, there are two assertions:

1. *It is not correct to say that the self-nature can be found in the conditions.*

2. *It is not correct to say that the self-nature can arise from conditions, because it would be something that is made.*

2. *What sense does it make to say
that the self-nature is something made?
A self-nature is something not made
and does not come about dependent on things other
than itself.*

性若是作者
云何有此義
性名為無作
不待異法成

How can you reason that self-nature is made? By definition, a self-nature is something not made. A self-nature does not need other things in order to come about. Something that has to rely on conditions other than itself cannot in principle have a self-nature. The Chinese character 待 in the last line means "wait for." If the flower had a self-nature it would not need to wait for the sun, the clouds, and the soil in order to come about. We cannot find a flower apart from non-flower elements so the flower does not have a self-nature. The same is true for Brother Minh Niệm; Brother Minh Niệm does not have a self-nature.

3. *If things do not have self-nature,*
   there cannot be an other-nature.
   The self-nature of one thing
   is the other-nature of another thing.

法若無自性
云何有他性
自性於他性
亦名為他性

There must be a self-nature for an other-nature to exist. For example, this is Brother Minh Niệm, and that is Brother Pháp Niệm. You believe that Brother Pháp Niệm has a self-nature inside, and his self-nature is not the self-nature of Brother Minh Niệm. As far as Pháp Niệm is concerned, the self-nature of Minh Niệm is an other-nature. What other people call their self-nature (*svabhāva*), we call other-nature (*parabhāva*). We call our self "self-nature." Other-nature goes along with self: we call the self of someone else other-nature. If our self-nature exists, the self-nature of the other also exists. If our self-nature does not exist, the self nature of the other does not exist either. From the no self-nature we realize the no other-nature.

If phenomena, things, have no self-nature, how can you conclude there is an other-nature?

What you call your self-nature is only a self-nature for you. As far as others are concerned, your self-nature is other-nature. Others have their self-nature; that is why they see us as other-nature. Therefore, if the self-nature of phenomena does not exist, the other-nature of phenomena also cannot exist.

4. *Without self-nature and other-nature*
   How can anything exist?
   When there is self-nature and other-nature
   phenomena are established.

離自性他性
何得更有法

若有自他性
諸法則得成

If self-nature and other-nature are not there, then how can things really be there?

Things are truly there because there is self-nature and other-nature. Observing Minh Niệm or the lily flower carefully, we do not see a self-nature or an other-nature. Therefore, we cannot be sure that things really exist. If we remove self-nature and other-nature, how can what we call phenomena be there? When self-nature and other-nature are there, things can formally be established, but because they do not have a self-nature and an other-nature, things cannot be formally established. They are not really there. It seems like they are there, but they are not real; they are false.

These verses teach us to begin to re-examine our view of being and nonbeing. Our daily activities are based on a foundation; that foundation is made of our ideas of being and nonbeing, self and other. Since these ideas are not in accord with reality, our actions of body, speech, and mind are mistaken. We have to look deeply to see that in truth we and others do not have a self-nature— which means that there is no self-nature or other-nature. We are there due to the conditions that allow us to manifest. The other person is there due to the conditions that allow them to manifest. Seeing this, we no longer get caught in the idea of what is self and what is not self. When we are able to see things in this way, our thinking is right thinking, our speech is right speech, and our actions are right actions. This is not a theory or philosophy.

A mother who lives with her daughter sees that she, the mother, is not a self-nature and that her daughter is not an other-nature. Both mother and daughter are free of a separate self-nature. The happiness and suffering of mother and daughter are closely related. The mother sees the no-self of herself and her daughter, and her thinking becomes right thinking.

The same is true for a young man. He sees that he and his father do not have separate self-natures. He is his father, and his father is him. He is the continuation of his father. Seeing this, all discrimination, anger and suffering disappear naturally. He wants to help his father to be free of his present state of mind, and he sees that in helping his father, he helps himself; likewise, in helping himself, he helps his father. In the same way, the father can be happy when he helps his child to breathe freely and to smile.

The suffering we incur comes from being caught in the idea of a self-nature, of a self. This kind of meditation is not philosophy, but a search for the truth. Once we discover the truth, discrimination and intolerance naturally disappear, and there is real harmony.

A teacher looks at his disciples and sees that they are his continuation. If they lose their way in the future, it is the teacher's responsibility; it is as if he, the teacher, has lost his way. He has to take care of the difficulties and weaknesses of his disciples just as he takes care of his own difficulties and weaknesses. When he resolves his disciple's difficulties, he resolves his own difficulties. With such an insight the teacher does not blame the disciple, and is not angry, upset, or prone to punishing the disciple; he is able to love them. This is the insight into no self-nature.

If we study the Verses on the Middle Way just to understand their philosophy and teach it to others, it will bring us no benefit. Our study of the Verses on the Middle Way is to help us meditate more effectively. During our practice of sitting meditation in the morning, at midday, in the evening, and while we do our work, we do not let our mind be carried away by our surroundings. We come back to ourselves and meditate to see that we and our father are not two separate realities. We meditate to see that we and our teacher are not two separate realities. When we can do this, the relationship between father and child, and between teacher and disciple, becomes very enjoyable. This is because of right view. The Verses on the Middle Way are not metaphysical speculation. They guide us to right view.

The morning sitting meditation is a precious time for us to nourish ourselves and our sangha. If you are present every morning and your presence is fresh, you nourish the sangha. Imagine if, in a sangha of three hundred people, only three or four were there for the morning sitting. When you are not present you yourself go hungry, and you make the sangha go hungry. You have to nourish the sangha and yourself with your practice. You are not present just for yourself; you are present for the sangha. Your physical presence is something beneficial. It nourishes the sangha and it nourishes you because when you sit amidst the sangha, you are able to open your heart and let the energy of the sangha enter you. Your energy also enters the sangha. The sangha nourishes you, and you nourish the sangha.

Say a mother goes into the garden to pick vegetables or dig potatoes. Her awareness that she is digging potatoes to cook a soup for her family brings her joy. You are the same. On the way from the monastic residence to the meditation hall, if you know that each step nourishes the sangha, just as the love of a mother nourishes her children, you will feel happy. If you say, on the other hand, "Good grief! Why do they make us go out in this freezing cold weather"? then there is no love. Just as a mother cannot let her child go hungry, we cannot let the sangha go hungry. When a mother nourishes her child, the child nourishes her mother. Although the child is still small and does not yet know how to dig potatoes or cook them, the child's presence and smile nourish the mother a great deal.

All of the sangha practices are designed to nourish the sangha and nourish you. While you are sitting in meditation, do not sit as an individual. Sit as a part of the sangha. You are aware that your older and younger brothers and sisters are sitting with you—like a flock of birds flying in the same direction—and this makes you overjoyed. You feel you are flowing as a river. You just have to be physically present and everyone already benefits—how much more so when your practice has real content. Real content means that the practice is correct: you follow your breathing, enjoying each in-breath and out-breath. In that way your energy nourishes the sangha even more. First, your physical presence nourishes the sangha; second, your mind is present as you breathe and smile, and this nourishes the sangha even more. This presence is something sublime. You have to open your body and mind for the energy of the sangha to enter you. Even if in the sangha there are a couple of people who are nodding off, you can love them because you also sometimes nod off. Someone nodding off is something normal; the fact that they are present is good enough already. The first thing to remember is to nourish the sangha and to nourish yourself. Whether it is walking meditation, sitting meditation, or eating mindfully in the sangha, the purpose of the practice is to nourish the sangha and you.

The practice of meditation has a use and a purpose. Its first benefit is to calm the body and mind. While sitting in meditation you relax your body and help it calm down. Your breathing plays an important role in this. First of all you sit beautifully, upright and relaxed. With the help of your breathing, your posture is at ease: beautifully relaxed. Tell yourself: *this is an opportunity to nourish myself and realize freedom.* Freedom means self-sovereignty. Usually we do not choose to live our lives. We allow our thinking and our feelings to drag us around in different directions. In this way we become nothing but the victim of our thoughts, our feelings, and our fear. A hoisted flag flaps in the wind; it is the victim of the wind. A cork thrown into the sea floats up and down on the waves; it is the victim of the waves. In your daily life you are the victim of the waves of feelings, thoughts, and mental formations.

Sitting meditation provides a chance to learn to be free. You learn to remain firm, to sit solidly, not allowing your feelings to pull you here and there. Your breathing is the anchor; you are the boat that keeps still in the middle of the ocean. Thirty or forty five minutes of sitting is there for you to learn how to be a free person. If you are not able to be free during that time, when will you be free? While working you are pulled away by the work. In conversation you are pulled away by the conversation. In your daily life you keep being pulled away. When can you be master of yourself? When can you have freedom and self-sovereignty? Sitting meditation is the time when you practice reclaiming your sovereignty. If at times you are pulled away, just smile and come back to yourself. You feel compassion; you recognize an old habit energy—pulling you after this or that—and you do not become angry with yourself. When you see that habit energy pulling you away you just smile and say: "Hey, stop pulling me away!" You return to your sitting and breathing; you reclaim your sovereignty. Your sovereignty comes back right away.

You use your abdomen and your lungs as you breathe in. Breathing out, you contract your abdomen to expel the air from your lungs. As you begin to breathe in, you can touch your index finger with your thumb as you follow the in-breath from beginning to end. When the lungs are full, you can smile and allow the air to flow out. Your mind is wholly with your breathing. When you can maintain your attention fully on the breath, thoughts and other mental formations can no longer drag you out to sea. You are sovereign of yourself on the island of mindfulness—the island of yourself. At that moment, you find yourself on the most secure island—the island of mindfulness and concentration—where you can gradually learn to reclaim your sovereignty. If you cannot do this, you will remain a victim, drifting and sinking without stability.

So sitting meditation time is precious. While you practice, you nourish the sangha. You deserve to be nourished because you are offering the sangha good food. You know that you are giving the sangha good food, because you are receiving good food. Every day you have more freedom and more sovereignty. You do not let things carry you away. You know where you are going and what you want to do. These are the preliminaries in the practice of sitting meditation. If you can bring harmony into your body and your breathing, and be stably present on the island of yourself, that is already a success. After that you can go further. You can look into yourself and ask: *"Do I have any difficulties with another person—with a friend, a parent, a partner, a brother or sister? Where do those difficulties come from? Is it because I believe in my own self-nature and the other-nature of that person? We both make each other suffer and say unkind things."* You may meditate like this towards that person:

"You suffer, and, at the same time, I suffer. How can we free ourselves from this situation? We need to see that we are both in the same boat. If you are happy I am happy. If you are at ease I can be at ease. If you want to abandon our relationship, that is partly my responsibility."

When you see you are both interrelated and that you condition each other, you will see there is no self-nature. The happiness of the other helps you to be happy, and the suffering of the other makes you suffer. It is crystal clear that your peace and joy contribute to the other's peace and joy.

In the beginning, the object of your mindfulness is the breath. As you continue to maintain awareness of your breathing, your mind stops wandering. It remains in one place. The object of your mindfulness can continue to be your breathing, or it can extend to your whole body. When you hold to that object and calm your mind, you cannot be blown away by the wind of your feelings and mental formations or swept away by the waves of your thinking. After this you gradually acquire the ability to look deeply. When the mental formations of anger and anxiety come up, you are able to recognize and look into them in order to discover their source.

The basic condition for these mental formations is ignorance. Craving, anger, and ignorance are the three poisons which rot the lives of human beings. Craving and anger, like the other unwholesome mental formations such as fear, hatred, and despair, arise from the basic mental formation of ignorance. Ignorance is the inability to see the truth because of confusion. We are brothers and sisters, teacher and students, father and son, but we behave as if the other were our enemy—a completely separate reality. That is ignorance, and it can only be shattered by the practice of looking deeply. The Verses on the Middle Way are like hammers that help us shatter the mass of ignorance.

The Vietnamese poet Vũ Hoàng Chương, in his poem "Fire of Compassion," written soon after Venerable Quảng Đức immolated himself, used the word *brotherhood*. Brotherhood is possible when we recognize that we are brothers and not enemies. We are of the same nation; we are brothers. So why does someone who is Catholic discriminate against someone who is Buddhist? Those flames that consumed the Venerable Quảng Đức were the message burning up ignorance, so that we could clearly see we are brothers:

> *The enormous mass of anger and ignorance has opened people's eyes,*
> *so they can look at each other and see the immensity of brotherhood.*

Anger and ignorance create so much separation and destruction because we are unable to see the truth—and the truth is brotherhood. One person immolated himself in order to remind everybody that we are brothers and sisters. Why do we make each other suffer?

> *Heaven is truly present today.*
> *Now is the splendid and propitious hour.*
> *The enormous mass of anger and ignorance has opened*
>   *people's eyes,*
> *so they can look at each other and see the immensity of*
>   *brotherhood.*

Suffering, jealousy, anger, fear, and despair all grow on a plot of land called ignorance. Ignorance goes by the name of coming and going, being and nonbeing, birth and death, self-nature and other-nature. This is not philosophy. This is a theme of our meditation, helping us see the truth in our own heart, in the heart of the other person, and in the heart of reality. Looking deeply, we see there is no self-nature and no other-nature. When we can see this, right view is there; when right view is there, right thinking, right speech, and right action are also there. We no longer make ourselves and the other person suffer.

When you teach your students the Verses on the Middle Way, teach them in such a way that they will be able to apply them in their daily lives. When I teach the Manifestation-only teachings, I teach in a way that my students can apply those teachings to transform their daily lives. When I teach the Diamond Sutra, I also teach in such a way that the sutra can become a companion for people on their path of practice. The sutra is related to your joys and sorrows and to your jealousy. It is not removed from your daily experience.

Yesterday, I received a letter from a German practitioner. He comes from the Christian tradition and says that his tradition gives him the feeling that he is living in a two-story house. The ground floor is for his everyday life, and the top floor is where there are peace, joy, and liberation, and he has been unable to find a staircase to go up to the top floor. Now that he has come to Buddhism, he has found the staircase. He wants to leave the Church and follow Buddhism. I did not agree with him, and told him that he should not abandon his religion. He was not happy, and he replied, "I have found my staircase in Buddhism. Why do you force me to be a Christian? Why don't you allow me to be a Buddhist?" I did not want to force him to be Christian; I wanted to help him not to lose his roots. Since he had found the staircase, I wanted him to bring it home, and install it in his house so that the people who had long been stuck on the ground floor would finally have a chance to go upstairs. If you are missing a staircase in your home it is better to make one rather than leave your home and go somewhere else.

Next year (2003) in May, I have been invited to attend a Christian conference in Berlin. This will be the first time in German history that the Catholic and the Protestant churches will meet in a conference. Four other spiritual leaders from different traditions and I have been invited to give an address. Each address can only last fifteen minutes, but because I will speak in English and need translation they are allowing me a little longer. After this conference I will speak to about 6,000 young people on the subjects of happiness, the future, and peace. The invitation letter impressed me; two sentences in particular especially moved me: "We would like to invite you to speak, in the spirit of interreligious dialogue, on how there can be peace in the world. We also would like you to make some concrete proposals which we could apply in our congregations."

I was delighted by their openness in this letter: they want a Buddhist to offer them a method of practice which they can apply in the heart of Christianity and in the spirit of the Christian teachings. They are open to learn. Many Buddhists do not have such a spirit of openness; they are closed and prejudiced. They are much less Buddhist than these Christians, who are eager to learn new practices which they can apply in their own tradition. These Christians are not proud and prejudiced. They are able to see the no self-nature and the no other-nature better than many Buddhists. Some Buddhists can talk until their throat is dry, but they are not open and they do not have the insight these Christians have. They may fight to the death for the sake of defining a term. They talk on and on about what they claim to be deep and mysterious teachings, but at the same time they are dying of hunger in their spiritual life. They think that they are rich, but in fact they have run away from home—they are lonely, homeless, and without food.

We have to make the Verses on the Middle Way, the Manifestation-Only teachings, and the Diamond Sutra into a way of practice in our daily lives. We need nourishment; we should not let ourselves or our sangha go hungry. We have to study and practice every day in such a way that we have the essence that nourishes ourselves, our sangha, and humanity.

In the first four verses of this chapter, Nāgārjuna uses the term *self-nature* (*svabhāva*). The self-nature is something permanent; it cannot become nothing from something or become something from nothing. It is a real substance, an entity.

There was once a king listening to a musician playing a sitar. The wonderful sound of the sitar moved the king's heart deeply. He wanted to find the original essence of the sitar's sound. How could the sitar produce sounds that could move him so deeply? He gave orders for the sitar to be sawn open so he could find the sound's essence. When this was done, however, he could not find anything. Scrutinizing each sawed-off piece, he could not find the original essence anywhere. The sound of a musical instrument does not have an original essence or a self-nature, so it is not possible to find it. That sound is mere manifestation.

In the sutras the Buddha sometimes used the image of a banana tree. When you take away the outer layer of the trunk, you come to the second and then the third layer. You can continue like this until the last layer— and then there is nothing inside! There is no core. The banana tree does not have a self-nature, a real substance, or an inner core. An onion is the same; you cannot find its heart. You remove one layer, then another, and when you have removed them all you find it has no core.

When you look at another person or at yourself, you believe that inside there is a core self-nature. Believing that there is this self-nature, you are afraid, you hate, and you are hurt. If you know that there is no self-nature, you are free and nothing can hurt you.

⚬⚬

To summarize: the third verse says that if there is no self-nature, there can be no other-nature. The self-nature is our own core, and the other-nature is the core of the other person. If the self-nature is not there, then how can there be an other-nature? We arrive at the knowledge that self-nature is an idea—not a reality. Its substance is emptiness. Emptiness is emptiness of a self-nature or a real substance; it is not the nonexistence of the banana tree, the sound of the sitar, or the onion.

The fourth verse says that only if there is a self-nature and an other-nature, can we establish the real existence of phenomena. If there is no self-nature and no other-nature, phenomena are a dream, a flash of lightning, foam, a magical appearance, or a bubble. Without a self-nature and an other-nature, you can still relate to phenomena; you can have an idea or a perception about them, but the object of that idea or perception does not have a substance or a core.

5. *If being is not established,*
   then how can nonbeing be established?
   Only because something exists
   can it cease to be.

有若不成者
無云何可成

因有有法故
有壞名為無

When we say "is not" we can become caught in the idea of nonbeing, and when we say "is" we can become caught in the idea of being.

If being is not established, then how can nonbeing be established? This is straightforward but very rich. When we hear the Buddha say that "this is not" we are caught in "is not," in the idea of nonbeing. Since we are not yet free of "is," we are caught in "is not." We hear it said that the sound of the sitar does not have a self-nature, and so we say that the sound of the sitar does not exist.

For a long time, people have been saying that the Verses on the Middle Way are a Mahāyāna commentary, and that Nāgārjuna is extolling the Mahāyāna. That is not so. The one sutra that is actually quoted—and other teachings that are referred to in the Verses on the Middle Way—all belong to Source Buddhism. Nāgārjuna does not cite one sentence from the Mahāyāna sutras. In later compositions he teaches the Prajñāpāramitā, but he did not write the Verses on the Middle Way as a Mahayanist. The verses are neither Mahāyāna nor Hīnayāna. In the Verses on the Middle Way we can see that all the deep and wonderful teachings of the Mahāyāna already lie in the teachings of Source Buddhism. The interesting thing about this text is that it manages to express the wonderful truth of the Mahāyāna without quoting any Mahāyāna sutra.

The Ratnakūṭa Sutra—a Mahāyāna text—says: You believe in being, but when you hear the Buddha teach that things are empty, you believe in nonbeing. You stop being caught in the one but are then caught in the other. It would be better to have attachment as great as Mount Meru to being, than to be attached to nonbeing.

In the Verses on the Middle Way Nāgārjuna also says, "If being is not, then how can nonbeing be? If being cannot be established, then how can we establish nonbeing?" Nonbeing can be there only thanks to being. Just like the right can only be there thanks to the left. If the left is not there, how could we have the right? Being is one extreme, and nonbeing is another extreme. The Middle Way transcends both extremes—pairs of opposites like being and nonbeing, birth and death, coming and going. This is elementary and clear:

If being is not established,
then how can nonbeing be established?

Nonbeing cannot be established for the very reason that:

Only because something exists,
Can it cease to be.

Because there is *being* and being ceases, therefore there is *nonbeing*. There are Buddhist scholars who say that Buddhism maintains nihilism: the idea that *nothing exists*. However, as long as you believe in nonbeing, you necessarily believe in being, because without being how can there be nonbeing? Therefore it is not a question of being or nonbeing; you do not have to choose between being or nonbeing but you have to *transcend* being and nonbeing. Being and nonbeing are not real. They are mere ideas and wrong perceptions.

6. *Someone who sees being, nonbeing,*
   self-nature and other-nature,
   cannot see
   the truth in the Buddha's teaching.

若人見有無
見自性他性
如是則不見
佛法真實義

If someone sees that there is being and nonbeing and that there is a self-nature and an other-nature, Nāgārjuna says that they have failed to understand the Buddha's teachings. The true meaning of the Buddha's teachings transcends both being and nonbeing.

7. *The Buddha refutes being and nonbeing*
   in the teachings given to Kātyāyana.
   He gave the teaching which removes
   [the concepts of] being and nonbeing.

佛能滅有無
如化迦旃延
經中之所說
離有亦離無

The Kātyāyana Sutra (SA 301, translated from Sanskrit into Chinese) and the Kaccānagotta Sutta (SN 12.15, the equivalent teaching preserved in Pali) belong to Source Buddhism and not to the Mahāyāna. In my translation* I have entitled this sutra *Discourse on the Middle Way*.

The Buddha is able to put an end to ideas of being and nonbeing. The word nirvāṇa means *to extinguish*, and first of all we extinguish ideas like being and nonbeing. Nirvāṇa means freedom from ideas. When we remove all our ideas, we have limitless freedom. With our ideas we imprison ourselves in the narrow frameworks of time and space. For example, we think that we only have a certain number of days, months, or years more to live.

---

* For the text, see *Chanting from the Heart*, Vol. 1, Parallax Press, 2023. For the text and commentary, see Thich Nhat Hanh, *Beyond the Self*, Parallax Press 2009.

These are simply ideas that imprison us. When we are in touch with nirvāṇa we extinguish those ideas—and with them the frameworks of time and space—and we are no longer imprisoned. We have no more fear and nobody can enclose us in frameworks anymore. We can translate nirvāṇa as freedom: freedom from all views and notions—including the notions of being and nonbeing.

Nirvāṇa also means cessation (*nirodha*). Cessation does not mean that from something things become nothing. It means the end of ideas of being and nonbeing. Therefore to enter nirvāṇa does not mean that you go from being to nothingness. It means to enter a realm which transcends being and nonbeing. When you hear that the Buddha has entered nirvāṇa and you think that means the Buddha no longer exists, it is completely wrong.

The teachings given to Kātyāyana are to transform wrong views, and the theme of these teachings is the removal of being and nonbeing. If you remove being but you do not remove nonbeing, you have not really removed being, because being and nonbeing are a pair of opposites that always go together.

8. *If phenomena had a self-nature*
   they could not become nothing.
   A self-nature that becomes something else
   is not reasonable.

若法實有性
後則不應無
性若有異相
是事終不然

If phenomena really have a self-nature—a core substance or a real existence—in principle, they cannot become nothing. By definition, a self-nature cannot become something from nothing or nothing from something. If the self-nature of things is being, how can it later become nothing? A self-nature that becomes something else is not possible. To say that the self-nature could change does not make sense.

As we learned already, there are four signs which all phenomena manifest in different moments: arising, abiding, decaying, and ending. The character 易, used to translate the Sanskrit *jarā* (decay), means "change." If there is a self-nature—a real existence—how can it change? The self-nature does not go through arising, abiding, decaying, and ending. Whatever goes through arising, abiding, decaying, and ending is not the self-nature, is not real existence. It is just a magic show. In the Vietnamese lyric poem Cung Oán Ngâm Khúc ("Complaint of a Palace Concubine"),* the concubine exclaims:

---

* A poem in the Nom script written by Nguyễn Gia Thiều (1741–98).

Just like the play of a drama on stage
this illusory lifetime is painful to see!

If things really exist, how, after a time, could they cease to exist? It is not possible for the self-nature of things to be subject to change; a self-nature has to be a constant reality.

In your sitting meditation, observe the five skandhas to see that they do not have a self-nature. The skandhas are there, but they do not have a self-nature. Once you can see this, you can transcend all ill-being. The Insight that Brings us to the Other Shore* tells us: *Avalokiteśvara, while practicing deeply with the insight that brings us to the other shore, suddenly discovered that all of the five skandhas are equally empty and with this realization he overcame all ill-being.* You also have to do that!

During the Han Dynasty in the south of that empire there was a king named Zhao Mo (reigned 137–122 BCE). He founded a country called Nanyue (Nam Việt), which included some of the southern provinces of mainland China† and central to northern Vietnam. The capital of Nanyue was Panyu, now Guangzhou, in the Guangdong Province.

---

* The author's most recent translation of the Heart Sutra. For text and commentary, see *The Other Shore*, Parallax Press, 2017.

† Guangdong, Guangxi, Hainan, Hong Kong, Macau, S. Fujian.

In 1983 the mausoleum of the king Zhao Mo and two of his bones were discovered. During one of our teaching tours in China, the Plum Village delegation had a chance to visit the mausoleum. With modern archaeological techniques, archaeologists of the site discovered many remains of the culture of Nanyue in the second century BCE, including the king's jade seal, other utensils he used in his daily life, his valuables, his medicine, and the food he liked. The remains of the king's doctors, his favorite concubines, and his cooks were discovered; they had been buried alive alongside him so that in the next world he would have people who could take care of his health and cook properly.

I went along with the monks, nuns, and lay friends in our delegation who visited the mausoleum and recognized how lucky we are to have been blessed by the grace of the Buddha. Thanks to the Buddha's wisdom we do not need to be caught in the view of a permanent self. We see that right in the present moment we are continuing in a cycle of birth and death and that we are being reborn at every moment—not only in the way we continue in the past and future but also how we are continuing right now—in many different forms. The insights of nonself, impermanence, and interbeing help us not be caught in the ideas that became beliefs for the people of Nanyue at that time. They believed that at death they took their whole self—their immortal self-nature—with them to the next world, and in that world they would need their doctors, attendants, and others.

Without the light of understanding like that of the Buddha, we could still be caught in these beliefs. We would suffer because of our own anxiety and fear, and then make others suffer by burying them alive. Since we have the chance to learn the Buddha's teachings on no-self, impermanence, and neither being nor non-being, we can be free from much suffering. We do not need to be the victims of beliefs like the ones of Nanyue. What a blessing! The gratitude we feel for the teachings of the Buddha is far greater than that we would feel for someone who might give us riches, houses, or honors. The Buddha sends out his halo of understanding and destroys all our blocks of ignorance so that we can see things as they are: interdependent and impermanent, without a self or essence. Since we can see this, we are no longer caught in the kind of belief that makes us want our loved ones to be buried or cremated with us when we die.

These teachings are paramount, and they are not mystical. They are for us to meditate on. What the Buddha has bestowed on us is so great that we cannot repay our gratitude for it in one lifetime. People in power, like Zhao Mo, are not fortunate enough to receive a drop of the compassionate nectar of the Buddha in their hearts. If they could, they would not act so cruelly. King Zhao Mo underwent all the hopes, fears, and anxieties of someone who does not know what will happen to them after death. If we are able to learn, understand, meditate on, and live our daily lives in the light of the right Dharma, we experience great happiness.

9. *If things have a self-nature,*
   how can they change?
   If things do not have a self-nature,
   how can they change?

若法實有性
云何而可異
若法實無性
云何而可異

If the self-nature of things were real, how could things change? If the self-nature of things were really existent, it would not need to be born, to abide, to decay, and to end. Therefore, to say that things really exist is not correct; if they really existed, they would never become nothing or be able to change.

The reasoning of the first two lines of this verse is: If things really are, how can they change and become nothing? The second two lines mean: If the essential nature of things doesn't really exist, then how could things change and become something?

When we hear the first two lines of this verse—*If things have a self-nature, how can they change?*—we might think that the author maintains that things do not have a self-nature, and so do not really exist. But it would be incorrect to think this, so we need to ask the second question: *If things do not have a self-nature, how can they change [and become something]?* "Change" in this verse means changing from something into nothing or from nothing into something.

This verse helps us to go beyond the ideas of being and nonbeing. As long as we are caught in nonbeing we are caught in being, and as long as we are caught in being we are caught in nonbeing. In Shakespeare's play *Hamlet* we read the sentence: "To be or not to be, that is the question!" But according to the teachings of Nāgārjuna, to be or not to be is not the question.

In the Kātyāyana Sutra the Buddha speaks clearly about this matter of being and nonbeing. He says: "Viewing the world as being is an extreme; viewing it as nonbeing is another extreme." He taught that the Middle Way transcends being and nonbeing. This is not a Mahāyāna sutra but a teaching of Source Buddhism. It is short, but of fundamental importance. The teachings of the Buddha tell us clearly to transcend being and nonbeing. Despite this, many people blame the Buddha for teaching nihilism. Western scholars, especially, continue to think of Buddhism as a doctrine of nihilism.

10. *To assert being is to be caught in eternalism.*
    To assert nonbeing is to be caught in nihilism.
    Therefore a wise person
    is not caught in being or nonbeing.

定有則著常
定無則著斷
是故有智者
不應著有無

If you assert definitively that things exist, you are caught in eternalism. If you assert definitively that things do not exist, you are caught in nihilism.

The first view we can be caught in is eternalism (*śāśvata dṛṣṭi*) and the second one is nihilism (*uccheda dṛṣṭi*). Eternalism is the view that *things are permanent*. Nihilism is the opposite view, which maintains that once things come to an end, *they are completely annihilated*. These views are connected to the idea of a soul.

Christianity believes that God is eternal and that the soul is eternal. Buddhism denies both eternalism and nihilism. It does not deny eternalism and then fall into nihilism. The reality of things is not eternal and is not annihilated. To say that the Buddha teaches nihilism is just not true. Normally people—and in particular Western people—will say that if something is not eternal, it must undergo annihilation. The truth is, once we are caught in nihilism, we are also caught in eternalism, because without eternalism how can there be nihilism? If we believe that things really exist, we are caught in eternalism; if we believe that things do not exist, we are caught in nihilism.

> *Therefore a wise person*
> *is not caught in being or nonbeing.*

有 (*asti*) means "being" or "existent" and 無 (*nāsti*) means "nonbeing" or "nonexistent."

We have to look at ourselves, at the person we love—and the person we hate—with the kind of eyes that are not caught in being or nonbeing. We have to look at the Buddha and at Jesus in the same way—with the eyes of the Middle Way.

> 11. *If things have a self-nature, and therefore are not*
> *nonexistent,*
> *that is eternalism.*
> *If they previously existed and now exist no more,*
> *that is nihilism.*

若法有定性
非無則是常
先有而今無
是則為斷滅

If we say that phenomena have a self-nature and that they are not nonexistent, we are caught in the view of eternalism. If we see that before something was and now it no longer is, we are caught in the view of nihilism.

We see someone sitting before us and we believe that they exist. When that person dies, we say they no longer exist. This is how people normally think when they do not practice or meditate. A large number of scientists have the tendency to think like this; they have scientific knowledge, but the way they see things is not scientific. Many scientists fall into the view of nihilism without knowing it, and yet a small number of outstanding scientists are capable of transcending this nihilistic view.

Let us consider saṃsāra and continuation. When a candle is lit, it begins to be alive. It produces light, heat, a smell, and chemical elements like carbonic acid. Anything that burns needs oxygen and carbon. Life is combustion; without combustion there is no life. The candle is a beautiful metaphor for life. First of all, it needs carbon, and then it needs oxygen. We are the same. Our food contains carbon; a cube of sugar $(C_6H_{12}O_6)$

contains a great deal of it. When we breathe in, we bring air into our lungs. In the air there is the oxygen (O_2) that is needed for combustion (respiration) to take place in our cells, and heat is produced. Without this combustion, we would not have a body temperature of 37 C (98.6 F). Inside us there is combustion at every moment. While glucose burns in contact with oxygen, we produce other elements—such as CO_2—as well.

The food we eat, the water we drink, and the air we breathe are inputs. We produce other things that are called outputs: excrement, urine, perspiration, and exhalation. While it burns, the candle eliminates carbon dioxide. A city like Paris eliminates huge amounts of carbon dioxide every twenty-four hours. If there were not large forests on land and green algae in the ocean this carbon dioxide could not be absorbed and people would die. Forests and algae are essential for human survival; they absorb CO_2 and produce oxygen (O_2). When you cut down trees or pollute the ocean, you are cutting down human life.

From the perspective of matter, the candle produces light, heat, and CO_2. We do not see it going anywhere or doing anything, and so when it is completely burnt we say that it no longer exists. The truth is that the candle goes into the universe under different forms. When we don't see it anymore, we say that it has gone from being to nonbeing. This is unscientific! There is nothing which can go from being to nonbeing, or from nonbeing to being. The same is true for us. From the perspective of our physical body, we are entering the cosmos with every out-breath.

From the perspective of the mind, we produce thoughts, words, and actions, each of which are our continuation. We call this continuation "the actions (*karma*) of body, speech, and mind." They precipitate a chain reaction of cause and effect in the cosmos. They are us. Therefore, when this body disintegrates, we do not disintegrate; we are still very much there in the cosmos. Only the eyes of science—the eyes of insight—are able to see our continuation.

When this body of mine perishes, it will be wrong to say that I am no more. I am alive in you and in many other people and places. If you have the eyes of science and of insight, you will be able to see that I am still there and that there is no way I could go from being to nonbeing. It would defy science. This is true for all people and all other species. A flower, a cloud, or a young child: none can go from being to nonbeing. If you imagine these things existed before and that now they have ceased to exist, you would be naïve and unscientific. A real scientist and a meditation practitioner both must be capable of seeing that in truth there is neither being nor nonbeing.

In the previous chapters we have learned about no birth and no death, no coming and no going, and in the present chapter we have learned that there is neither being nor nonbeing. Only when we can see this truth do we completely overcome fear and touch true happiness. If we are still anxious and afraid that one day we will go from being to nonbeing, our happiness cannot be complete. We practice in order to have the insight of "neither being nor nonbeing." The practice is not just a salve to soothe anxiety and sadness. It is essential to meditate on the reality of phenomena in order to see their nature of neither being nor nonbeing.

5

EXAMINATION OF FIRE AND FUEL

The tenth chapter of the Verses on the Middle Way is on fire (*agni*) and fuel (*indhana*). This chapter shows us that there is no enduring subject; there is no separate self lying inside us (a self-nature) or lying inside others (an other-nature). The way Nāgārjuna uses dialectics here is fascinating. The example of fire and fuel is found in other places, for example, in the theories of some of the mainstream Buddhist schools that use it to try to demonstrate that there is a subject, an enduring self in time and space.

1. *If fire were fuel*
   then actor and action would be one.
   If fire were other than fuel
   then without fuel there could be fire.

若燃是可燃
作作者則一
若燃異可燃
離可燃有燃

If fire (the burning) is fuel (that which is burned), this means that the action and the thing that produces the action—the actor—are one.

Here we are distinguishing two things: the subject that acts and the action. For example, in the phrase "I sit," we distinguish I and sit; in the phrase "I die," we distinguish I and die. Are I and sit, I and die one or two? Nāgārjuna demonstrates gradually that if the burning and the thing being burned are one, then the actor and the action are one.

On the other hand, if the fire is not the fuel which is being burned, then there could be something separate called fire apart from the fuel. If you say that the fire and the log are one, you are saying that the burning and the thing being burned are one. If you say that the fire and the log are two different things, you have to conclude that there can be burning without the thing being burned.

The candle that has not yet been lit cannot be said to be fuel. Normally we think that the fuel can exist separately from the fire, and that it is simply waiting for the fire to arrive. The fire cannot exist separately from the fuel; it is not possible to say that the fire can exist independently of the fuel. To say that the fire is the fuel is also wrong. Saying that the fire and the fuel are two different things means that the fuel can contain fire; this is also not reasonable. This is the beginning of the string that will lead us to the insight of nonself.

We have the tendency to think that there is a separate self, or an actor, who is always there, ready to perform an action. Brother Pháp Hữu must be there in order to be able to hold the umbrella or to make tea. We tend to separate Brother Pháp Hữu, who is the actor, from the action of making tea or holding the umbrella, but this is a mistaken way of thinking. Are Brother Pháp Hữu and the action of making tea the same thing or are they two separate things? We cannot prove either way. The actor and the action rely on each other. We always think that there is a real entity waiting there and that this real entity goes to this place to perform this action or to that place to perform that action. This is because of our ignorance.

We say: I know the wind is blowing. How absurd! Can the wind be a reality separate from blowing? Can there be a wind that does not blow? If it does not blow, it cannot be called wind.

When we say the wind blows, we witness the strangeness of the way we think and use words. The wind is always blowing; there is only one reality and that is the wind. There is a knowledge of what is happening. We think that there must be an I for a perception to take place. However, ask yourself: Can the perception be there without the I and can the I be there without the perception?

In the sentence "I know the wind is blowing," we can remove the word "is blowing." The wind is the object of perception. Are the object of the perception (the wind) and the subject of the perception (the knowing) the same or two different things? Can the two exist independently from each other? We can remove the knowing because wind is the object of the knowing. So instead of a long sentence like "I know the wind is blowing," we can simply say "Wind!" This one word includes the whole sentence, "I know the wind is blowing." In wind there is no self, no actor, and no action. There is just an event taking place. When you have a thought or a feeling, you do not think there has to be a person or a subject there first and then the thought or the feeling happens. You do not need an actor.

This is the skillful means used by Nāgārjuna to help us to see the irrationality of our thinking. We are caught in an idea of a self. Our thinking is based on a self—a separate reality. The principle of such thinking and reasoning is called "the principle of identity." A is A and A is not B. Once we are A we can only be A and we cannot be B. This is the basis of our cognition and thought: the principle of identity.

According to the dialectics of the Diamond Sutra, only when we recognize that A is not A can we recognize the true face of A. The Diamond Sutra says, "A bodhisattva is not a bodhisattva and that is why they are really a bodhisattva. Living beings are not living beings and that is why we call them living beings. The self is not a self and that is why we call it a self." We look deeply to see that the idea of self—of an unchanging entity—is not possible; it is simply an illusion. At that time we can see what it is; apart from that, there is only illusion.

Looking into a person we see they are made of non-human elements like earth, minerals, food, and other animal species. In the process of human evolution, these other species have played a role. When you look into a human being and see they are made of non-human elements, you know the human being is not an independent reality apart from those elements. Then you are able to see the real human being. A that is not A and is truly A.

The Diamond Sutra is one of the oldest texts on deep ecology. If you want to protect human beings, you have to protect the elements that help human beings manifest, such as earth, plants, and other animal species. When you look at a human being and you see the earth, plants, and other animal species, it is like looking at A and seeing that it is not A. Only then do you see the true human being; only then is A truly A. That is the insight of interbeing—seeing the true face of A.

The dialectics of Nāgārjuna are like the teaching of the Diamond Sutra. In the beginning we think that there is an actor who is separate from the action, but when we look carefully we see that it is not like this. Actor and action are not the same—nor are they two different things. This is the teaching of *not the same, not different.*

This verse is about the non-dual nature of what burns (i.e. the fire) and what is burned (i.e. the log). In our head we believe that the burning (fire) is one thing and what is burned (the wood) is something else. The nondual nature is crucial! Most of us believe that there is a soul that is separate from our body. When we die, that soul goes up to heaven or down to hell—as if the soul is something that can survive independently from the body (a disembodied soul).

The first lines of this verse assume that if the fire is the fuel, then the actor and the action are the same thing. We no longer need to distinguish between the subject and the object of the burning: the one who burns and the one who is burned are one. Yet this is not correct. The last two lines assume that if the fire is something other than the fuel, then fire will always be burning and will not need fuel. If we have a soul apart from our body, the soul will continue to live forever and will not need the body to survive. When we say there is no soul apart from the body, people might think we maintain that there is no soul.

2. *[If fire were other than fuel]*
   the fire would just keep burning.
   If fire did not need fuel,
   it would not need someone to set it alight,
   and lighting the fire would serve no purpose.

如是常應燃
不因可燃生
則無燃火功
亦名無作火

If without fuel, there would be fire, fire would always be burning. If without the body, a soul could survive, why would the soul need a body?

It would not need someone to set it alight.

To say that burning does not need fuel to set it alight is unreasonable. A soul that can survive without a body is unreasonable, although it is something most of us believe.

And lighting the fire would serve no purpose.

The purpose is the burning. In this case, you would not need to burn something because the fire has a self-nature.

It is there in and of itself and does not need the action of burning. When we light the stove in the Upper Hamlet, a monk is needed to strike a match. If the fire were there in and of itself, it would not need anyone to light a match. This is what is meant by *lighting the fire would serve no purpose*.

The first verse already destroyed the ideas of same and different. According to the dialectics of Nāgārjuna, to say that the fire and the fuel are the same or to say that they are different is absurd. The second verse destroys the idea that the fire does not need the fuel—that it could endure by itself.

3. *If the fire did not need fuel*
   then it would not arise from conditions.
   If the fire were permanently burning,
   there would be no need for anyone to light it.

燃不待可燃
則不從緣生
火若常燃者
人功則應空

If you say that the fire does not need the fuel in order to be there, the fire could be there all on its own and would not need conditions in order to arise. If fire were always burning, there would be no action of a person to set it alight.

This verse continues to destroy the idea that the fire is different from the fuel. It also teaches the idea of *waiting for each other*, that is, that the fire *waits for* the fuel and the fuel *waits for* the fire.

We could say that the unlit candle is a fuel that is waiting for the fire to come. Thus the fuel is there in and of itself and does not need the fire in order to be called "fuel." Looking in this way, it seems as if the fuel were there separately, on its own, and as if the fire were there separately on its own as well. This is a naïve way of thinking. Is the table fuel or not? If fire were to come, the table would burn. So should we call the table fuel? Is there anything on earth which is not fuel? Earth, rocks, and metal can burn. When a volcano erupts, the resulting fire can burn houses, earth, and stone. Looking at things in this way, there is nothing that is not fuel. Yet, *only when it is alight* can we see it as fuel. The unlit candle is like the table or a rock—we cannot call it fuel. The word fuel is only meaningful *when it is burning*; before that, it is not really fuel. When you are an aspirant you are not yet a novice, so we cannot call you "novice." The fire of the Ten Novice Precepts has to come along and burn for you to be called a novice. The unlit candle cannot be called fuel *because it is not yet burning*.

When your mother became pregnant, people thought that first of all, in her womb, there was a body, and that a soul then came and entered this body, after which there was a body with a soul. This is the dualistic point of view: fetus is one thing and soul is another. With this dualistic point of view, we have the impression that fire is an independent reality that comes to the fuel. However, based on what we learned above, we understand now clearly that *before it is burned something cannot be called fuel.* Is fire a reality separate from fuel? Just light a match and you will see. From a state where there is neither fire nor fuel, suddenly fire and fuel appear *at the same time.* As long as there is fire there will be fuel. The fuel is not waiting for the fire to come, nor is the fire looking for fuel. This is the insight of *no coming and no going,* of not coming from anywhere and not going anywhere.

The heat that is released by striking the match warms up the wax, which produces a kind of vapor. Before that there was no burning. The fuel has to heat up, become vapor, and then it becomes the condition that helps the fire arise. When a candle burns, it is the vapor that burns and not the wax itself. If you had a tube to siphon the vapor away from the candle, you could light a match and set light to this vapor. When the candle is burning it creates a hot air current, which draws in cold air from below. Thanks to this hot air current, the flame is long and beautiful.

If there were no oxygen around, then the candle could not burn. The fuel is one condition, and the oxygen is another. If we place a glass jar upside down over the candle, the flame will go out because it will no longer have enough oxygen. There are other conditions that contribute to the manifestation of the fire, and not just the fuel; there is the person who lights the match, the oxygen, etc. When the flame manifests it helps what we think of as fuel to become real fuel.

When you blow the candle out you see the smoke rise. That is a vapor that can burn. While the candle is burning, it produces carbonic acid and water without this smoke. The same is true of human beings. When the weather outside is frigid and five or ten people are sitting in a room with all the windows closed, after a while you will see water vapor. The vapor comes from people's breath. We are not different from a candle; the cells of our body are burning, and if we want them to burn properly we need to breathe in oxygen. The life of a person is a process of burning. If we compare ourselves to a candle, we see that we are not so different: the flame is the soul of the candle, while the wax is its body.

⚛

Let us ask: While the candle is burning, is the flame a separate reality from the candle, or the same reality? The question is: Are the fire and the fuel the same or different? Nāgārjuna replies: not the same and not different.

We are learning, gradually, that things do not come to other things. Fuel does not come to fire and fire does not come to fuel. Fire does not come to wood and wood does not come to fire. If they were to come to each other that would mean that *they would already be existing*. If you are not there how can you come to me? If I am not here how can I come to you?

If we meditate on our five skandhas, we shall see that they are like a candle. The lower part of the candle is dark, and the candle becomes brighter closer to its top. We have our body, and our feelings that arise from the body. The body is a foundation for our feelings. Feelings like well-being, tiredness, physical pain, or pleasure are based on the body. There are also feelings that are not based on the body, but rather on perceptions. Perception (*samjñā*) means recognition. When we look at a marker pen and recognize that this is a marker, it is a perception. When we have a wrong perception, we suffer. When another person does not hate us but we perceive that they do, we suffer. That feeling does not arise from our body, but from our perception. Perceptions are also connected with the body. If we did not have eyes and ears, how could we have perceptions? Feelings are based in the body, and so are perceptions. Depending on whether our perceptions are healthy or not, our body also becomes healthy or sick. When our perceptions are correct our mind is light and free, but if our perceptions are wrong and full of anxiety, it will harm our body as the days pass. Feelings and perceptions depend on the body, and the body depends on feelings and perceptions. The flame depends on the quality of the wax in order to manifest, and the wax also depends on the flame in order to melt and create light and heat. Our body contains conditions that give rise to feelings, perceptions, mental formations, and consciousness. Feelings and perceptions are two mental formations, and consciousness embraces all five skandhas. It arises from the body and it embraces the body. We can use the fuel as a metaphor for the body while feelings, perceptions, mental formations, and consciousness represent fire. Our mistake is to think that the fire is different from fuel or that fire is nothing but fuel.

According to the belief of a number of religious traditions, only human beings have a soul. Other animal species, plants, and minerals do not. For a long time, people have believed that animals only have instinct. Non-human animals survive thanks to their instinct, but they do not think like human beings. Do they have feelings? We know that animals have feelings; they suffer and feel sad. But do they have perceptions? If they did not have perceptions, how would they know where to go to find food, and how would they recognize what is edible or inedible? To say that they don't have perceptions is wrong. Still, we have the tendency to think that animals only have instinct. Nowadays ethologists—scientists who observe animals in their habitat—have discovered that animals have feelings, perceptions, and intelligence.

⚜

The American philosopher William James tells us about his friend who likes to go boating on a lake every Sunday, and who usually takes his dog with him. Every time he calls the dog to follow him the dog is pleased and knows that they are about to go boating. They have to walk approximately one kilometer to the lake. Normally, when they arrive at the boat the man uses a sponge to wipe it clean. One day he left the sponge at home, and when they arrived at the boat he saw that it was filthy. To go back to the house, though, was too far. He looked at the dog and made the gestures of wiping the boat, and then pointed in the direction of the house. The dog understood, galloped back home, and some minutes later returned with the sponge in its mouth.*

From numerous other experiences like this, people understand that dogs are astute. Yet, in everyday speech we say that "animal instinct" is something dark that we

---

* William James, *The Principles of Psychology* (New York: H. Holt and Company, 1905) pp. 349–50.

cannot see. Thanks to ethologists, we know that animals can transform. If humans have evolved from other animal species, then they benefit from the experience of those species. Animals also have intelligence and the capacity to think. The only difference is that they have it to a smaller extent than humans.

According to some psychologists, when there is intelligence, the perceptions in our head are like a cognitive map. For example, imagine a schoolboy who goes to school in the morning and returns home in the afternoon. One day on his way back he wants to buy a cake. He is intelligent and therefore he knows that the shop is on the way home, which means that he can stop by that shop and then continue on his way home. If he were to go home first and then go back to buy the cake it would not be intelligent at all. In the mind of the schoolboy there is a cognitive geographical map.

This cognitive map definition of intelligence was used by an ethologist to study bees.* He brought the beehive to a new place and left it there for a time so that the bees could discover the flowers in this new location. After this he chose a nearby location that he called point A, where he left a number of small containers full of food for the

---

* James L. Gould *The Locale Map of Honey Bees.* Science, 1986.05.16, vol. 232 pp 861–863.

bees. In just a few days, the bees discovered this location and began to go there regularly to feed. Once the bees became used to that source of food, the researcher took a number of bees from the beehive, put them into a box, and then brought them to a different location, which he called point B. He wanted to see if the bees would fly back to the beehive before going to point A, or if they were intelligent enough to go directly to point A before going back to the beehive. When he released the bees he noticed that there were a number of bees who did go back to the beehive, but some of them went directly to point A without needing to go back first. With this experiment he demonstrated that animals also have a cognitive geographical map and therefore their own share of intelligence.

Another ethologist one day found five small river rats, whose mother had died before they opened their eyes. He brought them back and fed them with flies for a little while. Eventually, when they were big enough, he released them in a lake. The five baby rats swam right away without needing to learn from their mother. Based on this, some people argued that humans' resourcefulness in dealing with their environment, as in the case of animals, is innate.

In the fifteenth and sixteenth centuries, people in Europe thought that, thanks to the five sense organs, human beings know the reality of the external world. This theory was based on the idea that, thanks to our past experiences, we can get to know the objective reality of the world outside. Later, in the eighteenth century, the German philosopher Immanuel Kant said that we cannot know the *thing-in-itself* (*Ding an sich*). We only see things in the way they manifest through our sense organs; in fact, out there things are not like that. We only see their representations. If we were to say this in the language of Manifestation-only we would say that we only get in touch with the "world of representations" and never see the suchness of things. Kant said that we have an idea of the outside world because we were born with this idea *a priori*. This *a priori* comes from experience; it is a frame in which the outside world is already contained, just like innate knowledge. If we didn't have it, we would not be able to cognize the external world.

The river rats were able to swim because their species had been transmitting that knowledge for many thousands of years. The same is true with humans. This theory is very much in accord with the theory of evolution. If a leopard cannot run fast, then it will not be able to chase a gazelle. In a situation of scarcity of food, if it isn't able to run fast it will certainly die of hunger. The giraffe that lives in the desert would not be able to eat the leaves of trees without its long neck. This is why when it is born its neck is already very long. This is because of the transmission of its parents, and the transmission happens both on a physical and psychological level. If a gazelle does not run fast, it will be eaten by a leopard. Without developing the ability to run faster, the species would not survive to produce the next generation. Those who run faster in each generation survive to reproduce, causing the legs of the species to change over time. This is the theory of evolution. This is not in fact *a priori*, it is *a posteriori*.* It is *a priori* for the generation that was just born, but from the perspective of the whole species it is *a posteriori*.

This verse concerns the problem of soul and body. Most people either think that the soul is something separate from the body, or that the body and the soul are the same thing. They do not see the realities of no coming and no going, of neither the same nor different, or of conditioned co-arising and interbeing—of which we speak in Buddhism. Beginning from here, we reach the deep insights of Buddhism.

4. *You say that when something is burning,*
   you can call it fuel.

---

* Here a *posteriori* means something that is because of what happened after a particular event.

If the fuel can only be fuel when it is burning,
what is it, then, that is burning it?

若汝謂燃時
名為可燃者
爾時但有薪
何物燃可燃

You say that at the time of burning, something can be called fuel. When the candle has not yet been lit, we cannot call it fuel. The table, the wooden floor, the air, and all other things can also be burned. If you call an unlit candle "fuel," why shouldn't we call everything else fuel? Everything, including our own body, can burn. We are looking for the fire and the fuel, but where should we look for the fuel? The answer is that something can be called fuel *while it is burning.*

When you just see the fuel, what is burning that fuel? In the third verse above, we looked for the fire but could not find its self-nature. Fire does not have a separate self-nature. In this verse we are looking for the self-nature of the fuel, and we are likewise unable to find it. In our head we think that the fire is what burns and that the candle is what is burned—the fire comes to the candle, or the candle comes to the fire—and that these two things can exist separately from one another. In truth it is not like this. Nothing is coming to anything. The third verse shows that the fire cannot exist independently; the fourth verse shows that the fuel cannot exist independently either.

"Coming" implies that that which is coming must already exist. For example we say: Sister Tuệ Nghiêm comes to Sister Định Nghiêm. There must be a separate Sister Tuệ Nghiêm and a separate Sister Định Nghiêm for them to come together. Before the fire and the fuel came together, did they already exist? If they already exist separately *then what need is there for the fire to come to the fuel?* If they already exist separately, the fire must always be burning, while the fuel must always be being burned. Therefore, to say that the fire is something independent outside of the fuel is wrong, and to say that the fuel is a reality outside of the fire is also wrong. It is wrong to imagine that one has to come to the other. To see this is to see *no-coming no-going.*

When the candle is burning, this generates heat which makes the wax melt. Sometimes, when we try to light a candle, it will not light and we must wait some time for the flame to catch. This is because there must be enough heat for the wax to melt and become a flammable vapor. Before this happens, the candle cannot burn. Heat is one condition, and the oxygen in the air is another as is the wick that conducts the vapor to the flame. The wax is just one of many conditions; to say that the flame comes from the wax is wrong.

When we extinguish the candle, we see vapor from the wax rise. This vapor is different from smoke. When the candle does not have enough oxygen, then it will not burn well and it makes smoke—which is not wax but tiny particles of carbon. The vapor from the wax is what floats up as we blow out the candle. That is what burns.

The same is true for our body. Our body also needs to burn; it needs fire and it needs to maintain a temperature of about 37 C. If it is a corpse that has grown cold it will not have what we call feelings, and since there are no feelings there can be no perceptions. A body with no heat is just like a candle that is not melting and releasing wax vapor to burn. All the cells of our body are experiencing combustion within, thanks to the oxygen we breathe. We have to breathe, bringing oxygen into our blood and shuttling it to our cells so they can burn, i.e., oxidizing glucose. This process produces CO_2, which is subsequently expelled by our lungs.

A candle is no different. When it burns, the candle gives off carbon dioxide, which contains oxygen and carbon. The cells of our body also need oxygen. As they burn, the temperature of our body rises; when the body is sufficiently warm, feelings and perceptions begin. In the same way, vapor appears just as the wax in the candle starts to heat up; with vapor, fire, light, and heat also appear.

If we sit in a room by ourselves, light a candle, and observe it, we will see that the candle is very much like ourselves. The candle is producing light, heat, and scent; we are producing thoughts, words, and actions. If the candle does not burn well, it will fill the room with smoke. We are the same. If we do not burn properly, we produce unwholesome thoughts, words, and actions that pollute our environment and ourselves.

⁜

The view that our body is the source of our mind or that our thoughts and feelings arise from our body is a dualistic view called "materialism." It is an incorrect view just as it is incorrect to say that the wax gives rise to the fire. Wax is just one of the conditions. If there are no other conditions like oxygen, the person who sets it alight, etc., the flame cannot arise. The wax is the same; it needs to rely on many conditions to manifest, and those conditions have to manifest simultaneously. There cannot be something that manifests before, and then something that manifests after it. This is also true of the notion of psychesoma (*nāmarūpa*). Psychesoma is a pair; it is not the case that psyche arises from soma or soma arises from psyche, or that they exist separately from each other and then come together in order to live.

To assume that there is a senseless body with no perceptions already there and from that senseless body a soul arises is naïve. It has been said: *toute connaissance a une origine corporelle, une origine biologique* (all knowledge has a physical and biological origin),[*] but that is not scientific. If feelings and perceptions have not arisen, what we call a body could not exist. A living body must have feelings and perceptions. To say that the body is the basis for consciousness comes from false reasoning. To say that the body comes first and then consciousness arises is like saying that the fire comes first and then the fuel comes afterwards, or the fuel comes first and the fire comes afterwards. This way of reasoning is wrong.

For example, when you hold your pen vertically, you see an above and a below. If you hold it horizontally, you see a left and a right. Ask yourself: Could the left be there first and be the basis for the right, or could the right be there first and be the basis for the left? Can we say that the above is there first and becomes the basis for the below, or that the below exists first and is the basis for the above? The fuel is not the cause of the fire, and the fire is not the cause of the fuel. If something is not there first, how can it be the cause for something else? The right has no self-nature and it cannot exist by itself. Only if it were

---

[*] See p. 27 of *Le Moment 1900 en philosophie* by Bruno Antonini et al., on Bergson and his contemporaries.

there first could it come to the left, but since it does not yet exist, then what is it that comes to the left?

This verse says: "I want to prove that what you call fuel does not exist. When it is not yet burning, you cannot call it fuel. But can it be called fuel when it is actually burning?" Nāgārjuna's question is: "If at that time there is only the fuel, then what is burning it?" If we want to have fuel, we have to have fire. This is the dialectics of Nāgārjuna.

5. If [the fuel] were other [than the fire], it could not
    reach [the fire].
    If it did not reach [the fire], it could not burn.
    If it does not burn, it could not cease.
    If it does not cease, it is eternal.

若異則不至
不至則不燒
不燒則不滅
不滅則常住

If the fire and the fuel are two different realities, it means that the fuel is there before the fire.

It is fuel by and of itself; but why would it then need to be used to stoke the fire in order to become fuel?

If the fuel does not reach the fire, it cannot be burned. If it cannot be burned, it cannot cease. If it cannot cease, it is eternal, and we fall into the view of eternalism.

However, fire is an impermanent thing. After something has been burning for a while, the fuel will burn up and the fire will go out. So we have to remove the idea that fire and fuel are something permanent that can exist by themselves. This is extremely important, because in this chapter we are not just talking about fire and fuel, we are also talking about our body and mind, and the existence of an eternal soul.

When you hold your pen in front of you, you see the left and the right end of the pen manifest. First there has to be a base, and then from that base there is a manifestation.

When you visit Plum Village in June and July you see many fields of golden sunflowers. That is a manifestation. Golden flowers and green leaves must come from a root. What is their source? Starting from April, the farmers plowed the earth, sowed the seeds, and fertilized them. This is the source. When you look into a manifestation you see its source. When body and mind manifest they manifest from a source. You cannot say that the sunflower comes from the sunflower leaves or the sunflower leaves come from the sunflower, that the body comes from the mind or the mind comes from the body, that the right comes from the left or the left comes from the right. By looking into phenomena you have to see their origin and source; by looking into external signs you have to see the nature of things.

❖

The word manifestation is better than the word birth. To be born means to be born from something: this is born from that or that is born from this. Manifestation, however, means that there does not need to be a birth or a death. The cloud was not born, it simply manifested. We tend to think that birth means that from nothing, we become something. Clearly, though, the cloud did not become something from nothing, it is a continuation of the vapor from the surface of the ocean, from the heat of the sun, and from other things as well. The cloud is just one of many manifestations—something continuing to manifest. Before that, it manifested as water and vapor. Now it manifests as a cloud, and later on it will manifest as rain. That is manifestation, not birth; it is the nature of no-birth and no-death. Therefore, to say that the body gives rise to the mind or that the mind gives rise to the body is not correct. Body and mind are both manifestations, which we call psychesoma (nāmarūpa).

In Lower Hamlet there is a calligraphy that says, "You are not a creation, you are only a manifestation." We say this because if there is creation (birth), then there must be destruction. Looking deeply into the heart of reality, though, we see that there is neither birth nor death; there is only manifestation and cessation of that manifestation followed by manifestation in a different form. Only this insight can help us overcome fear of birth and death.

These verses help us to see that there is no phenomenon with independent self-nature. All phenomena have to rely on each other in order to manifest.

6. *If the fire is different from the fuel*
   and can come to the fuel,
   it is like this person can come to that person,
   and that person can come to this person.

燃與可燃異
而能至可燃
如此至彼人
彼人至此人

If you say that the fire and the fuel are two different things, and that the fire can come to the fuel, it is like saying that this person can come to that person and that person can come to this person.

In Buddhist countries many monks register to study in Buddhist institutes, but what they learn does not have anything to do with their daily lives. People attach little importance to applying the meditation practices of sitting, walking, and breathing in their daily lives. Sometimes laypeople give more attention to the practice of meditation than monks do. There are elder monks who have seen this and want to change the situation. The Venerable Paññā from Sri Lanka, who visited Plum Village in 2001, is one of those who has seen that Mahāyāna Buddhism is vital to effect this change. Mahāyāna Buddhism has a penetrating insight into society and can make the teachings of the Buddha applicable for the modern-day. Venerable Paññā has translated a number of my books, including *The Sun My Heart, The Miracle of Mindfulness*, and *the Heart of Understanding: Commentaries on the Prajnaparamita Heart Sutra.** Nowadays many lay practitioners in traditionally Theravāda Buddhist countries are curious about and have begun to look into Mahāyāna sutras because these sutras express the desire to bring an engaged Buddhism into the world. In order to practice diligently, we do not need to go into the forest and cut off all contact with the outside world.

In Vietnam and China the program of studies is lavish, but what is taught and studied cannot be applied in daily life. In the temples we see a devotional practice that includes prayers for the alleviation of suffering offered in the hope that some sacred powers will help us escape our suffering. We do not see the practice of

---

* The new version of this book is titled *The Other Shore*, Parallax Press, 2017.

mindfulness, concentration, and insight. Although there is faith and religious freedom—the freedom to organize the practice—it does not take people far. Buddhism declines not because of external circumstances but because people who practice it profit from Buddhism for the sake of their own interest, status, or position. When we study the Verses on the Middle Way, the Vimala-kīrtinirdeśa, the Lotus, or the Śūraṅgama Sutras we have to ask ourselves whether these deep teachings have anything to do with our daily life. Can we apply them when we eat a meal, drink tea, get sad or angry, wish for something, or fall into despair?

If the fire is different from the fuel
and can come to the fuel,

In Sanskrit fire is *agni* and the fuel is *indhana*. You can make a compound word *agnīndhana*—fire and fuel. Only if the fire and the fuel are two different things can the fire come to the fuel. If they were not two different things, how could this one come to that one? It wouldn't have anywhere to go to!

When you light a candle you see the flame coming to the candle and you think that the fire is really coming to the fuel, but that is a mistake. You think that the flame and the fuel are separate things—quite different from each other. Is it true that the flame is not the fire? The fuel makes the fire possible. The fire cannot be by itself alone; it must have some fuel in it. So to say that the fire and the fuel can exist separately from each other is to express an impossibility.

We normally think that the sperm of the father and the ovum of the mother come together to form a fetus, and then a consciousness comes from somewhere to transform the fetus into a living being. This comes from the belief that, just as fire and fuel are two different things, so the fetus and consciousness are two different things. The sperm and the ovum, which combine to form a fetus, are the fuel, and the consciousness—which comes from we know not where—is the fire. This is completely wrong, and yet nearly all Buddhists believe in it.

We have to understand that Buddhism has different levels. There is popular Buddhism, practiced by the majority, and deep Buddhism, practiced by those with the means to go deep into the teachings. Those of us who have the chance to study the sutras have to let go of naïve beliefs and incorrect ways of looking in order to go deep into these wonderful teachings.

It is like this person can come to that person,
and that person can come to this person.

For example Brother Pháp Đôn comes to Brother Pháp Cần, or vice versa. Clearly—we think—they are two different people. Pháp Đôn is not Brother Pháp Cần, and Pháp Cần is not Brother Pháp Đôn. They are two entities separate from one another—we think—and this makes it possible for one to come to the other. However, if we want to go deep into the teachings we have to reexamine this idea and see that it is not correct. When we speak in this way we believe firmly that it is correct, but in our way of thinking there are errors of which we are unaware.

⚬

In the Āgamas and Nikāyas—the earliest Buddhist texts—the Buddha said, "This is because that is." It means that *all things rely on each other in order to exist*. The word "is" in this sentence doesn't denote absolute existence; it means that all things are interdependent: if this is, that is. Who would dare to deny this? When we hold the marker upright we see an above and a below, and when we hold it horizontally we see a right side and a left. We say that the left and the right arise simultaneously, each relying on the other, and we think that we are correct—that our premise is indisputable. Left and right, good and bad, nirvāṇa and saṃsāra all rely on each other in order to manifest. "Rely" is a verb and a verb must have a subject. What relies? It looks as if there has to be a cloud for there to be floating. If there were no cloud, how could there be floating? If there were no flower, how could there be blooming? If there is floating, there must be a subject that floats, and if there is blooming, there must be a subject that blooms. If phenomena are not yet there, how can they rely on each other? This relies on that, but what relies? To say "laugh" by itself is not enough. There must be someone for the laugh to be possible. If there were not a person in the sentence, then who would laugh? The verb "laugh" has to have a subject.

This chapter of the Verses on the Middle Way is closely related to the chapter entitled "Examination of Agent and Action." Action refers to the verb, and if we want a verb we have to have a subject of the verb. When we say: *all things rely on each other in order to exist,* all the things that rely have to *be.* But if they *are* already, they no longer rely on each other! Our way of thinking has many fundamental errors like this, and we are not aware to what degree we are victims of our naïveté. The aim of Nāgārjuna is to show us that *neither the fire nor the fuel have a separate being.* They do not have a separate self-nature. If they do not have a separate self-nature, *what do they rely on?* They are not something real; they only exist as notions.

If you describe a triangle ABC and describe a straight line from C to another point H halfway along the baseline AB, you will have two triangles: AHC and HBC.

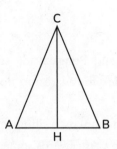

Ask yourself: does HBC arise from AHC, or does AHC arise from HBC? If you say that these two triangles rely on each other to arise, it is easy to understand. Yet, before they are there, how can they rely on each other? That is why the notion of birth is not as good as the notion of manifestation.

The words of the Vietnamese poet Xuân Diệu (1916–1985)—"I am sad and I don't know why I am sad"—imply that there is an "I" first and then there is the sadness. Sadness is a mental formation (*cittasaṃskāra*), and when that mental formation appears we provisionally designate a subject (who is sad) and the object (the sadness). A perception is always a perception of something. Say that all of a sudden a feeling of sadness or a perception arises. We can call this the *action*. We believe that if there is this action, there must be an *agent*. Therefore, the view that there must be a subject—the one who is sad, who sees, who goes, etc.—is captivating. The Buddha teaches, however, that that subject—that self—is not really there.

❖

The Sautrāntika and Pudgalavāda schools arose as a reaction to people who were too dogmatic about the teaching of no-self.

For example, a monk was sitting in meditation when a woman walked by. Afterwards someone else came that way and asked the monk:

"Venerable monk, did you see a woman pass by here?"

The monk, wanting to prove that he had understood no-self, said:

"I have not seen any woman go by. I have only seen a collection of bones, flesh, marrow, grease, and blood belonging to the thirty-six impure elements."

From a practical point of view, such a reply is bizarre; the man who asked the monk if he had seen a woman pass by was not looking for exalted teachings. He only wanted to know if a woman had walked by so that he could go and find her. A more intelligent and compassionate monk not caught in theory would have said, "Yes, a woman just went by." But the first monk wanted to prove that he was not caught in the idea of a self. The Sautrāntika school arose in response to this kind of dogmatic attitude.

The Sautrāntika school taught plainly that *there is something similar to a self* and quoted from the Ekottarika

Āgama to prove this: "Bhikshus, there is one person who arises in the world for the benefit of many people and the welfare of many living beings. Who is that one person? It is the Tathāgata, the Arhat, the World-Honored One."* So, the Sautrāntikas asked, Why do you not admit that the Buddha said that there *is* a person?

The Buddha also used everyday language. He used the words "me" and "you," but he had the insight of inter-being and nonself. When he used everyday language, he did so with freedom. We, however, are still ignorant, so when we use the words "me" and "you" we do not have that freedom.

Have you ever seen a dried squid? Our body is not very different from the body of a squid. Our human body contains between seven and ten liters of water. If you were to take all the water out of your body, in a few hours you would become a dried squid—you would be very light, and someone could lift you up with one hand. Nevertheless, in us are also the Dharma body (*dharma-kāya*), the retribution body (*saṃbhogakāya*), and the transformation body (*nirmāṇakāya*) of the Buddha. In us there is also the understanding of the Buddha and that of all our spiritual ancestors—together with the afflic-tions and the suffering of past generations. We believe

---

* EA 8.2 (corresponds to AN 1.XIII).

that when this body is a dry corpse, our spirit will separate itself and go somewhere else to be reborn. This is the belief in a Bardo or intermediate state. Here the body does not eat noodles or rice, but it can eat the fragrance of the food. This is a dualistic conception of our body and spirit. We think that the body is like fuel and the spirit is like fire, and that if the fire is not there, the fuel cannot come alive; we think there must be a consciousness that comes into the body and makes it a living reality.

❖

In Chapter Four I wrote about the mausoleum of the king Zhao Mo in Guangzhou. When the mausoleum was excavated in the 1980s, the archaeological team exhumed royal seals and gems and discovered remains of the members of the king's retinue (his doctor and his harem) thought to be needed by him, buried alive alongside him. The king's surviving subjects acted in this ruthless, inhumane way—burying his retinue alive—because they believed that after the body disintegrates, there is a spirit that goes to the other world and a fetus into which the deceased will be reincarnated.

Is there an immortal soul that leaves this body after it disintegrates in order to be reborn somewhere else, or not? If we do not understand the deep teachings of the Buddhadharma, we will not understand the idea of saṃsāra and rebirth, and we will be caught in popular beliefs. If we have a chance to go deeply into our study of Buddhism and we are still caught in these popular beliefs, all our time studying has been wasted. We all have an opportunity to study the deep teachings. If King Zhao Mo had had that opportunity, he would not have allowed his doctor and trusted servants to be buried alive.

The insight of the Buddha is very great. If we are able to realize this insight, we will overcome fear, suffering, and anguish. The grace of the Buddha is also great. This grace is the insight he transmits to us. Most Buddhists pray for the Buddha's grace, but many do not inherit the true understanding of the Buddha.

When we learn about consciousness we have the tendency to exclude what is *not* consciousness—like the body or the feelings. We do not realize that the body is also consciousness. How do we know that the body is there? Isn't it thanks to consciousness? When we think, "I know my body is here," this is a perception, and a perception can be wrong. Perception is always perception of something. The words "I know" refer to our knowledge of the object of our perception. Every perception must have an object.

In the Manifestation-only teachings we learn that all of our perceptions and mental formations have at least two parts: the perceiver and the perceived, or the subject and object of perception. In Buddhist terminology the perceiver, or subject, is called *darśanabhāga* (literally, "the part which sees") while the perceived, or object, is called *nimittabhāga* (the "sign part"). We say these two parts rely on each other to manifest and call their source the *svasaṃvittibhāga* ("the self-witnessing part"). We can compare the perceiver and the perceived with the heads and tails of a coin; both sides of the coin arise simultaneously, just like the left and right side of a pen. No side comes first before the other. The fuel is not already there waiting for the fire to come along; fire and fuel arise simultaneously. They do not come to each other. The sperm and the ovum are not there before consciousness arrives. Seeing this helps us to overcome the omnipresent dualism in our mind. The two sides of the coin symbolize the perceiver and perceived. The metal of the coin represents what we can provisionally call the self-witnessing part. It is the foundation from which both perceiver and perceived—subject and object of perception—arise.

When we hear the Buddha say that consciousness conditions the psychesoma, we tend to differentiate the body (soma) from the mind (psyche). In truth, psychesoma (nāmarūpa) is a composite; we could not possibly take a knife and cut it into two separate parts.

One notion is consciousness, another is psychesoma, and another is the five skandhas. The Buddha used these notions to teach and transmit the practice. We can talk in terms of one, two, or five. In the five skandhas the body (rūpa) is one skandha and the mind (nāma) is the remaining four (feelings, perceptions, mental formations, and consciousness). A toothache is a painful feeling. The painful feeling (belonging to mind) could never arise if there were no teeth (body). In the same way, you cannot say that fire can exist without fuel. In Plum Village we say: "You are not a creation, you are a manifestation." The manifestation has two parts: the perceiver and the perceived. This manifestation relies on a substratum just as the wave relies on the water. If you can accept the idea of manifestation you have taken a crucial step; although you are not completely free, the view that there is only manifestation helps you realize that there is no birth. Without birth there is no death. By removing the idea of birth, you remove the idea of death.

As you turn a kaleidoscope it manifests beautiful forms. When you turn it again, it manifests different forms—just as if the forms were being born and dying. In fact nothing is born and nothing dies. That which we call form (body) is not different from mind. All the wisdom and the experience of our ancestors is present in every cell of our body. An inheritance of experience has been transmitted to each of our cells—the suffering, despair, happiness, and wisdom of our ancestors. Modern science can prove this. Scientists have the capacity to recreate a whole person from one cell. In the one there is the all. Our ancestors were human beings, but they were also animal species, plants, and minerals. In Buddhism, when we look deeply we see that everything in and around us is consciousness (*vijñāna*).

A snail is not an architect and never went to a school of architecture, yet it builds a well-proportioned and wonderful shell. That is the talent of consciousness. Theists would call it God's creation, but students of Manifestation Only call it "the manifestation of consciousness." Looking at a snail we feel reverence and great respect. It has wisdom and experience. All the species on earth inherit the experience of their ancestors. There are animals that know how to camouflage themselves so that predators—thinking they are a piece of bark—will not come and eat them. Humans and all species aim at survival to avoid extinction. Although other species do not think like humans, they think in their own way. As we learned earlier, bees have the wisdom to return to the place where there is food without needing to find their hive first after being moved to a new location. The brain of the bee has a cognitive map. This talent arises from their consciousness and can be seen in the part we call body (*rūpa*). We as animals also benefit from the wisdom that other species have handed down to us.

We also can see the wisdom of plants. Trees produce brightly colored and fragrant flowers to attract bees and other insects, which come and collect the nectar; in this way the flowers may develop into fruit. As the insects collect nectar, their legs and wings are covered with pollen that they then carry with them and leave on other flowers, cross-pollinating the plants so they may fruit. Sometimes it is the wind that carries the pollen. Plants know how to create showy flowers to attract insects, and both parties benefit. The plants offer nectar, the bees offer a service. According to recent research on orchids, there are orchids with the scent and form of a female caterpillar or bee, which attracts the male insect of that species.

Going deeper, we see that consciousness is present in the clouds, the wind, the earth, and the hundreds of thousands of species of plants. We could say that *everything* is consciousness. We have to train ourselves to look at our body as something that cannot exist independently from our mind. The Buddha said explicitly, "If there is no form, then there are no feelings, perceptions, mental formations, or consciousness. And if there is no consciousness, there can be no form."* The idea that there is something that can exist separately from everything else is an idea

---

* Thus, Ānanda, with psychesoma as condition there is consciousness; with consciousness as condition there is psychesoma. DN 15 Mahānidāna Sutta.

of something impossible. Our own five skandhas are something wonderful. The Buddha said many times that, "looking deeply into the five skandhas we can go beyond birth and death.*" The Sutra on The Mindfulness of The Body† is an essential text that teaches us how to contemplate our own body. Do not look at your body as a mere house containing your soul. It is not like that. If we speak of containing, then we shouldn't say that the body contains consciousness, but rather that *consciousness contains the body*. In the 60, 80 or 100 years of our life we have to learn how to use and to take care of our body and our mind skillfully. In every moment of our life we create the future. The future is made of each instant of the present moment.

When a banana tree begins to grow, it has only two leaves. Subsequent leaves are still curled inside of the trunk. Let us provisionally call the first two leaves the elder sisters. The elder sisters open their bodies to receive rain, sun, water, light, and the minerals that rise from the roots of the tree to nourish both themselves and their younger sister leaves lying curled in the trunk of the tree. They are creating a future. They are living skillfully in the present moment and creating a future.

---

* Rohitassa Sutta AN 4.45.

† Kāyagatāsati Sutta MN 119, MA 81.

Whose future is that future? Are the younger sister leaves that are still rolled inside the banana trunk the same as the elder sisters, or are they different? There is not a moment when the elder sister leaves are not nourishing themselves and their younger sisters. This is because the younger leaves are part of them. There is a close relationship between the elder sister leaves and the younger sister leaves, whether they are present or have not yet manifested. How long will the elder sister leaves live? They might live for six or eight months, but then they will become torn, crumpled, and dried up. When we look at the capitulum we will be able to see the elder sisters in it, even though to all appearances they have dried up and died. The truth is that the elder sisters are plainly present and still green in the younger leaves and in the banana capitulum.

When our body is dry like the dried squid, we should not say that we have died. All our thoughts, words, and actions are continuing in future generations. We have to see ourselves in those generations and not fall into the view of nihilism—that after death we will be no more.

We often say that our children are our future. But how can they be our future? Is there something that can guarantee that our children can be our future? If we live our life in an irresponsible way—if our thinking is wrong thinking, our speech is wrong speech, and our actions are wrong actions—what kind of future will we have? If we have right thinking, right speech, and right action, they are gifts for our younger siblings, our children, and our students in every moment. Young people are not only our future; they are also our present. We have to live so that our students, our children, and our younger siblings become us in the present moment. We see that they are us and we are them. We are not caught in a separate self. Our happiness and suffering are not ours alone; they are also the happiness and suffering of our children, younger siblings, and students. We have to be them right now. When we have this insight of interbeing, we have enlightenment right away. What happens to our children and students happens to us and what happens to us happens to them. If young people are our present, there is no reason why they should not be our future. If in our daily life we do not allow the young people to be us in the present moment, how can we hope that they will be our future? Enlightenment is not something hard to see. It can be witnessed directly in our present-moment behavior.

⚬

Are there ways of practice that can help our thinking become right thinking? If we think in accord with impermanence, non-self, nirvāṇa, and interbeing, our words and actions will be loving and constructive. We can learn a great deal from the elder sister leaves. They know how to nourish themselves and display their beauty. They have lived well and deeply, while nourishing the banana tree every moment of their lives, including the younger sister leaves that have manifested or are still curled up in the trunk.

When we are disciples of a teacher, we may say that our teacher has enlightened understanding and that, therefore, whatever they do is correct—even if they make mistakes or break the precepts. We may believe that if someone has enlightened understanding they can do what they like: they can lie, steal, and have sexual relations with their disciples.

Enlightened understanding is something concrete. It is not something mysterious. You just need to look at someone for a little while, maybe only five minutes, and you immediately will see whether that person has enlightened understanding or not, because you can see the thinking, hear the words, and observe their behavior. Insight verses—the verses that a candidate Dharma teacher presents when they receive the lamp of transmission—are only four lines long, and yet that is enough to reveal someone's mind. Monks who have practiced in the monastery for a long time only need to look at a novice taking a step or inviting the bell to know how far along in the practice the novice is. They do not need to be with the novice for many months or years. From the way the novice speaks, works, stands, and closes the door they know his true attainment.

Enlightened understanding is something we can see, but it is not something we have to believe in. Belief in enlightened understanding leads many people to be deceived by their teacher. Their teacher claims to have achieved enlightenment—satori—but their behavior, the way they think, speak, and act, does not go along with the teachings on impermanence, no-self, and nirvāṇa. Nirvāṇa is an enlightened understanding. When you see that everything is a manifestation and that the foundation of manifestation is no birth and no death, no coming and no going, you have enlightened understanding. When a teacher's enlightened understanding is real, they have no more fear or discrimination. You do not have to believe that your teacher has enlightened understanding, and that whatever they do is right. Such a belief is extremely dangerous!

7. *If you say that the fire and the fuel*
   are two different things,
   then the fire would be able
   to come to the fuel.

若謂燃可燃
二俱相離者
如是燃則能
至於彼可燃

Only if the fire and the fuel can exist separately from each other could the fire come to the fuel.

As we have already learned, fire and fuel cannot be two separate realities. We have to reexamine our notions regarding rebirth, saṃsāra, hell and heaven; all our views are upside-down because they are based on the mistaken view that fire and fuel are two separate things. If when you study this verse you feel that something breaks apart inside of you, that is a very good sign! It is the breaking apart of a long-held intellectual belief. This verse provides an opportunity for you to re-examine your belief so that you can go deeper into the teachings and the practice.

8. *If thanks to the fuel, the fire exists,*
   and thanks to fire the fuel exists,
   which of them existed first
   for there to be fuel and fire?

若因可燃燃
因燃有可燃

先定有何法
而有燃可燃

We say that thanks to the fuel we have fire and thanks to the fire we have fuel—which is to say: this is because that is and that is because this is. If we say this, then which of the two determines the existence of the other by being there first? When we hold a marker horizontally we see that there are the left and the right tips. The left exists thanks to the right and the right exists thanks to the left. But which side was there first for the other side to rely on? If the other side was not yet present, how could it be relied on?

If thanks to the fuel, the fire exists,
and thanks to fire the fuel exists

This is precise, like mathematics. If you say that *thanks to the fuel there is the fire* and *thanks to the fire there is the fuel*, then you are saying that *these two things rely on each other*. But then we can ask the question:

which of them existed first
for there to be fuel and fire?

Did the fire exist first or was it the fuel? You say that thanks to the one the other exists, but does that one *already exist* for the other to depend on? If it does not already exist, what does the other depend on?

To say that the fire exists thanks to the fuel and that the fuel exists thanks to the fire is wrong. The sentence "All phenomena rely on each other in order to arise" sounds very good, but we cannot be sure it is correct. It would mean that there must first be one thing for the other thing to depend on and that *only then will there be two things*: the fire and the fuel.

9. *If thanks to the fuel there is fire,*
   what has already been burned, will be burned again,
   and in the fuel
   there could be no fire.

若因可燃燃
則燃成復成
是為可燃中
則為無有燃

If we say that in fuel there is fire, then something already burned has to burn a second time. If we say, "thanks to the fuel," this means that *the fuel is already there.* What, then, would be the point in burning it once more? This is not reasonable, and people could turn the argument around saying that *in the fuel, there is no fire.*

The eighth and ninth verses talk about "waiting." One thing is waiting for the other thing in order to manifest. Has the fire been waiting for the fuel? If the fuel is truly fuel, then it must have fire in itself. And if there is no fire burning it then it is not fuel. Therefore, to wait for something that has already manifested is absurd. This is just as if we said that the left was there first and that the right relied on it in order to be established. But if the left is not yet there, what is the right relying on in order to be established? The formula "this relies on that in order to exist" sounds correct at first, but in truth it is not so correct. That must be already there in order for this to rely on it, but if that is already there, then this is also already present in that and has no need to be born. In this way we come to the teaching of no-birth.

10. *If this waits for that in order to be,*
    this is also what that is waiting for.
    Therefore there is no cause for waiting,
    and there is nothing which comes to be.

若法因待成
是法還成待
今則無因待
亦無所成法

If something comes to be as a result of waiting for something else, that something is also what the other thing is waiting for in order to come to be. It is both the subject that is waiting and the object that is being waited for. If the fire is waiting for the fuel, the fuel is also waiting for the fire. They are both waiting for each other, but *there is nothing for them to wait for*. If we do not yet exist, how can the other person wait for us? And if the other person also does not exist, how can we wait for them? What are we waiting for? That thing which has to wait for something else in order to come into being is the very thing that that something else is waiting for in order to come into being.

"I have been waiting for you for thirty years" sounds like I have been waiting for you and you have been waiting for me. But say you do not exist and I do not exist. If phenomena come about because they wait for each other, those phenomena are waiting for other phenomena in order to come about. The right is waiting for the left in order to exist, but the left is also waiting for the right! If all phenomena are waiting for each other in order to manifest, then, the phrase "I have been waiting for you for thirty years," implies that I am the object waiting for you to make it possible for me to exist.

> *Therefore there is no cause for waiting,*
> *and there is nothing which comes to be.*

When we look carefully *we cannot see any object that is waited for,* and *there is no phenomenon that could arise or come about.* Are fire and fuel two separate phenomena?

Only if they are two separate phenomena can there be a situation in which this is waiting for that or that is waiting for this. This verse removes our mistaken idea of waiting.

11. *If something has to wait in order to come about,*
    how can it wait if it has not yet come about?
    If it has already come about and is waiting
    then what is it waiting for?

若法有待成
未成云何待
若成已有待
成已何用待

If something has to wait in order to come about,
how can it wait if it has not yet come about?

If we speak of waiting, then somebody needs to be waiting. If we have not manifested yet, how can we wait? If we say "I wait for you," there must be an "I" first that can perform the action of waiting. If we haven't manifested yet, who would be the one who waits? There must be a subject for the verb to have a real meaning. If we say "the cloud is floating," there must be a cloud present for the floating to have meaning; without a cloud how could there be floating? The same is true of waiting. There has to be someone waiting for "waiting" to have real meaning. If you say phenomena wait in order to manifest when they are not yet there, what is it that is waiting?

> *If it has already come about and is waiting*
> *then what is it waiting for?*

If a phenomenon has already come about, what does it need to wait for? How could phenomena wait for something in order to come about if they are not there? Thinking that they are already there *and* they are still waiting for something to help them come about would be absurd!

This whole chapter on fire and fuel is related to the ideas of an actor and an action. The connection between actor and action is an essential object of meditation. Whether we are liberated and can go beyond birth and death or not depends on whether we can succeed in the meditation on actor and action.

12. *The fire is not there because of the fuel,*
    but without fuel as a cause there is no fire;
    the fuel is not there because of the fire,
    but without fire as a cause there is no fuel.

因可燃無燃
不因亦無燃

因燃無可燃
不因無可燃

These four lines mean: it is not because of the fuel that the fire comes about, but, on the other hand, without the fuel there can be no fire; it is not because of the fire that the fuel comes about, but without the fire there can be no fuel. This verse looks into what we mean when we say "caused by" or "not caused by."

Normally we say that this depends on that in order to come about: the fire depends on the fuel in order to come about. Examining this carefully, we see clearly that it is not because of the fuel that there is a fire, and yet without the fuel as a cause there can be no fire. Neither "caused by" nor "not caused by" are appropriate.

> *The fire is not because of the fuel,*
> *but without fuel as a cause there is no fire;*

This means that if the fire is waiting for the fuel in order to arise, the fire does not have its own self-nature. If the fuel is waiting for the fire in order to manifest, then the fuel also does not have a self-nature. We cannot say "caused by that," neither can we say "not caused by that."

The last two lines of this verse are just like the first two, except that the words fire and fuel are reversed.

This formula applies in both directions and its aim is to take notions of causation out of our head.

We have already learned these things in the chapter on coming and going. If we can master the teachings of that chapter, this chapter will be easy to understand.

13. *The fire does not come from somewhere else,*
    and in the fuel there is no fire
    The same is true for the fuel,
    as we said in the section on coming and going.

燃不餘處來
燃處亦無燃
可燃亦如是
餘如去來說

If the fire does not come from somewhere else, then in the place where the fire is burning (i.e., the fuel) there is also no fire. This also applies to the fuel: it does not come from somewhere else, and so in the fuel there is also no fire. This whole problem is solved with the same reasoning that is used in the chapter on coming and going.

This verse refers to the place where the fire and the fuel originate. The fire does not originate from somewhere else, and the place where the fire is burning, the fuel, is not the place of origin of the fire.

In the chapter on coming and going we came to the conclusion that there is no coming or going and that there is no subject and no object. For example, our parents and grandparents grew up seeing such rivers as the Seine, Mekong, or another river. Now we have been born and grown up, and we have seen the same river as they did. In the future our children and grandchildren will be born, and they will also see this river. The river seems to be a real entity. We can say things like, "The river winds." To wind is a verb (action), and the river is the subject of the verb (actor). The river has been winding for many years, from the time before we or our parents and grandparents were born, and it will continue to wind until we die. We have the impression that there are rivers that we call Seine, Mekong, Gironde estuary, etc. that will be winding forever—as if they were a continuous, uninterrupted reality.

The collection of the five skandhas is just like a river. When we were small we had our picture taken. There are also photographs of us at twenty, thirty, forty years old and so on, and there are pictures of us now. Although these photographs are somewhat different from each other, they are in fact pictures of the same person. People think that there is an immortal and unchanging subject that is going through time in this way. We say "I live" just as we say "the river winds." I am the subject of the verb and live is the verb. If there is living without an I, who is living? We feel that the action of living must have an I or another subject.

When we observe a river deeply, we see that there is not a persistent subject in it. The river is made of many drops of water connecting with one another. We cannot bathe twice in the same river or get in touch twice with the same water. The river is changing at each moment. We ourselves are also changing at each moment. The cells in our body are like drops of water flowing in a river. The body is also a river, and if we look carefully at it we will not find something that can be called a subject.

Looking at the physical body, we see its cells are born and die at each moment. Looking at the mind is also like this. Our feelings, perceptions, mental formations, and consciousness are also like drops of water or cells of the mind. The mental formations of sadness, anger, worry, or happiness are drops of water in the river of consciousness. In this river there does not need to be an I, an actor, and an action—a subject and an object. Normally we think that the fire is a kind of subject and the fuel is a kind of object.

This verse is to help us contemplate the self—the ego. We say that consciousness makes the body alive, just like the fire comes from somewhere to burn the candle. This is a dualistic concept—that the candle cannot burn if fire does not come from somewhere else to burn it and bring it alive. Our body is a kind of fuel, and the soul is a kind of fire. We normally think that thanks to this kind of fire coming, the body can live. This chapter helps us to see that our dualistic idea concerning fire and fuel, body and spirit, actor and action is mistaken. As long as we are still unable to see this, we are not able to overcome fear, and we are not truly liberated. When the mental formation of anger arises, there is only that mental formation. If we analyze anger, we see that anger is always about something: our teacher, our friend, the cat, or the weather. Anger always has a subject and an object.

According to phenomenology, consciousness is always consciousness of *something—Toute conscience est conscience de quelque chose.*[*] Each of the fifty-one mental formations must have its own object. A mental formation arises; it lasts uninterruptedly for anywhere from half a minute to three minutes, and then gives way for another mental formation to arise just like successive drops of water in a river. There are only mental formations succeeding one another; this gives us the impression that there is a continuous self, but this self is an illusion. At night, when it is dark, we can light a torch and move it around in a continuous circle. Someone standing one hundred meters or more away will see a clear circle of

---

[*] Husserl, Méditations Cartésiennes (1929).

fire. In truth there is no circle; there are only dots of fire continuously succeeding one another giving us the impression that there is a circle.

What we call a soul, or self, is an illusion. In reality there is only a continuous succession of mental formations; a mental formation arises and then gives up its place for others to follow. There is an uninterrupted continuation that gives us the impression that there is a self (the fire) that makes the body (the fuel) alive. Looking carefully, we do not see an actor. When we talk about sadness, we are talking about a mental formation that arises and has an object. To be sad is to be sad about something. Sadness does not need an actor. Normally we say, "I am sad"; but who is sad? Actually we do not need the I. Sadness can be there by itself. Thinking is the same. When a thought comes up, there is no need for a subject sitting there who has that thought, i.e. "*Je pense, donc je suis*" ("I think, therefore I am"). There is a thought (*pensée*), but there is no I (*je*) because in the thought both subject and object are there. Earlier, we discussed how we tend to say: "I hear the wind blowing" and "I know the wind is blowing." Wind that does not blow is not wind. In the wind there is the blowing. It is absurd to say "The wind is blowing," when all you need to say is, "Wind."

In English there are verbs that are derived from nouns. House is a noun, but we can also use it as a verb, as in, "This building can house twenty people." In what we call subject or author, *there is already the action*. The house must house. If it does not house, it cannot be called a house—just like something that does not float cannot be called a cloud.

Remember the teaching of Confucius that we looked at earlier: "The king kings, the citizen citizens, the father fathers, the son sons."* The king must act as a king, citizens must act as citizens, fathers must act as fathers, and sons must act as sons. The noun is also a verb. Speaking about a monk you could say, "The monk monks." If you don't monk (verb) then you are not a monk (name). Monking is the practice of meditation and keeping the precepts. The verb and the subject of the verb are not two different things. In the same way we can also say, "The cook cooks." If he does not cook, we cannot call him a cook.

The thirteenth verse uses the example of fire and fuel in order to speak about all other things. A pot has the function of a pot, which is to contain something. Clothes have to clothe, which means they do the work of covering and warming the body. The function of a thing goes together with its nature. When we talk about something, we have to look deeply into it so that gradually we learn

---

* 官官, 臣臣, 父父, 子子.

and see clearly that in it there really is no distinction between subject and action. Actor and action cannot be two separate realities existing outside each other. There is a fundamental mistake when you say, "I live" or "I die." When you see this mistake you begin to see the truth and you can overcome fear and grief.

⊗

Geometry has a definition of a point and a line. What is a point? It is the meeting of two lines. The idea of a point is possible because of the idea of a line. Without the idea of a line there is no idea of a point. What is a line? It is a moving point. If we want to define the point we rely on the line, and when we define the line we rely on the notion of a point. This is a mere designation—an argument, a supposition—that we use to map out a strategy—a labyrinth. And we enter that labyrinth of speech and ideas. Nirvāṇa is the absence of all ideas—we are no longer controlled by ideas like self, human being, living being, or life span.

When we use the term psychesoma (nāmarūpa), nāma means the feelings, perceptions, mental formations, and consciousness, while rūpa means the body. There is a differentiation; nāma is not rūpa. The body is one thing and the mind is something else. This is exactly where we are caught. When we study the Manifestation-only teachings, we discover the truth that *both body and mind are a manifestation of store consciousness*—which sometimes manifests as nāma and sometimes as rūpa—*but that these two do not exclude each other.*

Researchers in particle physics have discovered, to their surprise, that elementary particles such as electrons sometimes manifest as waves and at other times manifest as particles. Particles are distinct from waves. How could a particle be a wave or a wave be a particle? It seems absurd; nevertheless, subatomic scientists have seen in their research that something can manifest as a particle at one moment and as a wave at another moment. In our macroscopic world we see that a wave cannot be a particle and a particle cannot be a wave. If we want to enter the microscopic world of particles and atoms, we have to put our normal way of looking behind us to enter that world where we see that particles are waves and waves are particles. In the West, the new word "wavicle" has been coined to describe this. It helps us transcend our dualistic notion of particles and waves—and likewise of body and mind.

We cannot realize liberation and enlightenment as long as we think that we leave our body here for our mind to be born again somewhere else—that our body is wholly other than our mind and our mind is wholly other than our body, or that the fire is wholly other than the fuel and the fuel wholly other than the fire. This does not mean that when our body disintegrates our mind also disintegrates. We have the impression that the body disintegrates, but this is not true. Though there is no candle left after we burn it for a few hours, this does not mean the candle is no longer there. It is still there in new forms. The disintegration of this body does not mean we are no longer there. The idea that after the dissolution of this body the consciousness wanders around and waits to enter a new body belongs to popular Buddhism. This is not deep Buddhism. We are fortunate to have the conditions to learn the teachings of deep Buddhism, so we must let go of the simplistic and naïve concepts of popular Buddhism. Looking again at verse 12:

> *The fire is not there because of the fuel*
> *but without fuel as a cause there is no fire;*
> *the fuel is not there because of the fire*
> *but without fire as a cause there is no fuel.*

When we read a verse like this, we should ask ourselves: Is it related to my suffering, fear, and craving? If we cannot see that it has something to do with us, we have not yet understood it. If it can shed a light that stops us from being attached, fearful, or worried, we know we have understood it. You should keep this fact in mind when you read the great Mahāyāna sutras such

as the Avataṃsaka Sutra, the Lotus Sutra, or the Vimala-
kīrtinirdeśa. You ask: "Are these deep and wonderful
ideas related to my suffering?" If the reply is "yes," you
have understood them. If all you can do is talk intel-
lectually in a superficial way about them, you have not
understood them.

*The fire is not there because of the fuel, but without fuel
as a cause there is no fire.* Again, imagine you are holding
a pen horizontally, viewing its right and its left end. To
say that the left arises because of the right is not correct,
but to say that it does not arise because of the right is
also not correct. The same is true for the fire and the
fuel. The fire does not arise due to the fuel, but without
the fuel it cannot arise.

*Phenomena are not born from themselves,
nor from others,*

Things do not arise from themselves. The egg is not born
of itself, but neither is it born from something else. These
are two ideas; the idea that something creates itself, and
the idea that something is created by something else.
Here it is the same; the fire is not created by the fuel, but
neither is it created by itself.

*Nor both from themselves and others, nor without cause.
Therefore we know they are unborn.*

All theories about creation are based on four ideas: the first, that the world arises by itself; the second, that the world arises because of something else (i.e. God); the third, that this world arises both from itself and because of something else; and the fourth, that the world arises without a cause. The idea of creation has to lie within one of these four categories.

However, Buddhism teaches us about *the unborn*, or *the uncreated*. The unborn is the highest fruit of the Buddha's teachings—the fruit that people like and desire most. What is the unborn? It is nirvāṇa. Nirvāṇa is unborn and undying. Birth and death are only ideas in our head; they are not the true nature of things. The unborn is the foundation of existence and of the world. It is the foundation of all of us, but since we are caught in an idea of birth and death, we worry and become afraid. The French chemist Lavoisier said something similar: *Rien ne se perd, rien ne se crée, tout se transforme.** He was not a Buddhist, and had never studied the Verses on the Middle Way; he observed reality and saw clearly that *nothing is created and nothing is destroyed*. Birth and death are ideas in our head; they are not real.

---

* "Nothing is lost, nothing is created. Everything transforms." *Traité Élémentaire de Chimie*, 1789.

We believe that the candle's life begins when we first light it and ends when it burns itself out. Birth is "becoming something from nothing" and death is "becoming nothing from something." There are, on the other hand, scientists who, while observing the object of their research, see that *there isn't anything that becomes something from nothing,* and vice versa.

A cloud could never become nothing; it can only become rain, snow, or ice. That is its no-death nature. No death always goes together with no birth. The cloud is not born; it does not come from nothing. Before it was a cloud it was water vapor and heat. That moment when we think it was born was the moment it manifested as a cloud. In Buddhism we can say, "You are not a creation, you are a manifestation." When Sister Trang Nghiêm was born she did not come from nothing. She was there before, only in different forms. What was called *the moment of her birth* was just *the moment of her manifestation.*

The cloud can hide its form of manifestation as a cloud to manifest in its new form of rain. This is not birth or death. Rain is not born and a cloud does not die. One manifestation follows the other. No-birth is nirvāṇa; we do not have to look for it in a far off place. It lies within our reach. When we realize no-birth we no longer have any fear.

Phenomena do not arise by themselves, but neither do they arise because of something else. *The fire is not there because of the fuel* means that fire does not arise from something else; *but without fuel as a cause there is no fire* means that neither does fire arise by itself. Phenomena do not arise from other phenomena and they do not give rise to themselves. It is wrong to talk about *this* arising because of *that,* but it is also wrong to talk about this not arising because of that. To say that the right is there because of the left is wrong, but it is also wrong to say that the right is not there because of the left. Why is this? Because if the right relies on the left in order to be there, the left must have been there already for the right to rely on it. But if the left were already there, it would be something independent of the right. In this way it would not need to rely on the right—it would be already there! Arising by oneself and arising because of another are both wrong.

Let us be concrete. Our dualistic concept of body and soul needs to be reexamined. Most of us believe that the body is different from the soul. Fire symbolizes *the soul,* or the metaphysical body—and fuel or wood symbolizes *the physical body.* We believe that thanks to consciousness or soul (fire) entering the body (wood), the body comes alive; without the soul the body is inert matter. Human beings have the wrong idea that the soul leaves or enters the body. This dualistic view is a fixed idea in human consciousness that is difficult to remove. These verses are like the very sharp strokes of a strong axe that help us to shatter our dualistic view of body and soul. If we do not understand this, we will not understand the chapter on the Examination of Fire and Fuel, though we may study it for a thousand lifetimes.

There are places in the world where, when someone dies, people still hope that they could come back to life. In Vietnam the corpse can be lowered on a mat to the ground in the hope that by receiving the substance of earth it will be able to live again. There is also the custom of taking some of the clothes of the deceased, climbing on top of the roof, and waving them around to call the soul back to the body. These customs arise from the belief that the body and the soul are two independent realities. In many religions—Buddhism included—we can find beliefs of this kind. Such dualistic beliefs of a body and a soul are not real or deep Buddhism, but rather an incorrect popular view.

This is because that is; the right arises from the left. If the left does not exist, however, how can the right rely on it to arise? If you want to rely on something, that thing has to be there beforehand. In the example of the fire and the fuel, neither thing is present first for the other to rely on it. If this does not rely on that, there is no such thing as *arising from the other*. Therefore the fire does not arise from the fuel, and yet it also does not arise from itself. This is the meaning of *The fuel is not there because of the fire / but without fire as a cause there is no fuel.*

⚜

Nothing has a self-nature, including fire and fuel. If one of them relied on the other to arise, that other would have to be there first. If it is already there it does not need to arise. Thus there is no possibility of something arising from something else; the argument that things arise from what is not themselves does not stand. In both cases—either things arise from themselves or arise from others—we come to the conclusion that *there is no birth or creation.*

Soul and body, fire and fuel both are without a separate self-nature. If they had a separate self-nature, they would not need to arise. So they are *unborn.* Nāgārjuna's reasoning is very keen. We talk and do not know what we are saying; we think and do not know what we are thinking.

We are deceived by our habits of speaking and thinking. We have already seen that there cannot be a wind that does not blow, and yet we still keep saying: "The wind blows." We say "Those practitioners are practicing," and yet, if they were not practicing, they would not be practitioners! The practice is already present in them.

We can conclude that the nature of reality is no birth and that the idea of creation is mistaken. There is only manifestation. When a marker is held horizontally, are the left and right born or do they manifest? If they are born, they have to be born from something. Do they rely on one another or are they born from themselves? Birth and death are an idea; *birth and death are manifestations.* If we go all the way with the deep logic of Nāgārjuna, we see that it renders all our ideas about reality absurd. Nirvāṇa is the reality that transcends all notions.

14. *In the fuel there is no fire.*
    Outside the fuel there is no fire.
    If the fire has no fuel,
    inside the fire there is no fuel.

可燃即非然
離可燃無燃
燃亦無可燃
燃中無可燃

The above verse is translated from the Chinese. Below is the translation of the equivalent verse from the Sanskrit text:

Fire is not fuel,[*]
And fire is not somewhere other than fuel.

---

[*] MN 62 Mahārāhulavāda.

> *Fire does not possess fuel.*
> *Fuel is not in fire and fire is not in fuel.*

Neither fire nor fuel have an individual self-nature. If there is no fire in the fuel, how can there be fire outside of the fuel? If there were fire in the fuel, why would you need to burn fuel? That is one aspect of the truth. The second aspect asks: How can there be fire apart from fuel? With this verse, we look into the matter of *inside* and *outside* and discover that our ideas about inside and outside are all wrong. If the fire isn't the fuel, then fire and fuel are two separate things. If they are two different things, how can one be in the other? Here there is the idea of *existing in each other*.

Once the Buddha taught his son Rāhula, "This body is not mine, I am not this body, this body is not myself." To say the self is the body is not correct; to say the body and the self are two separate things is also not correct; to say the self is in the body and the body is in the self is also not correct. The Buddha taught that all these three ideas are incorrect. The metaphor of fire and fuel helps us understand clearly the words of the Buddha in the sutras.

If *fire is not fuel,* then *fuel is not in fire and fire is not in fuel:* fire and fuel do not exist in each other. This is a kind of mathematics that seems daunting, but it isn't difficult. For example, if we take a number like 365 and we write it down as $(3 \times 100) + (6 \times 10) + (5 \times 1) = 365$ it looks as if it were some form of higher mathematics, but, actually, there is nothing to it.

15. *Fire and fuel are used*
    to explain grasping and the one who grasps,
    to explain the examples of a pot or cloth,
    and all the other examples.

以燃可燃法
說受受者法
及以說瓶衣
一切等諸法

We translate *upādāna* as "grasping"; it can mean clinging, grasping, or attachment. This term was initially translated into Chinese by a few monks as 受 and after that the character 取 became standard. The five skandhas are referred to as the skandhas of grasping (*upādāna-skandha*). Our body, feelings, perceptions, mental formations, and consciousness are the objects of our clinging or attachment. There is the subject that grasps and the object that is grasped. We grasp the five skandhas as our self (*ātmopādāna*). *Ātma* is the grasper—the self, the I, or the soul—and the five skandhas are the objects of grasping (*upādānaskandha*). We can think of the fire as ātma and the fuel as upādāna. This verse says we can take the example of fire and fuel in order to explain the self and its object of attachment, and also to shine light on all the other examples that have been given—such as a pot or cloth. Imagine a pot; looking deeply into it, we see the clay. The pot is like the fire and the fuel is like the clay; the relationship is the same as that between fire and fuel. We cannot say that one of them is what the other depends on to arise. The pot does not arise from itself, nor from something other than itself; it does not arise both from itself and something other than itself—and neither does it arise without a cause. The same is true for cloth. Looking at the cloth we see the cotton or silk threads. Does the cloth rely on the threads or do the threads rely on the cloth to arise? Just like the fire and the fuel, the cloth does not rely on the thread, or vice versa—and neither thread nor cloth arise from themselves. This principle holds true for other phenomena. Does the wind come first or the blowing come first? Our ways of thinking and speaking render us incapable of seeing reality! We must practice looking in such a way that we overcome notions—including the notions of birth and death. A good practitioner directs their attention inward. In their daily life—upon hearing or seeing something—they should look and listen in the light of no birth and no death.

We may reflect on the thought, while we are driving our car, that our grandmother was unable to drive. By looking deeply, though, we see that the truth is that our grandmother *is* driving the car because *she is in us*. We say that our grandfather did not practice, but in truth our grandfather *in us* is inviting the bell and breathing mindfully. We and our grandfather are not two different realities, but we need to have mindfulness and concentration in our daily lives to be able to see this. Once we are able to see, we will gradually overcome birth and death—and fear. This is not philosophy. This is a meditation to help us look deeply and get insight.

When we look at a lit candle we see that it offers light, heat, and fragrance at every moment. It also produces CO_2. Do not think that the candle is merely in the candle. The candle also lies outside the candle, because without the oxygen surrounding it the candle could not burn. We have to see the candle outside the candle. If we cover the candle with a glass jar, in just a few seconds the flame will go out. This demonstrates that the candle isn't only inside the candle. In Buddhism this insight is called "the body outside the body."

I wrote in *The Sun My Heart** something like this: "I have a heart inside my body. If that heart stopped beating I would die right away. But I also have many hearts

---

* Thich Nhat Hanh, *The Sun my Heart*, Parallax Press (1988, 2006, 2020), p. 66.

outside my body, and if any of those hearts stopped beating I would also die immediately. The sun is one of my hearts. Although it is outside of my body, if it were to go out, I would also go out." I have to look at myself to see everything inside me, and, at the same time, I have to look at what is *not* myself to see myself in those not-myself things.

The light and heat the candle offers we provisionally call *energy*. Matter becomes energy, but it is also said that matter is extremely condensed energy and that energy is extremely diluted matter. While the candle is burning, it is in a process of manifestation. We don't need to wait for it to burn itself out for it to manifest as something else. You do not need to wait until you bring me to the crematorium to see me manifest in a new form. Already in the present I have manifested in new forms, and you have to see this so that when the time comes you will not need to cry or feel sad. This is meditation! You have to see the light, the energy, and whatever else the candle is offering at each moment of its life.

We are the same; in each moment of our daily life we offer our thoughts, actions, and words, and we go in the direction set by them. We may offer something beautiful and wholesome or we may offer something unwholesome, like violence and hatred. When we light a stick of incense, it will continuously turn into smoke and fragrance. When it is finished, we shouldn't say that it is no more. It continues in the universe in the form of smoke and fragrance. The nature of the incense is unborn and undying. This is the kind of thing we need to contemplate in our daily life. As a monastic practitioner, if we spend all our time working and do not have time to look deeply, we are wasting our monastic life. Pots, clothes, candles, wind, and anything else can be contemplated on and understood in the light of the teachings on fire and fuel.

16. *If someone says that there is a self,*
    and that phenomena differ from one another
    you should know that this person
    has not tasted the essence of the Buddhadharma.

若人說有我
諸法各異相
當知如是人
不得佛法味

There is the notion of a *self* and the notion of *phenomena*. Self is an unchanging soul—a kind of fire that does not need fuel, but that still manages to manifest. Phenomena are things like pots, cloth, wind, or houses. All these things are not separate entities. If we are able to remove the notions of self and phenomena, we will be in touch with reality—with nirvāṇa—and experience no-birth. Once we have experienced no-birth, we no longer have any fear; we can smile as we die, because we know that we are not dying. Death is a moment of manifestation just as any other moment in life. An incense stick offers itself at each moment; likewise, the moment which we call "death" is also a moment of offering. Why should we worry about the last moment more than we do about the first? We have to be able to see our continuation right in the present moment. We don't wait for this body to disintegrate in order to continue; we are already continuing right now. If we can see this, we will die in peace—and we will live in peace. If we are not capable of living in a wholesome and happy way, there is no way we will be able to die in a wholesome and happy way. When we have experienced the unborn, we realize that life and death are illusions. There is the chant:

> *The Buddha is a flower of humanity*
> *who practiced the Way for countless lives.*
> *He appeared on this earth as a prince who left his*
>   *royal palace*
> *to practice at the foot of the Bodhi tree.*
> *He conquered illusion.*
> *When the morning star arose,*
> *he realized the great path of awakening*
> *and then turned the wheel of the Dharma.*

*All species together take refuge with one-pointed mind
to realize the path of no birth.
All species together take refuge with one-pointed mind
to vow to realize the path of no birth.*[*]

This is the ultimate aim of a monk or a nun—the most important thing a practitioner should realize. It would be a great shame not to realize this before our body disintegrates, because then we may experience a lot of worry, grasping, and attachment at the time of death. But if we can achieve no-birth, the moment of our death will be very joyful and utterly free of fear.

---

[*] From *Chanting from the Heart*, Volume II, Parallax Press 2023.

6

EXAMINATION OF NIRVĀṆA

1. *If all phenomena are empty,*
   they are unborn and undying.
   So what you call nirvāṇa
   is the ending and extinction of what?

   若一切法空
   無生無滅者
   何斷何所滅
   而稱為涅槃

This is the question of someone who has not understood nirvāṇa: "You teach no-birth and no-death, but
how can you speak about nirvāṇa?" When a candle is
blown out, we say that it is extinguished, and extinction is what we call nirvāṇa. "On the one hand," the one
who has not understood comments, "you say that all

things are unborn and undying, and on the other you say that there is extinction. There is clearly a contradiction in your teaching! If all dharmas are empty, unborn, and undying, then what is it that is extinguished in nirvāṇa?" This is a question based on precise reasoning. I had already read something about nirvāṇa at the age of fourteen or fifteen; I had heard people say that nirvāṇa is something that cannot be expressed, and I just believed it. It is partly true. There are things that we need to experience directly—to come to and be directly in touch with—if we want to see and know them. We cannot understand these things through language alone, no matter how much people speak about them. This is true not only for abstruse things. Take, for example, a tangerine. If someone has never seen one, peeled one to smell its fragrance, or put a segment in their mouth, they will never know exactly what a tangerine is—no matter how much you describe it.

It is correct that we cannot say anything about nirvāṇa. In theistic religions such as Christianity people ask, "What is God?" Theologians will reply that we cannot say anything about God, God can only be directly experienced. If we cannot say anything about God, we should remove theology as a subject of study and stop establishing seminaries to teach it. On the one hand, people say that you cannot speak about God, and on the other, they establish major and minor seminaries to teach about God, and they write countless books about God. There seems to be a contradiction in this.

When I grew up, my thinking matured. I saw that if you are skillful, you can speak about nirvāṇa without people becoming caught in what you say. If both the speaker and the audience are skillful, they will not be caught. The speaker does not lay a trap, and the listener is not caught in it. While speaking we can give clear instructions on how to get in touch with nirvāṇa. We can say, "Oh! You've never had a tangerine? It's small like this and orange. If you go out to the market you may be able to buy one." Although these words are not the tangerine itself, they can guide us to the tangerine and help us to recognize it. Words of guidance can be beneficial. If the speaker is skillful and the listener is skillful, neither of them will be caught. The listener will use the guidance to be able to touch nirvāṇa.

The Verses on the Middle Way use this approach. They know that we cannot describe the ultimate reality, but that if we use words skillfully—like a magician summoning up a phantom army—we will be able to make miracles happen. We will be able to help people remove their mistaken notions and ideas about reality. This chapter, just like all other chapters in the Verses on the Middle Way, uses the magic of words to help us do this. We should take care not to become attached to the words! In some of the Mahāyāna sutras* it is said that all the teachings of the Buddha are like a finger pointing at the moon. Although the finger is not the moon, it is thanks to the finger that we can see the moon. If we just grasp at the finger and believe it to be the moon, then we are caught. Someone who points their finger unskill-fully lays a trap, and someone who takes the finger to be the moon falls into it. In the end, both of them fail. The speaker and the one listening have to be skillful. A skill-ful listener should look up at the moon and not mistake the finger for it.

All Nāgārjuna's reasoning is a skillful means to help us experience something that cannot be spoken about or described in words. We cannot describe the insight of the Buddha or nirvāṇa, but we can still use language to help people remove their ideas about it. Nāgārjuna was a master of this magical language.

⊹

The term nirvāṇa in English can be translated as "extinc-tion," as in the extinction of a flame. Nirvāṇa is the high-est aim of the practice, just as a return to God—to sit at God's feet—is the highest aim of the Christian tradition.

---

* E.g. the Laṅkāvatāra and Śūraṅgama Sutras.

Some people ask: "What if you believe in heaven and God, but heaven and God do not exist, would you not lose out?" You invest your whole life and energy in something that does not exist. Would you not lose out? It is like gambling; if you win, you win big, but if you lose, you lose everything. Is theology just a game of chess? As Pascal* said, "You should keep having faith. If there is God and there is heaven, you will go there, and if there isn't, you won't lose anything. If you do not believe, and God and heaven do exist, then it would be a great loss! So, to have faith is much better." There is something quite sad about this kind of reasoning. If we were to apply this reasoning to Buddhism, how would it sound?

Is nirvāṇa something real, or is it something that we imagine? What if we spend our whole life going in the direction of our imagination, and in the end nirvāṇa does not exist? Would we not have wasted our time? There are people who ask, "Does nirvāṇa exist or not? Is nirvāṇa a reality or is it simply an idea, a wish, or the imagination of people who suffer and want to find a place they believe is free from suffering?"

In the teachings of Buddhism, nirvāṇa transcends being and nonbeing. Nirvāṇa is not being, but it is also

---

* See Pascal's wager (le pari de Pascal) in Blaise Pascal, *Pensées*, fragment 397.

not nonbeing. So doubt, in this case, is not appropriate—as it is in the case of God or heaven. The Buddhist tradition itself teaches that to say that "nirvāṇa is" is not correct because nirvāṇa transcends the idea of being. It is also incorrect to say that "nirvāṇa is not," because nirvāṇa also transcends the idea of nonbeing. Is and is not cannot describe nirvāṇa. Nirvāṇa is neither being nor nonbeing. If we existed and nirvāṇa also existed, something existing would be going towards something else which exists. If we existed, but nirvāṇa did not exist, then something existing would be going towards something which does not exist. In this case, wouldn't it be a waste of time? If you are business-minded then you will think, "Only if I know that nirvāṇa really exists will I invest in the practice, because if after I have practiced, nirvāṇa turns out not to exist, I will incur a loss." But right from the start you have to understand that nirvāṇa is the absence of the ideas of being and nonbeing. If we expect nirvāṇa to exist, we make a mistake right from the beginning.

⚬

The German theologian Paul Tillich wrote in one of his books that "God is the ground of being." All existing things—rivers, mountains, plants, minerals, animals, people, time, and space—belong to the category of being. But from the point of view of the Middle Way, the idea of being can only be born from the idea of nonbeing. Being is the opposite of nonbeing. The difference between being and nonbeing is like the difference between left and right. If there is being, there must be nonbeing. If nonbeing is not, how can there be being? So the question is, "If God is the ground of being, what is the ground of nonbeing?" Is God the ground of everything, or just the half which is being and not the other half which is nonbeing? Even on the level of language, "God is the ground of being" cannot be correct. Maybe in the future a Christian theologian will declare: "God is the ground of being and nonbeing." How can the concept of being stand without the concept of nonbeing? How can the concept of right stand without the concept of left?

The first verse of this chapter is an aperitif to whet your palate for the magic show of Nāgārjuna, and the next verse is the reply.

2. *If all phenomena are not empty,*
   they are unborn and undying.
   So what you call nirvāṇa
   is the ending and extinction of what?

若諸法不空
則無生無滅
何斷何所滅
而稱為涅槃

The second verse is perfectly symmetrical with the first. Nāgārjuna's opponents say that you cannot talk about nirvāṇa if all things are empty—and therefore are not produced or destroyed. They point out that it is wrong to say that all things are empty. For them, you only have the right to speak about nirvāṇa if you recognize that things exist. If all things are empty how can they end? Nāgārjuna, they say, your thesis is wrong! If things are not empty, nirvāṇa is meaningful. If they are empty, they are not produced or destroyed, so how can there be the ending that is called nirvāṇa? So, they declare, you should be saying that all things exist.

To this Nāgārjuna replies, "If things were not empty—which would mean that *they exist*—then they would also not be born nor die. In that case, what is there to be terminated or extinguished for there to be a nirvāṇa to speak of?" If things truly existed, they would be permanent. They would have a true substance or permanent entity—and could not be destroyed. They would be unborn and undying. "So what could end or be extinguished for you to talk about nirvāṇa?" Nāgārjuna asks in reply, using the same words as his opponent. The opponent, in the first verse, asks, "If all things are empty, how can there be nirvāṇa?" Nāgārjuna replies, "If all things are not empty, how can there be nirvāṇa?" With just one word he topples his opponent. "Not empty" means "exists" and if something exists, then it cannot become nonexistent.

> *It is not possible for something that*
> *existed yesterday evening not to exist*
> *this morning.*
>
> —VŨ HOÀNG CHƯƠNG

To exist means to exist permanently—to have a self-nature. By destroying the notion of nonbeing, Nāgārjuna destroys the notion of being. The idea of nirvāṇa is incompatible with ideas of being and nonbeing.

Reading this verse with our heart, we can understand how it is connected to our suffering and to our worries. There might be a person dear to us who is dying, and we may believe that this person is crossing the threshold from being to nonbeing. If we can realize the true nature of things, we will not suffer anymore.

3. *Not attaining and not coming,*
   not annihilated and not eternal,
   not born and not destroyed,
   this is what we call nirvāṇa.

無得亦無至
不斷亦不常
不生亦不滅
是說名涅槃

This verse tells us what Buddhism means by nirvāṇa: the extinction of all notions. It is not the extinction of phenomena, but simply *the extinction of our notions about them.*

Not attaining and not coming,

Nonattainment means *not coming into being from nonbeing.* Someone who had no children suddenly has a child. They ask: "Where did the child come from?" Buddhism replies: "The child does not come from anywhere." That is *no coming.* No coming is also no going. No coming and no going are one reality. Nonattainment also means no loss. The reality of nirvāṇa is the reality that transcends ideas of attainment and loss.

According to the Buddha's teachings, ideas of attainment and loss have nothing to do with reality. Coming from somewhere and going somewhere are just ideas. Attaining and coming mean from being nothing we come into existence and from being something we go to being nothing. Not attaining and not coming are the characteristics of nirvāṇa.

Not annihilated and not eternal

Eternal means existing, and existence cannot become nonexistence. *Annihilated* means complete destruction and nonexistence—an eternal nonexistence that can never become existence. The reality of nirvāṇa transcends eternalism and nihilism, attainment and loss, coming and going.

Not born and not destroyed,

Birth is the idea that something comes into being from nonbeing, and death is the idea that from being something goes into nonbeing.

Not attaining and not coming,
not annihilated and not eternal,
not born and not destroyed,
this is what we call nirvāṇa.

How strange it would be, then, to describe nirvāṇa in terms of being and nonbeing! If we say that nirvāṇa exists, we are wrong; if we say that it does not exist, we are also wrong. Ideas of being and nonbeing cannot be applied to nirvāṇa. It would be absurd to say, "I don't know for sure if nirvāṇa exists or not, so I'm not going to bother practicing." If we look for nirvāṇa in terms of being and nonbeing, we will never find it.

⁂

The Lotus Sutra presents the idea of a historical and an ultimate dimension. These two dimensions relate to each other like the wave and the water. In the historical dimension (the wave), there is birth and death, there are big waves and small waves. In the ultimate dimension (the water), ideas like birth and death, being and nonbeing, this wave and that wave, and big and small no longer apply. Imagine a wave suffering—afraid, anxious, and jealous. It is looking for a peaceful place. Someone tells the wave, "What you are looking for is *the water*. Once you know that you are water, you will no longer be afraid of going up or going down, of being big or small, beautiful or ugly."

The metaphor of the wave and the water is an example—a finger pointing to the moon. Nirvāṇa is like the water; being or nonbeing are like waves. In truth the wave does not need to go and look for the water because *its nature is already water*. We are the same. Nirvāṇa is our nature: not born, not dying, not coming, and not going. We rest already in nirvāṇa. How could we look for it? To say that nirvāṇa exists or does not exist, that we can look for it and then attain, witness, or realize it is mistaken and naïve—like a wave looking for the water. The wave is already water! What more does it need? That is nonattainment. In the sutras we read, "Witness the unwitnessed, attain the unattained"; this means we realize that there is nothing to realize, and we witness that there is nothing to witness, because we already are the object we want to attain or witness.

Imagine again a kaleidoscope, containing within it a number of mirrors and colored bits of paper. Shake it a little, and you will see a beautiful pattern of shapes and colors. Shake it once more, and that pattern will disappear, giving way to another. In this way children, spellbound by each new beautiful pattern, keep turning the kaleidoscope and don't regret the disappearance of one pattern as it gives way to another. This pattern differs from that one, but all the patterns arise from the little pieces of paper inside the kaleidoscope. Let these little pieces of paper represent the ultimate dimension and the patterns that manifest, the historical. If we know that everything manifests from the ultimate dimension, then birth and death and abiding and loss in the historical dimension cannot affect us.

A cloud—tired of being blown this way and that, and then dying—is lured by the hope of becoming water, and looks for it. Its dream of becoming water is needless because *it already is water*. When the cloud encounters cold air it becomes snow, hail, or rain. Although it no longer has the form of a cloud, it continues to be water.

I keep repeating these examples to help you understand, but I do not want you to become caught in them. The Buddha used many different examples when he taught, and said, "People of sharp intelligence, thanks to the example, will understand what I mean; people of dull intelligence will become caught in it."

When the cloud experiences itself as water, it is no longer afraid. It feels joy to be a cloud and joy to be rain, hail, or snow; it is carefree. Human beings worry, discriminate, and feel jealousy because they are not aware and cannot live the experience that they are nirvāṇa. If we can touch our reality of nirvāṇa—which is our nature of no birth and no death, no coming and no going, neither permanence nor annihilation—all of our worry, sadness, and jealousy will disappear. This is something that we can do. An enlightened person sees that our ground is nirvāṇa; and with this insight, going up or down, coming in or going out is a joy. Someone who has realized the path is a free person: they are free from ideas of being and nonbeing, gain and loss, coming and going.

Nowadays many scholars translate nirvāṇa as "freedom." In the past it has been translated as "extinction"—the extinction of notions like attainment and loss, coming and going, annihilated and eternal, and birth and death. Now we can translate it as "freedom from concepts." When our ideas no longer ensnare us and make us suffer, we have freedom—and that means we have nirvāṇa. This body does not have to disintegrate for us to realize nirvāṇa. Nirvāṇa is present right here and right now; it is called "nirvāṇa in the here and now" (*dṛṣṭadharmanirvāṇa*). In this way, Christians could say, "We are God and God is us. God is our ground of no-birth and no-death. We do not need to look for God because God is our ultimate reality."

Only the waves that know they are water can enjoy their time in a carefree way. When they finally break on the shore they can smile. Only those who realize nirvāṇa will know how to smile at their last breath; others, when faced with that moment, will be invaded by worries and fear. The best, most beautiful, and most wonderful aspect of being a practitioner is the realization of nir-vāṇa. Nirvāṇa is not something far away that we need to chase after. It is our own nature; it is found in every cell of our body. Nirvāṇa is the ground of everything.

Imagine someone who wants to locate space, who runs in search of it to the east, west, south, north, above and below, all the while blind to the space within and around them everywhere. We are just like that. We look for nirvāṇa in the past, in the future, in the east, and in the west. The truth is that *we are already in nirvāṇa*. This is called nirvāṇa in the here and now, and we can only see it when we wake up. Buddhism is called the path of awakening. When we wake up, we see we have no need to search for nirvāṇa. When we contemplate life deeply, we will be in touch with it. The French scientist Lavoisier—who had never studied Buddhism—could say, "Nothing is created, nothing is lost." The essence of all things is no-birth and no-death. If people like Lavoisier could go a little deeper, they would certainly realize freedom—the great freedom of nirvāṇa.

4. *You cannot say nirvāṇa exists;*
   existence is characterized by old age and death.
   There is ultimately no existence
   that is not characterized by old age and death.

涅槃不名有
有則老死相
終無有有法
離於老死相

If nirvāṇa exists, it must be characterized by decay and death. Everything that exists has to go through decay and death.

We say that a flower exists, and so it will wilt and die. If nirvāṇa existed, it would also have to go through old age and death. What good would it do to search for it? In the beginning we say, "The practice is to realize nirvāṇa, so if nirvāṇa does not exist, why practice?" If there were no God and no heaven, people might think "What a waste it would be to practice Christianity!" According to the teachings of the Buddha, nirvāṇa cannot be said to exist. If it existed, it would have to go through the doors of dissolution and death. In this case, it could not be called nirvāṇa. Ultimately there is no existence separate from old age and death.

5. *If nirvāṇa exists,*
   it would be conditioned.
   There is ultimately no existence
   that can be called unconditioned.

若涅槃是有
涅槃即有為
終無有一法
而是無為者

If you say that nirvāṇa exists, it has to be conditioned (*saṃskṛta*). But in principle, nirvāṇa is unconditioned (*asaṃskṛta*). All phenomena that are composed by the coming together of different conditions are called "conditioned." The forest, the rain, the carpenter, the nails, and so on come together for the table to manifest: the table is conditioned. Nirvāṇa is not conditioned because all conditioned things undergo decay and death, and a conditioned nirvāṇa subject to decay and death would not be worthy of our quest. If nirvāṇa is conditioned, what in the world would be unconditioned? Traditionally Buddhists divide phenomena into two: those that come about because of conditions—"conditioned dharmas"—and those that do not come about because of conditions—"unconditioned dharmas." In the sutras, nirvāṇa is always described as an unconditioned dharma.

6. *If nirvāṇa exists,*
   how could you call it independent?
   There is nothing independent
   that can be said to exist.

若涅槃是有
云何名無受
無有不從受
而名為有法

If you describe nirvāṇa as something that exists, how can you say it is independent? In Buddhism we learn: *What is dependent is subject to birth and death.* Nirvāṇa is independent—無受 (*anupādāya*).

Upādāya means receiving, acquiring, together with, appropriating, dependent. All the things that can be acquired and grasped that depend on other things to exist—can be called upādāya. They are conditioned and, as such, belong to the realm of birth and death. For example, working as a banker, farmer, or carpenter you are dependent; you are conditioned. The job is there now, but in the future it will not be there anymore. You could easily lose it. You have to depend on it and hold on to it. Your career relies on many conditions to manifest. If nirvāṇa relied on other things, it would not be nirvāṇa. If you say that nirvāṇa exists, how can nirvāṇa be independent? Independent means not tied to and relying on other things.

The third and the fourth lines mean that *there isn't a single existent that is not dependent*. All existents must be dependent on other things. There is not a single existent that does not rely on other things. Nirvāṇa is not dependent; it does not depend on being and nonbeing, going up or going down, abiding and loss, as do other things. Upādāya (dependent) and anupādāya (independent) should be understood in the light of the sutras, where dependent means being born and dying, and independent means nirvāṇa.

7. *If nirvāṇa is not existent,*
   how could it be nonexistent?
   Since existence does not apply to nirvāṇa
   how could nonexistence apply to it?

有尚非涅槃
何況於無耶
涅槃無有有
何處當有無

There are people who are willing to practice only if nirvāṇa exists. They think that if nirvāṇa does not exist, it would be a waste of energy to pursue it. This is our normal way of thinking. Nāgārjuna says, "Everything that we call existent, must change and decay. If nirvāṇa exists it will also change and decay." Is that the kind of nirvāṇa we want to look for? When people see that nirvāṇa does not exist then they have hopes that nirvāṇa is nonexistence. They go from the extreme of nirvāṇa existing to the extreme of nirvāṇa not existing. Is nirvāṇa nonexistent? Nāgārjuna replies, "Nirvāṇa is not existent. How much less so is it nonexistent!" Nāgārjuna demonstrates in the following verse how nonexistence is the opposite of existence.

8. *If nirvāṇa is nonexistent,*
   how could you call it independent?
   There is nothing independent
   that can be said not to exist.

若無是涅槃
云何名不受
未曾有不受
而名為無法

Independent means that it does not depend on other conditions to exist or not; to go up or down. If nirvāṇa is nonexistent, how could it be called independent?

Everything—whether existent or nonexistent—depends on other things.

Yesterday during sitting meditation I was looking at a log, and I saw it smiling to me. Everybody believes that this log is existent. Maybe tomorrow a novice will put it in the stove and—in two or three hours—it will become nonexistent. The existence of the log depends on the sun, the clouds, the earth, the weather, the novice, etc. So it is called dependent. When the log is burned in the stove and becomes nonexistent, its nonexistence is also dependent on conditions—the fire, the air, the novice, etc. Existence is dependent, but nonexistence is *also* dependent.

If nirvāṇa exists, then it is dependent, and if it does not exist, it is still dependent. As long as something is dependent it is not nirvāṇa. Nirvāṇa can only be independent.

> *There is nothing independent*
> *that can be said not to exist.*

This mirrors the sixth verse:

> *There is nothing independent*
> *that can be said to exist.*

In other words, everything that is described as existent depends on other things. The same is true for everything that is described as nonexistent: it has to depend on other things. Nirvāṇa is the only thing that is not dependent or conditioned. To say it another way, *there has never been any nonexistent thing that has the nature of independence.* Now the log exists thanks to the cloud, the sun, and the forest. It will become nonexistent thanks to the fire, the oxygen, and the novice. Nonexistence also needs conditions.

If we want to exist, we have to eat and drink. If we want not to exist we also need conditions for our nonexistence. Therefore, if nirvāṇa means nonexistence, that nonexistence is not independent or unconditioned. Existence and nonexistence are dependent; only nirvāṇa is independent.

9. *That which is dependent on conditions*
   comes and goes in the cycle of birth and death.
   That which is not dependent on conditions
   is called nirvāṇa.

受諸因緣故
輪轉生死中
不受諸因緣
是名為涅槃

This verse defines nirvāṇa and the cycle of birth and death. Birth and death is *saṃsāra* (literally "wandering through"); nirvāṇa means *we no longer wander*—we have arrived, we are home. We wander because we still depend on conditions. Once we no longer depend on conditions, we rest in nirvāṇa.

In the Chinese, 輪轉輪 means "to go in circles" and 轉 means "to change." The original Sanskrit is *ājavaṃ-javī*, which means coming and going—or to go in and out of birth and death. We depend on conditions, and this is why we come and go in the realm of saṃsāra. Once we no longer depend on conditions, then we are in nirvāṇa.

The nature of birth and death is dependence, while the nature of nirvāṇa is independence.

10. *As the Buddha said in the sutras,*
    one should end being and nonbeing.
    Therefore we know that nirvāṇa
    is neither being nor nonbeing.

如佛經中說
斷有斷非有
是故知涅槃
非有亦非無

We should give up being and nonbeing, as the Buddha has taught in the sutras. This is our practice. There is a craving or thirst for being (*bhavatṛṣṇā*). *Bhava* means being, while *tṛṣṇā* means craving. We thirst for existence—for a long-lasting existence or many existences. Alternatively, we are sometimes not satisfied with the quality of our present existence; we want to abandon it and look for a different one. We may want to go to heaven or be reborn in the Pure Land. That thirst for another existence is called *vibhava-tṛṣṇā*. We may find that we want to relieve our shoulders of the heavy burden of our present existence to look for nonexistence. This is the state of mind of someone who wants to commit suicide. Existence (*bhava*) and a different existence (*vibhava*) are both objects of our thirst. The Buddha said that neither of them should be followed and taught us what we should do to transcend them both. He did not teach us to abandon existence for nonexistence.

This is not a theory, but a practice to avoid being caught in becoming or non-becoming. In many sutras the Buddha taught not to crave being and not to crave nonbeing. We should not be attached to being or to becoming. Based on this teaching, we know that nirvāṇa is a state—a reality—that transcends being and nonbeing. In that state of nirvāṇa we are secure; we are not oppressed by the craving for being or nonbeing.

According to Christianity, the kingdom of God exists. If it did not exist, why would we hope to go there? But in the teachings of the Buddha, nirvāṇa is not something that exists. When we look carefully, we see that all that exists has to cease to exist. To look for the kingdom of God or for the Pure Land as something that exists means we are still craving. Existence and nonxistence—in any form—are not objects for a Buddhist to run after.

Therefore we know that nirvāṇa,
is neither being nor nonbeing.

To say that nirvāṇa exists or does not exist is not in accord with the Buddha's teachings.

Philosophers debate about being and nonbeing as something real. In the Sanskrit text of the Verses on the Middle Way, the second line of this verse uses the terms *bhava* and *vibhava* and the fourth line the terms *bhāva* and *abhāva*. In both cases the Chinese translation uses *being* and *nonbeing*, but there is a distinction that can be made. Bhava and vibhava are being and nonbeing as the object of the experience of our five skandhas in daily life. We can call them empirical events. Bhāva and abhāva belong to the realm of philosophy, to the essential. They are abstract or metaphysical assumptions—ideas that take us beyond the sphere of experience. When people want to talk about a deeper truth in Sanskrit they would use bhāva and abhāva.

11. If you say that being and nonbeing

together are nirvāṇa,
then being and nonbeing would be liberation,
and this is truly absurd.

若謂於有無
合為涅槃者
有無即解脫
是事則不然

Being by itself makes us suffer and nonbeing by itself also makes us suffer. If you combine these two notions, you will only suffer more; how can you call this liberation?

In these verses Nāgārjuna is looking at four propositions: something is, something is not, something both is and is not, and something neither is nor is not. Verse 11 looks specifically into the third proposition: something both is and is not. If truth is not found in *it is*, then it is found in *it is not*, but if it is not found in *it is not*, then it may lie in *it both is and is not*. Nāgārjuna shows that this is absurd.

12. *If you say that being and nonbeing*
    together are nirvāṇa,
    nirvāṇa would not be independent,
    since both being and nonbeing arise in dependence.

若謂於有無

合為涅槃者
涅槃非無受
是二從受生

If nirvāṇa were a combination of being and nonbeing, it would not be independent. Since being is dependent and nonbeing is dependent, nirvāṇa would be even more dependent. Nirvāṇa, however, does not depend on conditions. Being and nonbeing arise in dependence, while nirvāṇa is independent. The argument: "Nirvāṇa comes from a combination of being and nonbeing" does not stand firm. We are free from the third proposition of both being and nonbeing.

13. *How could we say that nirvāṇa*
    both is and is not?
    Nirvāṇa is unconditioned,
    while being and nonbeing are conditioned.

有無共合成
云何名涅槃
涅槃名無為
有無是有為

To take being and nonbeing, combine them, and say that together they are nirvāṇa is absurd because nirvāṇa is an unconditioned phenomenon, while being and nonbeing are both conditioned.

14. *How can being and nonbeing*
    together be nirvāṇa?
    Like light and darkness,
    they cannot occur together in the same place.

有無二事共
云何是涅槃
是二不同處
如明暗不俱

How can you call nirvāṇa the combination of these two things? Being and nonbeing are like light and darkness; they can never exist together at the same time.

15. *If you call nirvāṇa*
    neither being nor nonbeing,
    how could this neither being nor nonbeing
    be conceived of?*

若非有非無
名之為涅槃

---

* Kumārajīva, when translating into Chinese, reversed the 15th and 16th verses. The 15th verse in Chinese translates the 16th verse in Sanskrit, and the 16th verse in Chinese translates the 15th verse in Sanskrit. —Eds.

此非有非無
以何而分別

Neither being, nonbeing, or the combination of being and nonbeing, is nirvāṇa. Now we come to the fourth proposition, neither being nor nonbeing.

If that which we call "neither being nor nonbeing" is nirvāṇa, how are we to conceive of what is neither being nor nonbeing? It is not a concept, but merely words.

16. *You conceive neither being nor nonbeing*
    and call it nirvāṇa.
    Neither being nor nonbeing could only be established
    if being and nonbeing could be established.

分別非有無
如是名涅槃
若有無成者
非有非無成

It is wrong to consider neither being nor nonbeing to be nirvāṇa. If the concepts of being and nonbeing were apparent, the concept of neither being nor nonbeing would also be apparent. If the concepts of being and nonbeing are not apparent, the concept of neither being nor nonbeing would also not be apparent. If the left is not apparent, how can there be a right? If there is not an above, how can there be a below? If there is no being, how can there be nonbeing? The reasoning here is like that of the previous verses. Once we have toppled the idea of being, the idea of nonbeing, as the opposite of being, no longer has a leg to stand on. When one of them falls down, the other falls as well. We have already overthrown the idea that being and nonbeing together are nirvāṇa. When this idea is overthrown, the idea of neither-being-nor-nonbeing collapses; these two ideas contrast each other in the way that being and nonbeing, right and left, and above and below do. These are the dialectics of Nāgārjuna: since being and nonbeing together cannot be established, the idea of neither being nor nonbeing cannot be established either. As a result, it is mistaken to conceive of "neither being nor nonbeing" and then call it nirvāṇa.

These four propositions are presented in the Anurādha Sutta* as follows:

One day, as Anurādha was walking on the road a number of ascetics stopped him and asked: "Venerable Anurādha, the Tathāgata is often praised for having reached the highest fruit of awakening. He must have explained to you his understanding of these four propositions:

1. After death, the Tathāgata continues to exist.
2. After death, the Tathāgata ceases to exist.

---

* SN IV 380 in *Chanting from the Heart*, volume 1, Parallax Press, 2023.

3. After death, the Tathāgata both continues and ceases to exist.

4. After death, the Tathāgata neither continues nor ceases to exist.

Please tell us which of these propositions is true."

The Venerable Anurādha replied, "Friends, the Tathāgata, the World-Honored One, the one who has realized the highest fruit of awakening, has never proposed or spoken about these four propositions."

⚬

This was correct—and the Buddha confirms it to Anurādha later in the sutta—but the ascetics were not satisfied.

The seventeenth and eighteenth verses below reflect the essence of the Buddha's teaching in the Anurādha Sutta, which belongs to Source Buddhism and not the Mahāyāna.

17. *After the Tathāgata passes away,*
   you cannot say he exists, does not exist,
   both exists and does not exist,
   or neither exists nor does not exist.

如來滅度後
不言有與無
亦不言有無
非有及非無

We cannot force the Buddha into any of these four boxes.

In your busy daily life there could be moments when you wonder where you will go after death. Those moments are too short, because you have so much work and so many other worries. Many of us—including many Buddhists—believe that we have an immortal soul that remains just as it was when we were alive and goes looking for another body after this one disintegrates. This is how a number of Buddhists view saṃsāra. This view, however,—which we could call popular Buddhism—contradicts the teachings of the Buddha. It is a wrong view, according to the deep Buddhist teachings. For those who have a low level of understanding this can be a starting point from which they gradually progress. There are also other religions with a belief that there is an immortal soul which ascends to heaven or descends into hell after the death of the body.

There are also those who believe in materialism. Many scientists believe there is a soul that is not immortal; once the body disintegrates, the soul ceases completely to exist. Nothing remains. There are also scientists with a deeper insight who take exception to this materialistic view. "Nothing is created, nothing is lost," comes close to the Buddha's teachings. To say that there is something that can be totally annihilated goes against science.

To those who adhere to such nihilism, the Vietnamese poet Vũ Hoàng Chương wrote in the poem "Song of Liberation" the line,

> *It's absurd that what existed last night would become nonexistent this morning.*

As students of the Buddha practicing according to the insight of the Buddha, how should we see this matter? The story of the monks questioning Anurādha is recorded in many sutras, and questions like this were frequently asked in India at that time. Whenever the Buddha was asked these questions he, finding it impossible to validate or negate them, remained silent.

18. *While the Tathāgata is still alive*
    you cannot say he exists, does not exist,
    both exists and does not exist,
    or neither exists nor does not exist.

如來現在時
不言有與無
亦不言有無
非有及非無

The Anurādha sutra is wonderful! The ascetics ask what happens to the Tathāgata after death: does he still exist or not, or both exist and not exist, or neither exist nor not exist? At the time that the Tathāgata is present and alive he cannot be described by any of these four propositions. When Anurādha repeats the question to the Buddha, the Buddha replies, "Let's not speak about what happens after death. Let's talk about now! Right now, do I exist or not exist? Do I both exist and not exist? Do I neither exist nor not exist?"

Buddhist teachings always bring us back to the present moment so that we can observe things right now. If we can see things in the present moment, we can also see them in the future and in the past.

In the end Anurādha saw that it was not possible to describe the Buddha in the present moment by means of the four propositions. The Buddha said, "I am sitting here in front of you and you are unable to find me in terms of the four propositions; so how can you expect to find me by means of them after I have passed away?"

Imagine you have four containers in which you will put water or tangerines to carry them home. If you bring water home you will have water, and if you bring tangerines you will have tangerines. Bringing the four containers back successfully is called 得 *prāpta*—which means to be able to attain, conceive, comprehend, or grasp. But can you grasp the Buddha? You will never be able to grasp reality—including the Buddha—by using the four propositions, just as you cannot grasp the wind in your hand. We cannot grasp reality and so it is called ungraspable; as it says in the Heart Sutra, there is no object of attainment. This means *there is no object that can be grasped by means of the four propositions.* Even while the Buddha is alive you cannot grasp him. Only when you let go of these propositions can you be in touch with the reality of the Buddha.

Whatever really exists cannot become nonexistent. Whatever is really nonexistent cannot become existent. The things that manifest before our eyes do not have a self-nature; we cannot say that they exist or do not exist. The two categories—exists and does not exist—cannot encompass reality. To say that we have to choose to be or not to be is mistaken! In the light of Buddhism, "To be or not to be, that is not the question." To say that nirvāṇa, the Buddha, or the table exists, does not exist, both exists and does not exist, or neither exists nor does not exist, is mistaken.

19. *Between nirvāṇa and the world*
    there is not the slightest difference.
    Between the world and nirvāṇa
    there is not the slightest difference.

涅槃與世間
無有少分別

世間與涅槃
亦無少分別

The reality of birth and death—of being and nonbeing—is called "the world," or saṃsāra. When we speak
of nirvāṇa, we think of something completely different—
something that is unborn and undying, not coming and
not going, not the cycle of rebirth. Practitioners normally think that they have to let go of the world to find
nirvāṇa. Verse 19 booms like a thunderclap. It shows us
that there is no distinction whatsoever between nirvāṇa
and saṃsāra.

I often use the example of the wave and the water.
Water is a metaphor for nirvāṇa, and the wave is a metaphor for the world. In the world things go up and down,
exist and don't exist, are big and small, beautiful and ugly,
and so on. Water is not like that, but if we remove the
water there can be no wave, and if we remove the wave
there can be no water. Water and wave are one; they
cannot be separated from one another. Out of ignorance
we see something as saṃsāra. Without ignorance we see
the same thing as nirvāṇa. Nirvāṇa and saṃsāra are not
two separate realities. It is foolish to abandon one to find
the other. Only in the Buddhist tradition is this insight
presented in such a clear, direct, and powerful way. Our
dualistic conception of saṃsāra and nirvāṇa has to be

removed. Only then will we have a chance to get in touch with nirvāṇa.

The sentence, "Between nirvāṇa and the world there is not the slightest difference" is already very clear, but Nāgārjuna still adds a second sentence, "Between the world and nirvāṇa there is not the slightest difference." In the sutras, the Buddha uses this strategy to stress a point. The Heart Sutra also does this: "This body itself is emptiness and emptiness itself is this body."

20. *Between the true nature of nirvāṇa*
    and the true nature of saṃsāra
    there is not the slightest distinction.

涅槃之實際
及與世間際
如是二際者
無毫釐差別

The term *true nature* (實際) is translated from the Sanskrit *bhūta-koṭi*, which means "the boundary of reality." In Chinese 際 means boundary or limit. The true nature is the essence of reality, or suchness—the limit of the truth that we can be in contact with. When we look at things superficially from the outside, we only see their outer appearance and are unable to see their true nature. When we look with mindfulness, concentration, and insight, we discover this true nature. In Master Liễu Quán's poem (found on the Plum Village precepts' transmission certificates) there are the lines:

實際大導
性海清澄

The great way of reality is our true nature's clear ocean.

As descendants of Master Liễu Quán, we should be able to understand this sentence. The true nature of nirvāṇa is no birth and no death, no coming and no going, no existence, no nonexistence, no both existence and nonexistence, and no neither existence nor nonexistence. This is not only the true nature of nirvāṇa, it is also the true nature of the Tathāgata and all phenomena: the table, the novice, the stone, the cloud, and so on. To summarize, we cannot grasp the Tathāgata or any other phenomenon by means of the four propositions; all phenomena are ungraspable. When we look deeply into a cloud, a pebble, or a flower we see clearly that their true nature is emptiness: not being, not nonbeing, not born nor dying. In the beginning we discriminate between nirvāṇa and the world of birth and death, but when we look deeply into birth and death, we can touch nirvāṇa. Apart from birth and death we cannot find nirvāṇa, just as we cannot find water apart from waves. The teaching of Buddhism is that nirvāṇa and saṃsāra are one. When we are deluded, we discriminate between nirvāṇa and saṃsāra, but when we are enlightened, we see that saṃsāra and nirvāṇa are not the slightest bit different; they are identical.

21. *Views on existing after death or not,*
    being finite, eternal, and so on
    all rely on nirvāṇa,
    the past, and the future.

滅後有無等
有邊等常等
諸見依涅槃
未來過去世

In verse twenty we saw that the true nature of nirvāṇa and that of saṃsāra are not different: the idea of escaping saṃsāra to find nirvāṇa is mistaken. A Vietnamese Zen master* encouraged his disciples not to be attached to the world of birth and death, but to find nirvāṇa. A disciple stood up and asked the master, "Where can we find nirvāṇa?" The master replied, "You must find it right in the world of birth and death!" Outside of saṃsāra it is not possible to find nirvāṇa. Saṃsāra comes about

---

* Master Thiện Hội (d. 950).

because of our mistaken way of looking; when we can look with the eyes of insight and awakening, saṃsāra becomes nirvāṇa.

Verse 21 is about doctrines, 見 (dṛṣṭi). As we've learned from the Anurādha Sutta, these doctrines included the four propositions. Spiritual teachers at that time wanted people to choose one of the four, whereas the Buddha maintained that none of these four propositions contained the truth. When you pick plums you could bring four baskets to hold them, but the truth could never be put into a basket.

Nāgārjuna mentions twelve doctrines: the world is limited, limitless, both limited and limitless, or neither limited nor limitless; after death the Tathāgata continues to exist, ceases to exist, both continues and ceases to exist, or neither continues nor ceases to exist; the world is eternal, subject to annihilation, both eternal and subject to annihilation, or neither eternal nor subject to annihilation. All these doctrines rely on an idea of nirvāṇa and are connected with the two times of past and future; they lie within the frame of space and time.

Another matter for philosophical discussion in India during the lifetime of the Buddha and Nāgārjuna was the life force, 命 (jīva), and the body. Are the life force and the body one or two? Is the life force the body? If the body only exists for a certain time, does the life force only exist for a certain time? Altogether there were four-teen different theories. You were expected to select one of them and fit reality into it. The Buddha, however, taught that we cannot grasp reality by means of any of the fourteen categories. This is the teaching of Nāgār-juna in the verse 22 that follows.

We should note that verse 21 is not Nāgārjuna's teaching; he is merely listing the theories that people were putting forward and disputing.

The Buddha had a disciple named Mālunkyāputta* who asked him a great number of philosophical questions:

"Please teach me, World-Honored One. I want to know: Is the world eternal or annihilated? Does the universe have a limit or not? Is time infinite or finite? If you cannot answer me, I will leave the sangha and find the answers somewhere else."

The Buddha replied, "When you became a monk, did I ever promise you that I would answer these questions? Of course not. I never promised that I would reply to these questions."

The Buddha gave an example, which has become well-known: "Suppose a man walking on the road is struck by a poisonous arrow. Straightaway the poison

---

* Culamālunkyāputta Sutta, MN 63.

enters his body and people nearby summon a doctor. When the doctor is about to remove the arrow, the wounded man says: "Stop! Stop! Do not pull it out yet. First, you have to tell me who shot this arrow: What is his name? What clan does he belong to? Why did he shoot me? Only after I know the answers will I allow you to remove the arrow."

The Buddha said, "Mālunkyāputta, if the doctor were to keep sitting there answering all those questions, the wounded man would die before the wound could be treated. I don't speak about these metaphysical subjects because I see that doing so would be of no advantage to you. I teach about suffering, the nature of suffering, the causes of suffering, and the path for overcoming suffering. I am a doctor; I'm not here to answer these kinds of questions. If I were to reply to them, you would die before having a chance to practice and to transform."

We become a monk or a nun first of all to heal our wounds, not to satisfy our curiosity about metaphysical or philosophical questions.

22. *Since all phenomena are empty*
    how can they be limited or limitless,
    both limited and limitless
    or neither limited nor limitless?

一切法空故
何有邊無邊
亦邊亦無邊
非有非無邊

We have learned that all phenomena are without a self-nature. Limited and limitless are qualities that people apply to the self-nature of phenomena. Only when the self-nature of something really is, however, can we talk about it being limited or limitless! If it is not really existing, how can we say it is or is not limited, both is and is not limited, or neither is nor is not limited?

23. *How can there be same and different,*
    permanence or impermanence,
    both permanence and impermanence,
    or neither permanence nor impermanence?

何者為一異
何有常無常
亦常亦無常
非常非無常

If all phenomena are empty, why do we have to find out whether they are the same or different—as in the case of life force and the body, or matter and spirit? Here we speak of the characteristics of phenomena: Are they the same or different? Are body and mind the same or different? There are four doctrines: same, different, both the same and different, and neither the same nor different.

If phenomena are empty, how can we call them permanent, impermanent, both permanent and impermanent, or neither permanent nor impermanent? Nāgārjuna's answer is clear in the following verses.

24. [Realizing that] phenomena cannot be grasped,
    we remove all speculation.
    There is no person and no location,
    and the Buddha did not teach anything.

諸法不可得
滅一切戲論
無人亦無處
佛亦無所說

As we cannot describe phenomena as being or nonbeing, why do we waste time finding out if they are permanent or impermanent, limited or limitless, the same or different? Meanwhile we forget to practice breathing and walking meditation, and we don't know how to recognize our feelings and internal knots in order to calm and transform them. We are like that man struck by an arrow who did not want to remove it. After the Buddha gave that teaching, Mālunkyāputta accepted it. He stopped asking questions and began to practice.

Phenomena have the character of being ungraspable. We cannot grasp the Buddha because he is a phenomenon, an object of our mind. With what do we grasp the Buddha? We do not grasp him with our hands, but with our thoughts, our ideas, and with mental categories— like being, nonbeing, both being and nonbeing, neither being nor nonbeing, permanence, impermanence, both permanence and impermanence, neither permanence nor impermanence, limited or limitless, both limited and limitless, or neither limited nor limitless. These are all mental categories, and you cannot grasp reality with mental categories. This is what is meant by, *phenomena cannot be grasped.*

Therefore, we have to remove all of our speculation. The Chinese 戲論 (*prapañca*) means "useless speculation," the questions, answers, and theories. 戲 means to play with and 論 means speculation.

Our life is short, and we waste it with vain speculations that lead nowhere.

There is no person and no location.

We cannot find a person's self or their location in time or space. If, when observing a person and their location, we are able to transcend our ideas about them and their location, then we can see them as they really are. If we only hold on tight to our sense of "here is that person" or "here is that location," we cannot see the interbeing nature—the nirvāṇa nature—of all things. We allow our brain's ideas to dominate us, and we are still blind.

The Buddha did not say anything means that the Buddha remained silent before questions like those mentioned above. The Buddha's silence is referred to in many places in the sutras; we can call this silence *noble silence* or *thundering silence*.

One day a very intelligent ascetic called Vacchagotta came and asked the Buddha: "World-Honored One, is there a self? Is it true that there is a self?"

The Buddha smiled but did not say a word. Ānanda was surprised that the Buddha did not reply—even a disciple ordained for only two or three days could have answered this.

After a long while Vacchagotta asked "So there is no self, right?" The Buddha again smiled as he sat in silence. After a while, Vacchagotta left.

Ānanda asked the Buddha, "World Honored One, why did you not answer the ascetic? You normally say that there is no self."

The Buddha replied: "Ānanda, Vacchagotta was looking for an answer to his intellectual questions. I am not foolish enough to fall into his trap. If I had told him that there is a self, I would have contradicted what I teach. If I had told him that there is no self, it would not have helped. He would have understood 'no self' to be a theory contradicting the theory of a self. I do not accept the doctrine of self, so I teach no self; but when I teach no self it is not for people to be caught in it. The purpose of the teachings on no self is to shatter our notion of a self. If I talk about no self with the result that people grasp it and are caught in it, there is no benefit. This is why I was silent."

That is thundering silence. When we find ourselves in a situation where there is speculation, we can do just as the Buddha did. We can sit quietly, in silence, and simply smile—by doing so, we will be worthy students of the Buddha. When people were caught in a vicious cycle of speculation, the Buddha said nothing, and we, his descendants, can do the same.

APPENDIX

The following Appendix includes only the sections of the Verses on the Middle Way that the author has translated and commented on for this book. Numbers preceding the title indicate the chapter in this book; each title is followed by the original chapter name and number.

VERSES ON THE MIDDLE WAY
MŪLAMADHYAMAKAKĀRIKĀ

Unborn and undying,
neither permanent nor annihilated,
neither the same nor different,
neither coming nor going—
the Buddha thus proclaims conditioned co-arising
that puts an end to all speculation.
I bow down to him,
the supreme and excellent teacher.

anirodham anutpādam anucchedam aśāśvatam
anekārtham anānārtham anāgamam anirgamam
yaḥ pratītyasamutpādaṃ prapañcopaśamaṃ śivam
deśayām āsa saṃbuddhas taṃ vande vadatāṃ varam

1 EXAMINATION OF CONDITIONS
PRATYAYAPARĪKṢĀ (CHAPTER 1)

1. *Phenomena are not born from themselves,*
   nor from others,
   nor both from themselves and others, nor without cause.
   Therefore we know they are unborn.

2. *Seed condition, condition of continuity,*
   object of cognition as condition and supportive condition:
   These four conditions give birth to all dharmas,
   and there is no fifth one.

3. *The self-nature of phenomena*
   is not found in the conditions.
   Since there is no self-nature,
   how could there be an other-nature?

4. *Does the effect arise out of the conditions,*
   or does it arise out of a non-condition?
   Is the effect contained in the conditions,
   or is there no effect in the conditions?

5. *A seed condition that gives rise to an effect*
   is called a condition.
   When the effect has not yet arisen,
   why then don't we call it a non-condition?

6. *To say that the effect, prior to arising,*
   exists or not within the conditions, has no meaning.
   If it does not exist, then what does the condition condition?
   And if it does exist, then why do we need a condition?

7. *If the effect is already present before it arises,*
   or if it is not present before it arises,
   or if it is both present and not present before it arises,
   how can we say that it is conditioned?

8. *When the effect has not yet arisen*
   its cause cannot cease.
   How can a phenomenon that has ceased condition
   *   something?*
   Therefore there is no continuity condition.

9. *As proclaimed by the buddhas,*
   the true and wonderful Dharmadhātu
   transcends subject and object of cognition,
   So how could there be an object of cognition as condition?

10. *If phenomena are without a self-nature*
    they do not have the mark of "being."
    For this reason we cannot say
    this is because that is.

11. *Looking into conditions, at length or in brief,*
    we are not able to see the effect.
    If it is not found in the conditions
    how can we say the effect arises from the conditions?

12. *If you say that the effect is not in the conditions,*
    but that the effect arises from the conditions,
    then why does not that effect
    arise from what are not its conditions?

13. *If the effect comes from conditions,*
    those conditions do not have a self-nature.
    If, then, the effect comes from conditions that do not
        have a self-nature,
    how can it be said to come from those conditions?

14. *There is no effect that arises from conditions,*
    nor an effect that arises from non-conditions.
    Since there is no effect,
    there are neither conditions nor non-conditions.

2 EXAMINATION OF COMING AND GOING
  GATĀGATAPARĪKṢĀ (CHAPTER 2)

1. *That which has already gone is not going;*
   that which has not yet gone is not going.

Besides already-gone and not-yet-gone,
the present going cannot be known.

2. When the act of going is taking place,
   there is going;
   There is no having-gone nor not-yet-gone at the time
      of going,
   but there is going at the time of going.

3. How could the fact of going be there
   during the time of going?
   If there is no fact of going
   how can there be a time of going?

4. It is a mistake to say that there is going
   during the time of going.
   Without going, how could the time of going
   go by itself?

5. If there is going in the time of going,
   then there are two goings:
   the first is the time of going,
   and the second is the act of going.

6. If there are two goings,
   there must be two subjects who go.

Without a subject who goes,
how can we establish the fact of going?

7. If there is no subject who goes,
   the act of going will be impossible.
   When there is not an act of going,
   how can there be someone who goes?

8. The goer does not go;
   the non-goer does not go.
   Apart from goer and non-goer,
   there is no third possibility.

9. How can we conceive
   of the goer going?
   Without the act of going,
   how could there be a goer?

10. If you say that there is a goer going
    there would be two kinds of going:
    the going of the goer
    and the going of the act of going.

11. If you say that the goer goes
    that would be a contradiction:
    there would be a goer apart from the going
    that the goer undertakes.

12. The starting point is not in what has gone,
    nor is it in what will go,
    nor is it in the present going.
    So when does the starting point happen?

13. When going you do not begin to go,
    nor do you begin to go when you have already gone.
    If the beginning is not found in these two cases
    how can you begin to go before you have gone?

14. When going you do not begin to go,
    nor do you begin to go when you have already gone.
    If the beginning is not found in these two cases,
    how can you begin to go before you have gone?

15. The goer does not abide anywhere.
    The non-goer does not abide anywhere either.
    Apart from goer and non-goer
    how could anything abide?

16. It would be absurd to say
    that it is the goer that abides.
    If the act of going is not
    how can a goer be possible?

17. Someone who has gone or has not yet gone does
       not abide.
    Someone who is going also does not abide.
    Similarly, someone who is going, has gone, or has not
       yet gone
    does not arise, decay, or end.

18. It is absurd to say that
    the goer is the act of going.
    It is also absurd to say that
    the goer is not the act of going.

19. You cannot say the act of going
    is the goer.
    If so, the author of the action and the action
    are the same thing.

20. If you say that the act of going
    is different from the one who goes,
    then apart from the goer there is the act of going
    and there is a goer apart from the act of going.

21. Whether you say that the goer
    and the act of going
    are the same or two different entities
    your argument cannot stand.

22. Because of the going you recognize the goer.
    How does the goer use the act of going?
    Before the act of going, the goer was not going
    therefore there is no goer who uses the act of going.

23. You recognize a goer because there is going.
    The goer cannot use another kind of going.
    For one goer
    there cannot be two kinds of going.

24. If you insist there is a real goer
    they could not use the three times of going.
    If you insist there is no real goer
    they also could not use the three times of going.

25. Whether the going is or is not,
    the goer does not go.
    Therefore there is no goer going,
    and no destination.

3 EXAMINATION OF THE FOUR NOBLE TRUTHS ARYASATYAPARĪKṢĀ (CHAPTER 24)

1. If everything is empty,
   unborn and undying,
   the teaching on the Four Noble Truths
   cannot exist.

2. *Without the Four Noble Truths,*
   seeing suffering, cutting off its causes,
   attaining extinction, and practicing the path,
   could not take place.

3. *Since all these things don't exist,*
   the four fruits also don't exist.
   And if the four fruits don't exist
   then the four kinds of orientation also don't exist.

4. *If the eight kinds of holy people do not exist,*
   then the Sangha jewel does not exist.
   If there are no Four Noble Truths,
   then there is no Dharma jewel either.

5. *If the Dharma and the Sangha jewels don't exist,*
   then there is no Buddha Jewel.
   Therefore the teaching on emptiness
   undermines the Three Jewels.

6. *The teaching of emptiness undermines the teaching of*
       causality
   as well as that of merit and demerit.
   It also undermines
   worldly conventions.

7. You really do not understand
   emptiness and the reasons for teaching emptiness.
   You do not understand the meaning of emptiness
   and so are troubled by it.

8. The buddhas rely on the two truths
   in order to teach the Dharma to beings.
   One truth is the worldly truth,
   the other is the ultimate truth.

9. If someone is not able
   to distinguish one truth from the other,
   they will not be able to understand
   the deep meaning of the Dharma.

10. Without relying on conventional truth,
    you cannot realize ultimate truth.
    Without realizing ultimate truth,
    you will not attain nirvāṇa.

11. Without a right understanding of emptiness
    a dull-witted person does harm to themselves,
    like someone who does not know how
    and grasps a poisonous snake the wrong way.

12. The World-Honored One knew that this teaching,
    so deep and subtle,
    would be out of the reach of those of meager intelligence,
    so he did not want to teach it to them.

13. You say that I am caught in emptiness,
    and so have made many errors.
    But the things you call errors
    have nothing to do with emptiness.

14. Because emptiness is possible,
    everything is possible.
    If emptiness were not possible,
    nothing would be possible.

15. The mistakes you make,
    you attribute to me,
    just like someone who rides a horse
    forgets the horse he is riding.

16. If you see that all things
    must have a self-nature,
    then you also maintain
    that they have no causes and conditions.

17. You deny cause and effect,
    action, the actor, and what is made.

You also deny
the arising and ceasing of all things.

18. *I call empty*
    things that arise from conditions.
    They are conventional designations
    and they are the Middle Way.

4 EXAMINATION OF BEING AND NONBEING SVABHĀVAPARĪKṢĀ (CHAPTER 15)

1. *The existence of something's self-nature*
   is not evident in its conditions.
   A self-nature that arises from conditions
   is something that is made.

2. *What sense does it make to say*
   that the self-nature is something made?
   A self-nature is something not made
   and does not come about dependent on things other
       than itself.

3. *If things do not have self-nature,*
   there cannot be an other-nature.
   The self-nature of one thing
   is the other-nature of another thing.

4. *Without self-nature and other-nature*
   How can anything exist?
   When there is self-nature and other-nature
   phenomena are established.

5. *If being is not established,*
   then how can nonbeing be established?
   Only because something exists
   can it cease to be.

6. *Someone who sees being, nonbeing,*
   self-nature and other-nature,
   cannot see
   the truth in the Buddha's teaching.

7. *The Buddha refutes being and nonbeing*
   in the teachings given to Kātyāyana.
   He gave the teaching which removes
   [the concepts of] being and nonbeing.

8. *If phenomena had a self-nature*
   they could not become nothing.
   A self-nature that becomes something else
   is not reasonable.

9. *If things have a self-nature,*
   how can they change?

If things do not have a self-nature,
how can they change?

10. To assert being is to be caught in eternalism.
To assert nonbeing is to be caught in nihilism.
Therefore a wise person
is not caught in being or nonbeing.

11. If things have a self-nature, and therefore are not
     nonexistent,
that is eternalism.
If they previously existed and now exist no more,
that is nihilism.

5 EXAMINATION OF FIRE AND FUEL
AGNĪNDHANAPARĪKṢĀ (CHAPTER 10)

1. If fire were fuel
then actor and action would be one.
If fire were other than fuel
then without fuel there could be fire.

2. [If fire were other than fuel]
the fire would just keep burning.
If fire did not need fuel,
it would not need someone to set it alight,
and lighting the fire would serve no purpose.

3. *If the fire did not need fuel*
   then it would not arise from conditions.
   If the fire were permanently burning,
   there would be no need for anyone to light it.

4. *You say that when something is burning,*
   you can call it fuel.
   If the fuel can only be fuel when it is burning,
   what is it, then, that is burning it?

5. *If [the fuel] were other [than the fire], it could not*
        reach [the fire].
   If it did not reach [the fire], it could not burn.
   If it does not burn, it could not cease.
   If it does not cease, it is eternal.

6. *If the fire is different from the fuel*
   and can come to the fuel,
   it is like this person can come to that person,
   and that person can come to this person.

7. *If you say that the fire and the fuel*
   are two different things,
   then the fire would be able
   to come to the fuel.

8. *If thanks to the fuel, the fire exists,*
   and thanks to fire the fuel exists,
   which of them existed first
   for there to be fuel and fire?

9. *If thanks to the fuel there is fire,*
   what has already been burned, will be burned again,
   and in the fuel
   there could be no fire.

10. *If this waits for that in order to be,*
    this is also what that is waiting for.
    Therefore there is no cause for waiting,
    and there is nothing which comes to be.

11. *If something has to wait in order to come about,*
    how can it wait if it has not yet come about?
    If it has already come about and is waiting
    then what is it waiting for?

12. *The fire is not there because of the fuel,*
    but without fuel as a cause there is no fire;
    the fuel is not there because of the fire,
    but without fire as a cause there is no fuel.

13. The fire does not come from somewhere else,
    and in the fuel there is no fire
    The same is true for the fuel,
    as we said in the section on coming and going.

14. In the fuel there is no fire.
    Outside the fuel there is no fire.
    If the fire has no fuel,
    inside the fire there is no fuel.

15. Fire and fuel are used
    to explain grasping and the one who grasps,
    to explain the examples of a pot or cloth,
    and all the other examples.

16. If someone says that there is a self,
    and that phenomena differ from one another
    you should know that this person
    has not tasted the essence of the Buddhadharma.

6 EXAMINATION OF NIRVĀṆA
NIRVĀṆAPARĪKṢĀ (CHAPTER 25)

1. If all phenomena are empty,
   they are unborn and undying.

So what you call nirvāṇa
is the ending and extinction of what?

2. If all phenomena are not empty,
   they are unborn and undying,
   So what you call nirvāṇa
   is the ending and extinction of what?

3. Not attaining and not coming,
   not annihilated and not eternal,
   not born and not destroyed,
   this is what we call nirvāṇa.

4. You cannot say nirvāṇa exists;
   existence is characterized by old age and death.
   There is ultimately no existence
   that is not characterized by old age and death.

5. If nirvāṇa exists,
   it would be conditioned.
   There is ultimately no existence
   that can be called unconditioned.

6. If nirvāṇa exists,
   how could you call it independent?
   There is nothing independent
   that can be said to exist.

7. *If nirvāṇa is not existent,*
   how could it be nonexistent?
   Since existence does not apply to nirvāṇa
   how could nonexistence apply to it?

8. *If nirvāṇa is nonexistent,*
   how could you call it independent?
   There is nothing independent
   that can be said not to exist.

9. *That which is dependent on conditions*
   comes and goes in the cycle of birth and death.
   That which is not dependent on conditions
   is called nirvāṇa.

10. *As the Buddha said in the sutras,*
    one should end being and nonbeing.
    Therefore we know that nirvāṇa
    is neither being nor nonbeing.

11. *If you say that being and nonbeing*
    together are nirvāṇa,
    then being and nonbeing would be liberation,
    and this is truly absurd.

12. If you say that being and nonbeing
    together are nirvāṇa,
    nirvāṇa would not be independent,
    since both being and nonbeing arise in dependence.

13. How could we say that nirvāṇa
    both is and is not?
    Nirvāṇa is unconditioned,
    while being and nonbeing are conditioned.

14. How can being and nonbeing
    together be nirvāṇa?
    Like light and darkness,
    they cannot occur together in the same place.

15. If you call nirvāṇa
    neither being nor nonbeing,
    how could this neither being nor nonbeing
    be conceived of?

16. You conceive neither being nor nonbeing
    and call it nirvāṇa.
    Neither being nor nonbeing could only be established
    if being and nonbeing could be established.

17. After the Tathāgata passes away,
    you cannot say he exists, does not exist,
    both exists and does not exist,
    or neither exists nor does not exist.

18. While the Tathāgata is still alive
    you cannot say he exists, does not exist,
    both exists and does not exist,
    or neither exists nor does not exist.

19. Between nirvāṇa and the world
    there is not the slightest difference.
    Between the world and nirvāṇa
    there is not the slightest difference.

20. Between the true nature of nirvāṇa
    and the true nature of saṃsāra
    there is not the slightest distinction.

21. Views on existing after death or not,
    being finite, eternal, and so on
    all rely on nirvāṇa,
    the past, and the future.

22. *Since all phenomena are empty*
    how can they be limited or limitless,
    both limited and limitless
    or neither limited nor limitless?

23. *How can there be same and different,*
    permanence or impermanence,
    both permanence and impermanence,
    or neither permanence nor impermanence?

24. *[Realizing that] phenomena cannot be grasped,*
    we remove all speculation.
    There is no person and no location,
    and the Buddha did not teach anything.

中論 ZHONG LUN
MŪLAMADHYAMAKAKĀRIKĀ

不生亦不滅	能說是因緣
不常亦不斷	善滅諸戲論
不一亦不異	我稽首禮佛
不來亦不出	諸說中第一

1 觀因緣 (GUAN YIN YUAN)
PRATYAYAPARĪKṢĀ (CHAPTER 1)

1. 諸法不自生	4. 果為從緣生
亦不從他生	為從非緣生
不共不無因	是緣為有果
是故知無生	是緣為無果
2. 因緣次第緣	5. 因是法生果
緣緣增上緣	是法名為緣
四緣生諸法	若是果未生
更無第五緣	何不名非緣
3. 如諸法自性	6. 果先於緣中
不在於緣中	有無俱不可
以無自性故	先無為誰緣
他性亦復無	先有何用緣

7. 若果非有生
　亦復非無生
　亦非有無生
　何得言有緣

8. 果若未生時
　則不應有滅
　滅法何能緣
　故無次第緣

9. 如諸佛所說
　真實微妙法
　於此無緣法
　云何有緣緣

10. 諸法無自性
　故無有有相
　說有是事故
　是事有不然

11. 略廣因緣中
　求果不可得
　因緣中若無
　云何從緣出

12. 若謂緣無果
　而從緣中出
　是果何不從
　非緣中而出

13. 若果從緣生
　是緣無自性
　從無自性生
　何得從緣生

14. 果不從緣生
　不從非緣生
　以果無有故
　緣非緣亦無

2　觀去來 (GUAN QU LAI)
　GATĀGATAPARĪKṢĀ (CHAPTER 2)

1. 已去無有去
　未去亦無去

離已去未去
去時亦無去

2. 動處則有去
   此中有去時
   非已去未去
   是故去時去

3. 云何於去時
   而當有去法
   若離於去法
   去時不可得

4. 若言去時去
   是人則有咎
   離去有去時
   去時獨去故

5. 若去時有去
   則有二種去
   一謂為去時
   二謂去時去

6. 若有二去法
   則有二去者
   以離於去者
   去法不可得

7. 若離於去者
   去法不可得

以無去法故
何得有去者

8. 去者則不去
   不去者不去
   離去不去者
   無第三去者

9. 若言去者去
   云何有此義
   若離於去法
   去者不可得

10. 若去者有去
    則有二種去
    一謂去者去
    二謂去法去

11. 若謂去者去
    是人則有咎
    離去有去者
    說去者有去

12. 已去中無發
    未去中無發
    去時中無發
    何處當有發

13. 未發無去時
    亦無有已去
    是二應有發
    未去何有發

14. 無去無未去
    亦復無去時
    一切無有發
    何故而分別

15. 去者則不住
    不去者不住
    離去不去者
    何有第三住

16. 去者若當住
    云何有此義
    若當離於去
    去者不可得

17. 去未去無住
    去時亦無住
    所有行止法
    皆同於去義

18. 去法即去者
    是事則不然
    去法異去者
    是事亦不然

19. 若謂於去法
    即為是去者
    作者及作業
    是事則為一

20. 若謂於去法
    有異於去者
    離去者有去
    離去有去者

21. 去去者是二
    若一異法成
    二門俱不成
    云何當有成

22. 因去知去者
    不能用是去
    先無有去法
    故無去者去

23. 因去知去者　　　不決定去者
　　不能用異去　　　亦不用三去
　　於一去者中
　　不得二去故　　25. 去法定不定
　　　　　　　　　　去者不用三
24. 決定有去者　　　是故去去者
　　不能用三去　　　所去處皆無

3　觀四諦 (GUAN SI DI)
ARYASATYAPARĪKṢĀ (CHAPTER 24)

1. 若一切皆空　　4. 若無八賢聖
　　無生亦無滅　　　則無有僧寶
　　如是則無有　　　以無四諦故
　　四聖諦之法　　　亦無有法寶

2. 以無四諦故　　5. 以無法僧寶
　　見苦與斷集　　　亦無有佛寶
　　證滅及修道　　　如是說空者
　　如是事皆無　　　是則破三寶

3. 以是事無故　　6. 空法壞因果
　　則無四道果　　　亦壞於罪福
　　無有四果故　　　亦復悉毀壞
　　得向者亦無　　　一切世俗法

7. 汝今實不能
   知空空因緣
   及知於空義
   是故自生惱

8. 諸佛依二諦
   為眾生說法
   一以世俗諦
   二第一義諦

9. 若人不能知
   分別於二諦
   則於深佛法
   不知真實義

10. 若不依俗諦
    不得第一義
    不得第一義
    則不得涅槃

11. 不能正觀空
    鈍根則自害
    如不善咒術
    不善捉毒蛇

12. 世尊知是法
    甚深微妙相
    非鈍根所及
    是故不欲說

13. 汝謂我著空
    而為我生過
    汝今所說過
    於空則無有

14. 以有空義故
    一切法得成
    若無空義者
    一切則不成

15. 汝今自有過
    而以迴向我
    如人乘馬者
    自忘於所乘

16. 若汝見諸法
    決定有性者
    即為見諸法
    無因亦無緣

17. 即為破因果
    作作者作法
    亦復壞一切
    萬物之生滅

18. 眾因緣生法
    我說 即是空
    亦為是假名
    亦是中道義

4 觀有無 (GUAN YOU WU)
SVABHĀVAPARĪKṢĀ (CHAPTER 15)

1. 眾緣中有性
   是事則不然
   性從眾緣出
   即名為作法

2. 性若是作者
   云何有此義
   性名為無作
   不待異法成

3. 法若無自性
   云何有他性
   自性於他性
   亦名為他性

4. 離自性他性
   何得更有法
   若有自他性
   諸法則得成

5. 有若不成者
   無云何可成
   因有有法故
   有壞名為無

6. 若人見有無
   見自性他性
   如是則不見
   佛法真實義

7. 佛能滅有無
   如化迦旃延
   經中之所說
   離有亦離無

8. 若法實有性
   後則不應無
   性若有異相
   是事終不然

9. 若法實有性　　　　是故有智者
　 云何而可異　　　　不應著有無
　 若法實無性
　 云何而可異　　11. 若法有定性
　　　　　　　　　　非無則是常
10. 定有則著常　　　　先有而今無
　 定無則著斷　　　　是則為斷滅

5 觀燃可燃 (GUAN RAN KE RAN)
　 AGNĪNDHANAPARĪKṢĀ (CHAPTER 10)

1. 若燃是可燃　　　4. 若汝謂燃時
　 作作者則一　　　　名為可燃者
　 若燃異可燃　　　　爾時但有薪
　 離可燃有燃　　　　何物燃可燃

2. 如是常應燃　　　5. 若異則不至
　 不因可燃生　　　　不至則不燒
　 則無燃火功　　　　不燒則不滅
　 亦名無作火　　　　不滅則常住

3. 燃不待可燃　　　6. 燃與可燃異
　 則不從緣生　　　　而能至可燃
　 火若常燃者　　　　如此至彼人
　 人功則應空　　　　彼人至此人

7. 若謂燃可燃
二俱相離者
如是燃則能
至於彼可燃

8. 若因可燃燃
因燃有可燃
先定有何法
而有燃可燃

9. 若因可燃燃
則燃成復成
是為可燃中
則為無有燃

10. 若法因待成
是法還成待
今則無因待
亦無所成法

11. 若法有待成
未成云何待
若成已有待
成已何用待

12. 因可燃無燃
不因亦無燃
因燃無可燃
不因無可燃

13. 燃不餘處來
燃處亦無燃
可燃亦如是
餘如去來說

14. 若可燃無燃
離可燃無燃
燃亦無可燃
燃中無可燃

15. 以燃可燃法
說受受者法
及以說瓶衣
一切等諸法

16. 若人說有我
諸法各異相
當知如是人
不得佛法味

6 觀涅槃 (GUAN NIEPAN)
NIRVĀṆAPARĪKṢĀ (CHAPTER 25)

1. 若一切法空
   無生無滅者
   何斷何所滅
   而稱為涅槃

2. 若諸法不空
   則無生無滅
   何斷何所滅
   而稱為涅槃

3. 無得亦無至
   不斷亦不常
   不生亦不滅
   是說名涅槃

4. 涅槃不名有
   有則老死相
   終無有有法
   離於老死相

5. 若涅槃是有
   涅槃即有為
   終無有一法
   而是無為者

6. 若涅槃是有
   云何名無受
   無有不從受
   而名為有法

7. 有尚非涅槃
   何況於無耶
   涅槃無有有
   何處當有無

8. 若無是涅槃
   云何名不受
   未曾有不受
   而名為無法

9. 受諸因緣故
   輪轉生死中
   不受諸因緣
   是名為涅槃

10. 如佛經中說
    斷有斷非有
    是故知涅槃
    非有亦非無

11. 若謂於有無
    合為涅槃者
    有無即解脫
    是事則不然

12. 若謂於有無
    合為涅槃者
    涅槃非無受
    是二從受生

13. 有無共合成
    云何名涅槃
    涅槃名無為
    有無是有為

14. 有無二事共
    云何是涅槃
    是二不同處
    如明暗不俱

15. 若非有非無
    名之為涅槃
    此非有非無
    以何而分別

16. 分別非有無
    如是名涅槃
    若有無成者
    非有非無成

17. 如來滅度後
    不言有與無
    亦不言有無
    非有及非無

18. 如來現在時
    不言有與無
    亦不言有無
    非有及非無

19. 涅槃與世間
    無有少分別
    世間與涅槃
    亦無少分別

20. 涅槃之實際
    及與世間際
    如是二際者
    無毫釐差別

21. 滅後有無等
    有邊等常等
    諸見依涅槃
    未來過去世

22. 一切法空故
    何有邊無邊
    亦邊亦無邊
    非有非無邊

23. 何者為一異
    何有常無常
    亦常亦無常
    非常非無常

24. 諸法不可得
    滅一切戲論
    無人亦無處
    佛亦無所說

ALSO BY THÍCH NHẤT HẠNH

The Admonitions and
Encouraging Words of
Master Guishan

Anger

At Home in the World

Awakening of the Heart

Be Free Where You Are

Being Peace

Beyond the Self

The Blooming of a Lotus

The Bodhisattva Path

Breathe, You Are Alive!

Call Me by My True Names

Chanting from the Heart

Cultivating the Mind of Love

The Diamond that Cuts
through Illusion

Enjoying the Ultimate

Fragrant Palm Leaves

The Heart of the Buddha's
Teaching

Hermitage among the Clouds

Interbeing

Joyfully Together

Living Buddha, Living Christ

Love in Action

Love Letter to the Earth

Master Tang Hoi

The Mindfulness Survival Kit

The Miracle of Mindfulness

No Mud, No Lotus

Old Path White Clouds

The Other Shore

Our Appointment with Life

Peace Is Every Step

Silence

Stepping into Freedom

The Sun My Heart

Teachings on Love

Thundering Silence

Transformation and Healing

Two Treasures

Understanding Our Mind

Vietnam: Lotus in a Sea of Fire

The World We Have

Zen and the Art of Saving the
Planet

Monastics and visitors practice the art of mindful living in the tradition of Thich Nhat Hanh at our mindfulness practice centers around the world. To reach any of these communities, or for information about how individuals, couples, and families can join in a retreat, please contact:

PLUM VILLAGE
33580 Dieulivol, France
plumvillage.org

LA MAISON DE L'INSPIR
77510 Villeneuve-sur-Bellot, France
maisondelinspir.org

HEALING SPRING
MONASTERY
77510 Verdelot, France
healingspringmonastery.org

MAGNOLIA GROVE
MONASTERY
Batesville, MS 38606, USA
magnoliagrovemonastery.org

BLUE CLIFF MONASTERY
Pine Bush, NY 12566, USA
bluecliffmonastery.org

DEER PARK MONASTERY
Escondido, CA 92026, USA
deerparkmonastery.org

EUROPEAN INSTITUTE OF
APPLIED BUDDHISM
D-51545 Waldbröl, Germany
eiab.eu

THAILAND PLUM VILLAGE
Nakhon Ratchasima
30130 Thailand
thaiplumvillage.org

ASIAN INSTITUTE OF
APPLIED BUDDHISM
Lantau Island, Hong Kong
pvfhk.org

STREAM ENTERING
MONASTERY
Porcupine Ridge, Victoria 3461
Australia
nhapluu.org

MOUNTAIN SPRING
MONASTERY
Bilpin, NSW 2758, Australia
mountainspringmonastery.org

For more information visit: *plumvillage.org*
To find an online sangha visit: *plumline.org*
For more resources, try the Plum Village app: *plumvillage.app*
Social media: *@thichnhathanh @plumvillagefrance*

THICH NHAT HANH FOUNDATION

planting seeds of Compassion

THE THICH NHAT HANH FOUNDATION works to continue the mindful teachings and practice of Zen Master Thich Nhat Hanh, in order to foster peace and transform suffering in all people, animals, plants, and our planet. Through donations to the Foundation, thousands of generous supporters ensure the continuation of Plum Village practice centers and monastics around the world, bring transformative practices to those who otherwise would not be able to access them, support local mindfulness initiatives, and bring humanitarian relief to communities in crisis in Vietnam.

By becoming a supporter, you join many others who want to learn and share these life-changing practices of mindfulness, loving speech, deep listening, and compassion for oneself, each other, and the planet.

For more information on how you can help support mindfulness around the world, or to subscribe to the Foundation's monthly newsletter with teachings, news, and global retreats, visit tnhf.org.

PALM LEAVES PRESS aims to develop a complete catalog of the scholarly works of Thich Nhat Hanh to contribute to the study and practice of Engaged Buddhism and Applied Buddhism, to share what spiritual practice can offer to counteract social injustice and climate change, to develop a global ethic, and to facilitate the awakening of the collective consciousness. Infused with the rich tradition of Vietnamese Buddhism, the mission of Palm Leaves Press is to preserve Thich Nhat Hanh's legacy so his teachings can continue to nourish practitioners now and for many generations in the future.

THE MINDFULNESS BELL is a journal of the art of mindful living in the Plum Village tradition of Thich Nhat Hanh. To subscribe or to see the worldwide directory of Sanghas (local mindfulness groups), visit mindfulnessbell.org.